CURRENT

A MILLION FIRST DATES

Dan Slater contributes to *The New York Times* and *Fast Company* magazine. He is a former legal affairs reporter for *The Wall Street Journal*, and his work has also appeared in *The Washington Post*, *The Boston Globe*, *GQ*, and *Men's Health*. Slater is a graduate of Colgate University and Brooklyn Law School. His favorite date remains dinner and a movie.

A Million First Dates

SOLVING THE PUZZLE OF ONLINE DATING

DAN SLATER

PREVIOUSLY PUBLISHED AS *LOVE IN THE TIME OF ALGORITHMS*

CURRENT

CURRENT
Published by the Penguin Group
Penguin Group (USA) LLC
375 Hudson Street
New York, New York 10014

USA | Canada | UK | Ireland | Australia | New Zealand | India | South Africa | China
penguin.com
A Penguin Random House Company

First published in the United States of America under the title *Love in the Time of Algorithms*
by Current, a member of Penguin Group (USA) Inc., 2013
This paperback edition with a new preface published 2014

Portions of this book first appeared in *GQ* magazine.

Author's Note
This book attempts to be a factual inside account of the development of an industry, and a
chronicle of how that industry has affected the lives of the people whose stories I've told. The
casual nature of online interaction, however, required taking liberties with some of the secondary material quoted—namely, the conversations, profiles, and messages pulled from online dating sites and the Phantasy Tour forum. Occasionally, I relocated or transposed a
sentence or paragraph, adjoined remarks written by the same person at different times, removed words or phrases from quotes without inserting marks of ellipsis, and cleaned up
spelling and grammar. None of these changes are intended to alter meaning or make the material more interesting, but rather to privilege clarity and narrative flow over fidelity to the
precise original. Also, the names of most online-dating users have been changed to protect
their privacy.

THE LIBRARY OF CONGRESS HAS CATALOGED THE HARDCOVER EDITION AS FOLLOWS:
Slater, Dan.
Love in the time of algorithms : what technology does to meeting and mating / Dan Slater.
p. cm.
Includes bibliographical references and index.
ISBN 978-1-59184-531-7 (hc.)
ISBN 978-1-61723-009-7 (pbk.)
1. Online dating. 2. Courtship. 3. Dating (Social customs)—Technological innovations.
4. Marriage brokerage—Technological innovations. I. Title.
HQ801.82.S58 2013
306.730285—dc23 2012036921

Printed in the United States of America
10 9 8 7 6 5 4 3 2 1

Set in Diverda Serif Com with Aroma No. 2 LT Pro
Designed by Daniel Lagin

For G & G

The Internet did not develop in order to facilitate relationships, any more than newspapers were invented to publish personal ads. Like the panda's thumb, evolution, whether natural or technological, takes unexpected directions.

—**Monica Whitty and Adrian Carr,** *Cyberspace Romance*

CONTENTS

PREFACE TO THE PAPERBACK EDITION

STRAPPING IN

I met my wife in the most modern of ways: a yoga class. After a week or three of hemming and hawing, I collected my courage and asked her out. I was thirty-one, licking the wounds of a recently failed relationship, and about to be laid off from my job. Who wouldn't want to date me?

Yes—believe it or not—she declined this incredible opportunity. She had a boyfriend. Rats.

So I began dating people, some of whom I met online, and started working on this book. Time passed. Then, one sunny day, my wife-to-be popped up in that right-hand column on Facebook as "A Person You May Know." As it turned out, the boyfriend had since been banished—much to my delight!—and eighteen months later we were married.

Hardly any of that was predictable or formulaic, particularly when you add those other relationships that came before. Were those other relationships—with all their joy and scarring—necessary for this one to work out?

When this book was published, the most common question I got was: Why a book about online dating? I'd explain that the book was really about modern relationships and how they're affected by all this technology we're using to find new relationships and keep old ones going. Okay, fine. But why? And the answer I never gave, maybe because it seemed so unsophisticated, but would like to give now is this: I wrote a book about relationships because I never understood books about relationships.

Not novels. I love a good romance. I'm talking about all those "how-to" books, the ones with lots of peppy lists and cheery chapter titles. They tell you what you're doing wrong, how to improve your appeal, and are general enough to apply to pretty much anyone. A lot of the advice makes sense. For instance, brush your teeth before a date. That's helpful. But once you get past the common-sense stuff, these books' usefulness sort of ends. Why is that?

My opinion is that relationship manuals fail because they start from the premise that finding a good relationship is reducible to a formula of dos and don'ts—one that worked for the author or for the author's friends and is guaranteed to work for you, too, if only you can learn to do it right.

The reality of dating, of course, is far from formulaic. It's more like riding a rollercoaster, blindfolded, while the track ahead is still under construction. The original plans for the track were abandoned, and now the engineers are working with whatever materials they can get, hoping to finish the next loop-the-loop before you fly off into orbit. Your stomach drops when you're plunged into a horrifying encounter one day and you scream to be let off. But wait. That memory is quickly erased when the dating rollercoaster rockets you up to a moment of hopefulness the next day, a peak of joy that was so unforeseeable but makes perfect sense! Except . . . maybe it doesn't make sense. Because another plunge awaits, the worst kind of sinking feeling: that no call back (or text back) after the date that seemed to go so well. You swear you'll never ride that fucking rollercoaster again. But you will.

I think the rise of online dating heightens the impression that finding love is a formula, that love is literally a matter of filling out lists and doing a bunch of mechanical things on your laptop or phone. You'll know you've mastered the formula when your dating site spits out the perfect mate.

The dating rollercoaster is moving fast these days, along with the other aspects of life that have been accelerated by the Internet. A new mate is always, potentially, a click away. But it's not all sunny days. This unprecedented efficiency in the dating market solves some old problems and raises many new ones. If it's become easier to move on from relationships, should you? If you can use the Internet to meet people in foreign countries, should you? If dating sites promise to find you the perfect mate (if only you follow their formula!), should you believe them? If you can monitor a new boyfriend 24/7 on Facebook and Twitter and Instagram and Match.com, should you? How can you make this new efficiency work in your favor?

My goal in *A Million First Dates* is to provide hints, clues, and even some answers to these questions. Not in a checklist format or in a formula, but rather through the lessons of the online daters and online-dating entrepreneurs whose stories I tell.

As you'll see in the mix of uplifting, cautionary, and downright pathetic tales that follow, online dating doesn't make the rollercoaster any less harrowing. But if you know how the ride works and how others have traveled it well and traveled it poorly, then maybe you can come up with a formula of your own—one that, in hindsight, makes all the sense in the world.

In the meantime, enjoy the ride.

D.S.
Easton, CT
2013

INTRODUCTION

Liquidity in the Market

THE iDATE AWARDS

It's January 2011, and Sam Yagan and Markus Frind are trying to chat casually by the pool behind Miami's National Hotel. Their reflections shimmer in the water as a humid evening breeze shakes the palm fronds. The two men, both in their early thirties, are dressed identically in blue button-downs, navy blue blazers, and khakis. But these similarities belie their true relationship. They are stiff competitors, and the presence of the other unnerves them both. Yagan and Frind shift on their feet, beers in hand, waiting for the other to speak.

"Why didn't they ask you to give the talk on free dating?" asks Yagan.

"Because," says Frind, "I hate public speaking."

This is true: Despite running what's believed to be the largest online-dating site in the world, Frind is loath to appear on television or radio. When he does, he speaks of "programming languages" and rattles off statistics. In a 2009 appearance on a Toronto-based talk show, Frind said the average online dater "needs about 3.8 dates for a relationship."

Yagan, meanwhile, has been a media fixture since college. Cable, newspapers, magazines, tech-news sites, investors, Silicon Valley—they all love Yagan and he loves them right back. His question to Frind barely conceals his excitement that his rival was not asked to speak.

"Then why not get one of your illustrious team members to do it?" responds Yagan, his quip divided evenly between mockery and jealousy over Frind's entourage of beautiful female executives, all of whom are mingling a few feet away. Some tension is released as Frind and Yagan gaze appreciatively.

Yagan is a slender man, about five feet eight inches tall, with a narrow chin, an aquiline nose, thick eyebrows, a broad forehead, and cropped hair that's gone prematurely gray. With friends Yagan is intensely congenial but turns quickly to disgusted and derisive when a subject or viewpoint arises that conflicts with his agenda.

Frind is taller, paler, more reserved. He tends to press his chin in while casting his bespectacled eyes down, as if expecting an insult or a punch to the face. His look, wrote *The Globe and Mail*, is that of a "true coder," his style reminiscent of men "twice his 33 years, boomers whose only exertion is to toddle to the first tee." Frind uses his fame to surround himself with attractive women, including his new wife, Annie, a charming and radiant blonde.

They've come to Miami to attend the iDate Awards dinner, the featured event of the online-dating industry's annual conference in South Beach. Yagan, a cofounder of OkCupid, and Frind, the sole founder of Plenty of Fish, are celebrities in this place where relationships are the business, a very lucrative business that has reached $2 billion in North America, with billions more being made abroad, as millions of customers join, and return to, dating sites every day. From New York, Los Angeles, Quebec, Vancouver, Sydney, Moscow, Kiev, London, and Rio de Janeiro, the one hundred dating executives who turned up at the conference are here to show their faces and shore up their interests in an industry that has arrived at a crossroads, saturated with players and facing an uncertain future. The online-dating industry may service thirty million of America's ninety million single adults, but momentum is slowing. Following a period of explosive growth between 1998 and 2005, the Facebook-led rise of social networks began stealing market share. Meanwhile, popular matchmaking sites like eHarmony and Chemistry face attacks from academics who say the science behind their algorithms is bunk.

For three days, the dating execs have been cutting advertising deals, buying and selling dating sites, and arguing over the future of the industry. Now they're ordering drinks, posing on a red carpet, and waiting for the awards dinner to begin.

Yagan, the son of Syrian immigrants and a graduate of Harvard and Stanford Business School, is CEO of OkCupid, a dating site known for its community of urban-creative types. Frind, a Canadian who comes from German-farmer stock, attended a vocational school before starting Plenty of Fish. Frind's site is thought to attract a certain kind of customer, one who feels at home among grammar-free profiles comprised largely of text-speak and emoticons—a sizable population, as it turns out: Frind owns 20 percent of the world's online-dating traffic.

Yagan says Plenty of Fish, because of its unmanageable size, is infested with "romance scammers," people who create fake dating profiles to wring money from the desperate. Frind dismisses Yagan's OkCupid as a "niche site" with a limited following among "the writer-slash-hippie-slash-whatever crowd." Frind says Plenty of Fish grows an OkCupid a day. All sallies are partially correct: Plenty of Fish is much larger than OkCupid, and therefore more vulnerable to infiltration by scammers.

But as antagonistic as they fancy themselves, Frind and Yagan are aligned when it comes to one key element of the business: They both believe online dating should be free. Yagan's anger over not being asked to give the conference talk about the state of free online dating is palpable. He campaigned to give the talk. When the conference organizers refused him, citing the need to let others in the industry speak, he nearly boycotted the conference, agreeing to make the trip from New York only after the organizers hinted that OkCupid would receive several honors at tonight's ceremony.

That Frind and Yagan are two of the savviest entrepreneurs in an industry that markets human relationships is, to put it mildly, totally bizarre. Both are married. Neither has dated online. Yagan often jokes that he and his OkCupid partners know nothing about dating. They are business-minded, unemotional math guys. Dating, relationships, and love, on the other hand, are irreducible products riddled with variables

Or are they?

My phone buzzes with a text: "Just walked in. You here?"

When I asked the conference organizers about the possibility of bringing an online date to the awards dinner, I expected some pushback. The one-hundred-dollar-per-head event was sold out, after all, and I was lucky to get a last-minute press pass. But instead of resistance, my request met with universal encouragement. I was in Miami for three days and had lined up a date through Match.com. This, I suppose, was precisely the kind of dating adventure their business models encouraged.

I walk through the hotel's foyer and find my date standing patiently beneath the chandelier. I don't know much about RedPepper—her online-dating nom de plume—other than a few dating vitals: thirty years old; a Jew of Dutch descent; Michigan-raised; the director of marketing for a global ice cream brand. Two weeks before my trip to Miami, she'd written to me via Match's messaging system:

> So, you're probably thinking: Why is this girl from Florida e-mailing
> me on Match? Well, I was sitting here alone in South Africa on a
> business trip in the middle of the night and talking to my best friend
> in Brooklyn. She said why don't you switch your search parameters to
> Brooklyn and see who shows up. You showed up first, we match on
> all the green bubbles, and you made me laugh. Anyway, you should
> write me back. What have you got to lose?

There was something serendipitous about getting this message so close to my trip. South Africa, Florida, New York: What were the chances? Yet after nine months of online dating from my home base of Brooklyn, the situation didn't *seem* that unusual. I'd become conditioned to the message-in-a-bottle randomness of it all, having received queries from London, Hanoi, San Francisco, and even the Upper East Side.

RedPepper is tall and slender, with large blue eyes, a cheery disposition, and long frizzy hair that is almost platinum. We greet in one of those slapstick ballets of mistimed lunges and errant cheek kisses. The awkwardness contains itself, and we make for the pool. "I'm always up for an adventure," says RedPepper. "But I did wonder why you didn't respond to my second message asking what brings you to Florida." Indeed, I had needed some time to figure out how to ask an online date to an online-dating conference.

While RedPepper and I wait for the awards dinner to start, we sip our drinks beneath the palm fronds that wrap around the pool. Nearby is Markus Frind's entourage, led by Kate Bilenki, Plenty of Fish's chief operating officer. Doe-eyed and porcelain browed, Bilenki gets hit on by pretty much every heterosexual male at iDate. Particularly relentless is a team of British dating executives, one of whom boasted that he was flying Bilenki to England in the spring to take her to "the polo." When he said this I wondered if he was referring to a business meeting or a cross-continental date of some kind. But this was the point. Nowhere else in corporate life do work and play merge so shamelessly as they do among these dating mavens.

Whereas prior to RedPepper's arrival I was an interloping reporter with too many questions and uncertain motives, I am now part of a couple, one half of which is inarguably attractive. As such, we begin drawing dating execs to our area beneath the palm fronds. A Chinese American man introduces himself as Jason Du, the founder of MillionaireMatch, whose members include "professional athletes, beauty queens, fitness models, and Hollywood celebrities." The actor Charlie Sheen, he says, was an early customer. Du also runs PositiveSingles, a dating site for people with sexually transmitted diseases. "Because of privacy concerns, it's very tricky for people with STDs to date," he explains. "So on the site we have a button labeled Quick Exit for those times when your pesky boss walks by."

A post-forty-five-ish blonde drifts over. She's Julie Ferman of Cupid's Coach, an offline matchmaker. Ferman flashes a toothy smile and looks like a cross between Julia Louis-Dreyfuss and Glenn Close. "It's very hard to find good guys for my great women," she laments. "These are women who live in great million-dollar homes, have great careers, and just need that great special someone, that great relationship with that great stable guy."

"Like what's an example?" asks RedPepper.

Ferman purses her lips, happy to be asked, and relates a recent conflict: "I matched up a client in L.A. with a great guy. But then the client went out of town. When the client returned, the guy was not calling her. So the client called me, and I told her she had two options. Either she could wait it out, or she could take the situation into her own hands and call *him*."

When RedPepper realizes this is the sum of the facts, she becomes slightly hostile, asking Ferman whether it's "problematic" that a forty-year-old woman is paying thousands of dollars for advice that "seems kind of basic." Ferman turns to me and says she loves to take care of her friends in the media, and that she recently arranged a very successful date for Dr. Phil. This name drop piques the interest of Jason Du, who appears to be envisioning Dr. Phil as MillionaireMatch's next celebrity dater.

After Du and Ferman leave, RedPepper says, matter-of-factly, "Me and my friends, we're well-educated and successful and all that. But I guess we focused on other things after college. Career stuff. Now it's hard to find anyone. Some are already resigned to waiting for a divorce to pop up. Or just marrying guys they're not very excited about."

The gist of what RedPepper describes happens to be highly relevant for the online-dating industry. The ascension of women at work and their rising financial status, the lagging prospects of men, the ebb of the marriage rate, and the ever-rising marriage age—these are societal trends that have dovetailed with, and been a boon to, online dating in recent years. "My friends think I'm crazy for being on Match," she says. "They tell me I don't need it. But quote unquote need isn't really the point, is it? It's about taking control."

On and off, for the last nine months, I, like RedPepper, had been taking control. Three events accounted for my foray into online dating: I turned thirty-one, got out of a long-term relationship, and then lost my job. I was single at a point in life where all my friends were married or settled down, and I suddenly had a lot of free time on my hands.

Then, a few months into my online-dating adventure, a fourth thing happened. A package, sent from my father, arrived, containing a stack of old letters and postcards dated 1966 and addressed to him at Harvard University, where he'd gone as an undergraduate. The correspondence had been written by my mother, a student at Mount Holyoke College, during the early months of their courtship. My parents had separated in the eighties, when I was three. I'd always just assumed they met at a dance, or were introduced by a friend, but I'd never bothered to ask.

Among the materials was an annotated cartoon booklet given to my father on his twenty-second birthday. On the first page, adjacent to a drawing of a girl and her dog, my mother had written, in her neat tight scrawl: "Thank you, you old mathematically-minded-can't-mind-your-own-business-mass-production-post-card-instigating-work-of-art-in-stainless-steel computer. Thank you."

What computer could she possibly have been thanking, and why?

Flipping through the rest of the pile I came upon a questionnaire entitled "CONTACT Personality Preference Inventory."

"Oh yeah. You didn't know?" my father said, when I called to ask him what CONTACT was. "Your mother and I met through a computer dating service. These days they're all over the Internet. I think they're mostly for desperate people though."

There were a few flops in my online-dating experience. But most of the people I met were, like RedPepper, the kinds of people I might've pursued had we run into each other "IRL," in real life. The main difference was that I no longer had to rely on real life. From the convenience and privacy of my laptop (or cell phone), I could browse through hundreds or thousands of people I would likely never meet otherwise. In the past I'd had to rely on my social circle—family, friends at school and work, friends of friends—or the occasional chance encounter in the subway or on the street. But even at my most outgoing, opportunities to make a connection were limited; potential partners, rare.

For virtually all of human history the search for a mate has been predicated on scarcity: One met only so many people in his or her lifetime. They optimized their options within a circumscribed pool, chose someone, settled down, and, in the best of cases, found something they called happiness. Even when women's lib came along, and the legal and cultural restraints surrounding divorce began to ease in the 1960s and 1970s, making it easier to leave failed relationships, many chose to stick with the devil they knew because of scarcity, believing it was better to be in a so-so relationship than no relationship at all.

Today, however, companies in the online-dating arms race are building ever more efficient, "frictionless" systems for bringing together people who are likely to like each other. By posing hundreds or thousands of questions and quizzes—or asking nothing at all—these sites offer endless choice, combining to form a vast mate-seeking arena I came to think of as the "date-o-sphere," not a physical construct but not an entirely virtual one either, a special category of social media that yokes together enormous online communities for the purpose of offline relationships. So in 2010, when I discovered that thirty million single adults in the United States—about one-third of all American singles—had an online-dating profile, and that I couldn't sit through a dinner party without meeting at least one couple, if not several, who'd met online, I became hooked by a simple question: What does all this connective technology mean for the future of relationships?

This isn't a book about me, or my parents. It's about how online dating—as both a revolutionary medium and a quirky, virginal industry—is remaking the landscape of modern relationships. It's about a man in Oregon whose plans to settle down took a detour when he discovered how easy it was to meet new women online. It's about a young woman in New York whose compulsion to broadcast her online-dating adventures in social media seemed to foil her offline relationships, and about another online dater in San Francisco whose Facebook monitoring had become the enemy of her new relationships. It's about an asthmatic in Atlanta who realized, thanks to a cutting-edge algorithm, that he could be happy with a smoker; and about a cancer survivor in southern California whose isolation inspired her to start a niche dating site for people, like herself, who can no longer have sex. Authenticity, deception, commitment, intimacy, paranoia, sex, and trust—technology is changing all these aspects of relationships. Those changes are what this book is about.

It's also about how, over the last half century, a bunch of geeks reengineered romance and serendipity, redefined our values around meeting and mating, and fought through a heavy societal stigma in the process. Beginning with the early computers of the 1950s and 1960s, the video cameras of the 1970s, the bulletin board systems of the 1980s, the Internet of the 1990s, and the smartphones of the last decade, every new format of electronically intermediated introductions has faced a stigma of some kind.

Only recently has the discredit that's dogged traditional online-dating sites like Match.com begun to dissolve, only to pop up elsewhere in the date-o-sphere. Today, more risqué incarnations—from sites that facilitate marital affairs to those that connect Western men with women in the developing world—are hoping to travel a similar path toward wide acceptance. The profits made by these companies tell a fascinating (and, for some, disturbing) story of shifting sexual mores, as easy access to hitherto unimagined liaisons slowly erodes the taboos that surround them. This, too, is the subject that *A Million First Dates* explores: how these new means of connection are threatening the old paradigm of adult life.

My journey took me to the headquarters of dating sites around the country, where I saw dating executives struggle with how to balance their business interests with the interests of their users; into the private lives of dozens of online daters across America; and then abroad, to England, France, Russia, and Colombia, where Latin women, many of whom don't own a computer, use online dating to meet men from North America.

I also went back in time, to understand how technology has influenced our relationships throughout history. As it turns out, this is not the first time that technology has upended the old ways. In the past these changes have been fueled by the personal ad, the bicycle, the car, the movie theater, and contraception. Today it's the Internet. In all cases the narrative is similar: One generation considers its social norms around meeting and mating to be inviolable, only to see them disregarded by the next.

When the awards dinner begins, the emcee, playing to the supposed proclivities of his audience, tells a series of jokes featuring his mother and sister in outlandish sexual scenarios. RedPepper and I laugh. Nothing will come of our date. She's great. But the chemistry isn't quite right. Sparks would really need to fly to pursue a long-distance relationship with someone in Miami.

For the moment, however, we're still on a date, and seated next to Sam Yagan, who's treating the event as a kind of companion-media to his smartphone, which he thumbs furiously while at the same time telling us how much he dislikes his rivals. A special hatred is reserved for Match, the oldest and largest online-dating site in the paid category. Yagan claims Match has built a business around bamboozling its customers. But his contempt masks the truth about his own business: OkCupid, in spite of its loyal following, hasn't performed very well in terms of revenue. Without the enormous traffic of Plenty of Fish, it's hard to be profitable as a free site, depending wholly on advertising to make money. With around 1.5 million paying subscribers, and many million more free users to fill out its database (more on that later), Match makes nearly $350 million a year in revenue. OkCupid makes less than $5 million.

For the last year, Yagan has been quietly courting potential buyers, including AOL, MSN, Google, Yahoo, Viacom, and the Hearst Corporation. Viacom's MTV and Hearst's magazines are all about relationships and sex. AOL owns the domain name Love.com but doesn't use it. A dating site, he's tried to convince these companies, would fit perfectly in their empires. But no luck. "The idea is interesting enough for them to talk to me for thirty minutes," says Yagan. "But the conversations end the same: 'no thanks.'" The only major acquirers of online-dating sites are other online-dating sites, namely Match, the company Yagan and his partners have made a sport out of slamming publicly.

He's called up to accept OkCupid's first award of the night, for Best

Up and Coming Dating Site. "Seven years in business and we're still 'up and coming,'" he mumbles on his way to the podium, where he graciously accepts the award.

Next up is offline matchmaker Julie Ferman, who wins for Best Matchmaker. Ferman remarks that the award—a long, arcing glass statuette—looks like a giant dildo, which it sort of does, and then proceeds to frog hop off the stage while pretending to ram the award into her rear end.

During a lull, I ask Yagan a version of the same question I'd posed to other dating execs: "If dating through the Internet becomes more and more popular, and sites become more efficient, what do you think will happen to commitment when people discover how much easier it's become to find new relationships?"

"That's really a point about market liquidity," Yagan replies, "which I like."

His answer is technical but not surprising. Even though Yagan and his Harvard pals created one of the industry's top dating sites, he distances himself from the notion that they're relationship gurus. Yagan married his high school sweetheart. His OkCupid cofounders are also married. "We're a bunch of math guys," he told the *Boston Globe* in 2007. "We don't know anything about dating."

OkCupid wins four awards, including Best Dating Site—the iDate equivalent of a Best Picture Oscar. At the podium, Yagan thanks the conference organizers and bows to his industry colleagues. "What I like most about this business," he tells the crowd, "is that all of us here are committed to helping people find love."

CHAPTER ONE

Your Pleasure Is Our Business

THE BIRTH OF THE ORIGINAL SOCIAL NETWORK

It is clearly the most unusual entry on the resume of Judge Douglas H. Ginsburg, President Reagan's nominee for the Supreme Court.

According to a spokesman, Judge Ginsburg left college for more than a year in the mid-1960s and founded a nationwide computer-dating service known as Operation Match.

—**"Nominee Left College to be Matchmaker,"**
New York Times, **October 30, 1987**

Before he achieved notoriety for his crazy handlebar mustache and film criticism on the *Today* show, Gene Shalit was a journeyman culture reporter for *Look* magazine. A general-interest publication and a runner-up to *Life*, *Look* was trying to stay on top of the computing revolution when, in 1965, it spotted a good story coming out of Boston. Some industrious Harvard students were putting computers to novel use. *Look*'s editors dispatched Shalit, then twenty-nine years old, to investigate.

It was still several decades before Facebook and the phrase "social media" would come into vogue, but the earliest pioneers were still aware of the computer's social implications. In 1959, two Stanford engineering students who were known to throw epic parties, complete with home-brewed beer and nurses from the veterans' hospital in Menlo Park, designed a class project around using the IBM 650 to match up the people in their readymade mating pool: forty-nine men and forty-nine women. Jim Harvey and Phil Fialer called their project Happy Families Planning Services and wrote a questionnaire asking about age, height, weight, religion, hobbies, and personality traits. They programmed the IBM to measure differences in their respondents' answers. But the pool was small, making for some odd couples. Although the project received an A, and even produced one marriage, it never moved beyond the classroom.

In the early sixties, some colleges used computers to optimize the meeting potential at dances. In 1963, Ed Lewis, a psychology professor at Iowa State University, served as "personality consultant" in an initiative to match up one thousand students. Answers to a lengthy questionnaire were transferred onto punch cards and fed through an IBM. Short on females, the university had to bus in nursing students from Des Moines. The value, said Lewis, was simply pairing people up; the question of why they'd been matched was a good icebreaker. There was also scientific value. Iowa State professors squeezed in some research, and the results surprised them: Men tended to fall in love more quickly and less deliberately than women; men also reported feeling more romantic attraction and were more optimistic about the prospect of marriage. One or two happy couples emerged. *Time* published a story. *Life* planned a big spread for its November issue but had to scrap it to cover the JFK assassination.

Back then, computers occupied entire rooms and were prohibitively expensive, and therefore were owned mostly by universities and corporations. Harvard had owned computers since 1944. Weighing in at ten thousand pounds, the steel frame of the Harvard Mark I was fifty-one feet long and eight feet high. The machine used five hundred miles of wire with three million connections: 3,500 multipole relays with 35,000 contacts; 2,225 counters; 1,464 tenpole switches; and tiers of 72 adding machines. The Mark I's dizzying complexity tended to obscure its function. It could perform long computations automatically. Basically, it was a giant calculator.

Even while more companies, such as Xerox, entered the computing market, the potential of computers remained a matter of speculation in the sixties, making them a subject of sci-fi fantasy. In the fall of sixty-five, when *Look* sent Gene Shalit to Harvard, the film director Stanley Kubrick was starting work on what would become his most enduring film, *2001: A Space Odyssey*. The story starred a sentient computer named HAL 9000 and even featured a tabletlike device. As for the Internet, it was still in seed form. In sixty-three, a Defense Department employee named J. C. R. Licklider had sent a memo to the nation's top computer scientists ("Members and Affiliates of the Intergalactic Computer Network") in which he suggested it might be "interesting and important . . . to develop a capability for integrated network operation."

But how interesting or important was it? How different might this integrated network be from telephones or wireless transmissions?

Of course it was quite different. By merging these old technologies with a new search-and-discovery tool, the Internet would endow users with a degree of control and decision-making power unprecedented in the history of the communication and information industry. It was this idea of control that interested Gene Shalit. At the pre-Internet Harvard of sixty-five, the computer's human-augmenting effects were finally being revealed to the masses. Two rival companies, both student-run, were making money hand-over-fist by using what Shalit called the "Great God Computer" to help college students find dates.

The concept had taken root at Harvard earlier that year, when a junior math major named Jeff Tarr decided he was fed up with coming home alone from the same mixers with Radcliffe, the women's college across the way. Despite Tarr's towering stature in the math department, he was, at five feet seven inches, less than a heartthrob. Tarr's eureka moment, like that of so many innovators before and after him, reflected the desperation of a guy who couldn't get a date. That he could also make a fortune by expanding the mating pool from Wheaton to Wellesley, from Pembroke to Mount Holyoke, was an afterthought. His primary goal was meeting girls.

Tarr raised $1,250 in start-up capital, and recruited classmate

Vaughan Morrill. Tarr wrote a matching questionnaire that asked students to answer seventy-five questions about themselves and another seventy-five about their "ideal date," and passed it around. Feedback was good. Then the plan hit a snag: Tarr knew nothing about computers. He was just a math guy; computer science did not yet exist as a major. So he paid a friend one hundred dollars to program an IBM 1401 to match up the responses to the questionnaire. Tarr and Morrill distributed the questionnaire to Boston-area colleges. Students filled it out and returned it with a three-dollar subscription fee. Tarr then paid "punch-card ladies" to transfer the answers from each questionnaire onto Hollerith punch cards—similar to voting cards—which were then run through the 1401, which was a little smaller than a library bookcase and could be rented from an IBM susdidiary across town in Roxbury. Within days the student would receive a sprocket-fed computer printout with the names, phone numbers, addresses, colleges, and graduation years of six people. Tarr and Morrill gave their parent company a scientific-sounding name: Compatibility Research Inc. They called the dating service Operation Match.*

In March, just weeks before the official launch, a science editor and future Pulitzer Prize winner at the *Boston Globe* received a tip from his alma mater. Timothy Leland ('60) rushed over to Tarr's corporate headquarters—dorm room G-35, Winthrop House—where he was greeted by a sign on the door: YOUR BUSINESS IS OUR PLEASURE. YOUR PLEASURE IS OUR BUSINESS. Half naked and shaving when Leland barged in, Tarr improvised. Operation Match, he jested, had done a study on which kinds of women prefer which kinds of aftershaves.

"And?" Leland asked.

Tarr explained that Old Spice attracts the All-American ladies, while Royall Lime gets the preppy types. Fascinated, Leland jotted this down and put it in the *Globe* article, the first in-depth piece ever produced on the computer-dating industry, which ran under the front-page headline, "2 Harvard Men Replacing Cupid With Computer." The breathless Leland wrote that Tarr was "masterminding the cleverest business enter-

---

* No relation to today's Match.com.

prise since J.D. Rockefeller invested in oil." The computer, Leland explained, would "analyze all the personality profiles and match the couples up scientifically in less time than it takes to blow a kiss."

"A computer," Tarr told Leland, "can find the right date for a person in a split second, when it might take him or her three years to do it alone." Leland wanted to know if Tarr planned to run his own questionnaire through the computer. "Darn right I do," said Tarr. "Two or three times at least. That's the beauty of being a company president."

The idea, to use modern parlance, went viral. Tarr had tapped into a vein of loneliness and frustration at single-sex schools in the Northeast, and beyond. Operation Match hit colleges across the country.

"This is the greatest excuse for calling up a strange girl that I've ever heard," wrote a computer dater from Williams in a letter to the company.

"No dogs please!" wrote another from Dartmouth.

"The girl you sent me didn't have much upstairs," wrote a third, from Northwestern, "but what a staircase!"

A female computer dater from Connecticut College suspected "that boys don't level" on their questionnaires. "I was honest with mine," she told Shalit, "but I wonder if some guys fill out theirs to see if they can get a first-nighter."

By the fall of sixty-five, six months after the launch, some ninety thousand Operation Match questionnaires had been received, amounting to $270,000 in gross profits, about $1.8 million in today's dollars. Not bad for a scholarship student from small-town Maine. Tarr would need a bigger staff. He pulled in another classmate, a chemistry major named David Crump. Then, walking through Cambridge one day, Tarr struck up a conversation with a dropout from Cornell University named Douglas Ginsburg. A pot-smoking free spirit looking for a cause, Ginsburg was not yet on his way to becoming a Harvard Law School professor and Supreme Court nominee. "A computer-dating service?" laughed Ginsburg, whose friends called him Fug. He signed on right away.

Profits aside, Gene Shalit wanted to know the same thing as the rest of the world: Did it work? Did the computer really make good matches? Was Operation Match a gift from the Great God or mere technogimmickry? "I approve of it as a way to meet people," said an Operation Match subscriber from Yale, "although I have no faith in the questionnaire's ability to match compatible people. The machine has no way of telling whether or not the girl has pizzazz!" By pizzazz, the student referred to that mysterious aspect of romantic connection, chemistry. How could such an elusive quality be quantified and commercialized?

Tarr made no claims. "We're not trying to take the love out of love," he told Shalit, "we're just trying to make it more efficient. We supply everything but the spark." It was an honest response, one rarely heard from today's online-dating companies, which like to differentiate their brands based on scientifically groundbreaking algorithms.

Operation Match might get ten thousand questionnaires returned from any given geographical area. Tarr and his partners would then do a series of "sorts"—sorting the questionnaires, for instance, according to age, then height, then religion, etc. After five or six sorts, the pools would become too small to further differentiate. The vast majority of the 150 questions never came into play. Computer dating was about *more* dates, not better dates.

Harvard being Harvard—a place where students have historically evaded traditional career paths by creating their own jobs—it didn't take long before Operation Match met its first competitor. In the summer of sixty-five, an MIT graduate named David Dewan was preparing to enter Harvard Business School. Having followed the success of Operation Match as it was chronicled in the pages of the *Harvard Crimson*, Dewan thought he could steal some market share.

Over the summer he drafted his own dating questionnaire and taught himself how to write matching code for the Honeywell 200, a car-sized contraption that, at around three o'clock in the morning, could be rented for thirty dollars an hour from a small Boston-based mutual fund company called Fidelity.

Unlike Tarr, whose main interest in computer dating was as a means of self-help, Dewan came to the business with a seriousness that Harvard people associate with their more buttoned-up geek rivals at MIT. Dewan played the part: A rich kid who wore Brooks Brothers and drove a Jaguar, he borrowed ten thousand dollars from his grandfather to start his own computer-dating service. He called the service Eros and its parent company Contact Inc.

Shalit called Dewan "a brilliant math and engineering student" and "a frugal man" who "runs deep in the black." With no full-time employees, Dewan operated Contact out of his grandparents' home near Cambridge. In one distribution of questionnaires, he drew eleven thousand responses at $4 each, or $44,000 in gross profits, about $250,000 in today's dollars.

Dewan entered the fledgling market with guns blazing, telling the *Crimson* that Operation Match's questionnaire was "less sophisticated, appealing to the big, Mid-west universities." In truth, very little distinguished Contact from Operation Match. Operation Match sold its questionnaires for three dollars while Contact charged four dollars. The questions reflected the politics and preoccupations of the era. Both offered three options for race: Caucasian, Oriental, or Negro. Contact's questionnaire was more straight-laced, seeking daters' opinions on whether civil rights laws should be strengthened, whether censorship of students is justifiable, and, prophetically, whether the computer is invading too many aspects of personal life. Dewan asked daters to correlate qualities in themselves with the qualities they desired in a date, such as sociability (friendly versus reserved), conformity (conventional versus eccentric), role in the group (center of attention versus spectator), and sexual history (limited versus experienced).

Operation Match took a more playful approach with its questionnaire. Question 69 posed this dilemma:

Your roommate gets you a blind date for a big dance. Good looking, your roommate says. When you meet your date, you are sure it's your roommate who is blind—your date is friendly, but embarrassingly unattractive. You:

1) suggest going to a movie instead.
2) monopolize your roommate's date, leaving your roommate only one noble alternative . . .

3) dance with your date, smiling weakly, but end the evening as early
   as possible.
4) act very friendly the whole time and run the risk of getting
   trapped into a second date.

"If there's some chick I'm dying to go out with," Tarr told Shalit, "I can drop her a note in my capacity as president of Operation Match and say, 'Dear Joan, You have been selected by a highly personal process called Random Sampling to be interviewed extensively by myself . . .'"

Tarr may have been a jokester, but he wasn't going to stand by while Dewan cornered the industry that he had pioneered. In retaliation for Dewan's trash-talking to the *Crimson*, Operation Match alerted authorities that Dewan intended to paper Harvard Yard with questionnaires for Contact. Things got ugly, fast. On September 29, 1965, campus police collared Dewan for the dubious crime of "distributing questionnaires without a permit." The next day the *Crimson* splashed the news across its front page: "University Police Eject Man from Winthrop House."

"Funny," an Operation Match employee later recalled. "The last I heard you didn't need a permit to distribute questionnaires in a dorm. I think our guys were messing with Dewan."

Dewan's enthusiasm was unmarred. "The way I envision things, in 50 years computers may well have reduced our work week to zero hours," he told the *Sarasota Journal*. "We'll date through computers, mate through computers, select our home with the help of computers, and plan our recreation with computers. It will be a fantastic time and my company and I hope to be a large part of it."

Going back to the Newtonians, Dewan's exuberance echoed earlier eras of intellectuals and scientists who believed man's innovations would liberate him from pain and drudgery. Today we can laugh about the zero-hour workweek Dewan predicted. What an idealization to think the machine would supplant the workaholic in us rather than accentuate him! But even while Dewan turned out to be a visionary (everything else he predicted came true, after all), his first taste of utopia was bittersweet.

"Back then I was going out with a girl from Wellesley," he recalled four decades later. "I gave her a free questionnaire, because she helped me distribute in the dorms there. When we ran it through the computer, she and I matched. That was exciting! But I forgot that she also received five other matches, including a guy from Amherst, whom she later dumped me for."

Somewhere in there lurked a lesson about the relationship between technology and the people who use it. Did the machines remain ours to control? Or did they control us?

Meanwhile, on campus, a political science major named Gerry coasted through his last months in Cambridge, pondering his own relationship future. Gerry kept himself busy with bartending jobs, membership in the Hasty Pudding Club, and a term paper about the psychology of speech impediments. Gerry stuttered. He'd come to Harvard via boarding school, where he was mocked savagely for the way he spoke. Despite good looks and charisma, he was, by his own admission, a late bloomer when it came to girls. He tended to seek out self-esteem and identity through friendships with professors.

So when David Dewan swung by Adams House with questionnaires for Contact, Gerry carefully answered all one hundred questions. Accuracy of self-assessment varied. Gerry ranked himself as assertive and said he was looking for someone who was more submissive. He said he was uninhibited and wanted someone more restrained. He preferred security, as opposed to risk taking, and was looking for the same. He was sexually experienced and wanted his date to be similarly experienced. He thought of himself as particularly perceptive, considered himself highly self-confident, and said he appreciated "the aesthetic experience." When asked about verbal fluency, the inveterate reader marked himself inarticulate. He returned the Contact questionnaire with the four-dollar subscription fee.

On Halloween, Gerry received a computer printout in the mail: "Dear Gerry," it began, "My name is Eros. I'm the Contact computer. In the last minute I have introduced you to 4,122 people. Here is your first group of computer matched dates." The list included six Boston-area coeds: Mimi of Wheaton; Ellen of Simmons; Pamela of Wellesley; Romana of Pembroke; Hinda of Boston University; and finally—just for good measure, it seemed, given the distance—Nancy, a nineteen-year-old English major at Mount Holyoke, an all-women's school located ninety miles west of Boston.

Gerry went out with Pamela and Hinda because they were nearby. Both dates were unimpressive.

He set his Contact sheet aside and returned to his studies. In December, as final exams approached, he received a one-line postcard from the sixth girl on his Contact sheet. "Dear Gerry," she wrote, "Do you exist?"

Intrigued, Gerry poured himself two fingers of Prunier, a hard-to-get cognac he enjoyed, and sat down to compose a response.

Dear Nancy:

First let me say that I think it was ingenious of you to write post-cards to the negligent boys on your Contact list. I confess that because Mt. Holyoke is so far away, I probably would not have pursued your name. However, your postcard really impressed me. Either you are a very inventive, outgoing girl, or the social life in South Hadley is horrible. Whichever it is, I will look forward to meeting you.

Ten days later, a reply:

Dear Sir Gerald:

How are you so sure you weren't the only guy privileged with receiving a post card? As a matter of fact, you're right. I sent them to everyone, except for 3 names that had already "come to life." "Flop" is a good word for two of them. The other was successful enough, but nothing special. "Contact" seems to have been pretty much a failure for everyone—except for one girl in my dorm who is now pinned, thanks to Eros.

After weeks of correspondence, Gerry drove to Mount Holyoke for a Saturday date. Nancy wrote to him the day after: "I did have a very nice day—and want you to know that I appreciate very much your having driven ¾ of the way across the state and back again! Thanks for showing me around my home town area. Hope you didn't find it all unbearably bucolic."

If he did, the correspondence didn't say. But he enjoyed himself enough to return the invitation, responding that when Nancy visited him in Cambridge, she should be prepared to do "some horseback riding very early on Sunday morning." Pulling out all the stops, he added: "I usually follow that up with bagels and lox in some Jewish restaurant."

Sure, people debated whether Operation Match and Contact worked, whether the chance of meeting someone you liked "via the punch cards" was any better than trolling at a mixer. On campus there was little embarrassment or shame. Odd, given that thirty years later online dating would encounter a strong stigma; to "date online" suggested an inability to meet people in real life. But in the sixties, when Jeff Tarr and David Dewan brought the first incarnations of computer dating to college kids, stigma didn't surround the medium as it later would.

For one thing, a celebrated singles culture was emerging outside Harvard's walls. In urban areas across the country, the energetic young were spending disposable income in "singles bars." Maxwell's Plum, on Manhattan's Upper East Side, was one of the first bars that "respectable" single women could visit alone. (Dorrian's Red Hand, more familiar to today's UES singles, opened in 1960.)* City papers announced upcoming singles events. The *New York Review of Books*, known for its highbrow readers, began its famous personals column in 1965. Developers con-

---

* Project TACT—an acronym for Technical Automated Compatibility Testing—was New York City's first computer dating service. TACT's founders, a young accountant and a programmer from IBM, got their inspiration from Tarr, figuring that the Upper East Side would be a good testing ground: "The demolition of the Third Avenue Elevated subway line set off a building boom and a white-collar influx, most notably of young educated women who suddenly found themselves free of family, opprobrium, and, thanks to birth control, the problem of sexual consequence," Nick Paumgarten later wrote in *The New Yorker*. "Within a year, more than five thousand subscribers had signed on."

structed youth-oriented apartment complexes. Guidebooks helped the unattached navigate the scene.

In some ways this world of urban nightlife and go-go courtship resembled the post–World War I era, when young people took to cars and movie theaters and other commercial amusements. The Roaring Twenties and the Freewheeling Sixties shared an enthusiasm over new technology. Again, though, a taboo greeted one but not the other. The youth of the 1920s "had elicited pity, scorn or fear from the middle class who sought to control their behavior and made them the object of reformation efforts," wrote John D'Emilio and Estelle Freedman in *Intimate Matters: A History of Sexuality in America*. By contrast, in the 1960s "young adults of the middle-class were glamorized; they embodied the unspoken fantasies of a consumer society extended to the sphere of sex."

Rebelling against their parents' suburban sprawl and soulless conformity, youth of the sixties saw staying single as an exciting adventure for those up to the challenge. The new singles culture, said one commentator, was regarded as a "privileged, spotlighted, envied group."

As for computer dating, it's possible that whatever stigma existed at the time was outweighed by the medium's novelty, a coolness factor that comes with being in the know about new gadgetry, particularly for a generation that was reveling in the first film adaptations of Ian Fleming's James Bond series, featuring colorfully blinking walls and programmable computer boards, as well as a dashing Sean Connery carousing his way through a world of killer fountain pens and sports cars with ejector seats, not to mention an endless stream of beautiful women.

"I wanted people to see Operation Match as a novelty," Jeff Tarr remembered, "something neat. I advertised it as a social experiment."

Certainly it was a social experiment. But finding dates via the punch cards was a much different proposition than today's online dating. The pool to which computer dating provided access had known limits: college students in your area. So what if a guy from Harvard was driving ninety miles to date a girl from Mount Holyoke? How much different might she really be from the Radcliffe chick across the Yard? Yes, computer dating brought a new efficiency to the college mating scene. But it merely extended the connections within an already cloistered world. It was not too surprising, then, when early correspondence between the budding lovers revealed that Gerry knew Nancy's brothers from summer camp.

Their relationship progressed into the summer of 1966, with vigorous correspondence between Europe, where Gerry was taking a graduation trip, and the Rocky Mountains, where Nancy spent the summer vacationing with her family. She wrote of her "cumberless rovings" in the woods and of her thoughts on books she was reading, such as *Love Without Fear*, a 1947 marriage guide by Dr. Eustace Chesser, billed as "one of England's most reputable marriage counselors" and "the foremost authority on sex technique."

From Goose Prairie, Washington, Nancy reported on a special guest: "William Douglas, the Supreme Court Justice, came for dinner last night with his new wife—#4, age 23. I'd always expected a Supreme Court Justice to be a very imposing person, but he's not. He's just an ordinary, nervous individual—especially when I spoke to him. He knows people are thinking about his marrying a girl 1/3 his age."

Despite her precocious acuity, the twenty-year-old Nancy did not know that her dinner guest was, in both his private and public lives, a crusader for the liberalization of relationship politics in America, not unlike Nancy was, albeit unwittingly, when she decided to write to the negligent boys on her Contact list. In June of sixty-five, two months after Jeff Tarr opened for business, the Supreme Court handed down one of its most progressive decisions. In *Griswold v. Connecticut*, the sixty-six-year-old Justice Douglas reasoned that even though "privacy" is mentioned nowhere in the Bill of Rights, a "right to privacy" could be divined in the "penumbras" and "emanations" of other constitutional protections. The holding in *Griswold*, which struck down Connecticut's ban on contraception, established a right to marital privacy. While state laws against sodomy and abortion remained on the books, the Court's decision in *Griswold* sent a strong message to state legislatures: Mating decisions are sacrosanct. Two years later, in *Loving v. Virginia*, a unanimous Court struck down Virginia's antimiscegenation statute, the Racial Integrity Act of 1924, ending race-based legal restrictions on marriage. In 1972 the Court expanded *Griswold*'s holding to unmarried couples; that case, *Eisenstadt v. Baird*, established a more fundamental right to control reproduction and laid groundwork for the Court's landmark abortion decision in *Roe v. Wade* the following year.

For a culture whose courtship practices were undergoing rapid liberalization, these Supreme Court rulings can be seen as a response to, an accommodation of, or just the obvious result of recent developments in American mating. In the 1950s, the crude competition of dating's early years—when men showed off their assets and expressed their interest in terms of resource expenditure, while women worked hard to cultivate an aura of popularity—was giving way to the postwar generation's desire for security in an uncertain world. This desire for security transformed dating into the custom of "going steady." Many young people, by going steady, did not expect to marry but to act as if they were already married: The boy gave the girl some visible token (class ring, letter sweater, etc.); he had to call her a certain number of times per week and take her on a certain number of dates; and exclusivity was assumed. Under the new going-steady complex, a "beleaguered system of sexual control based on the resolve of young girls to say no, at least to the final step of actual intercourse, was further breaking down," writes Beth Bailey in *From Front Porch to Back Seat: Courtship in Twentieth-Century America*.

The old dating system versus the new going-steady complex: both located power in the control of the scarce resource—access to sex. "Through at least the first two-thirds of the twentieth century," writes Bailey, "Americans thought of courtship as a system governed by laws of scarcity and abundance, and acted in accordance with that perception." Regardless of which courting system reigned at a given time, *scarcity* would always be the natural social control reinforcing the system du jour. Scarcity would always be the irrefragable regulatory device that—along with religion and moral dogma—would keep the youth in line with certain expectations, forestalling the doomsday scenario of a society run amok in the pursuit of unchecked desire.

But wait. Suppose some Harvard math whiz came along with an idea to harness technology in a way that was so big, so fresh, that it could change the game entirely? Not by solving some riddle of scarcity, but by smashing the whole concept of scarcity to pieces, eradicating its relevancy altogether. Why settle for the smug and entitled Cliffies, asked the height-challenged Jeff Tarr, when I can meet every girl at every school?

Like the *Griswold* case, the revolutionary technology that brought Nancy and Gerry together was a portent, if not a precursor, to what would become the sexual revolution of the late 1960s and 1970s. And yet, in the narrative of that sexual revolution, from the Pill to *Playboy* magazine to the North American Swingers Club to the countercultural battle cry of "free love," computer dating never became a character. This is probably because the technology faded out before it could spread past college campuses. There was no Internet to optimize matching or let users search for themselves, discreetly.

When Gene Shalit left Harvard to write his article, Tarr planned to install hundreds of "special typewriters" around campus, all linked to "a centralized mother computer." A boy typing in his requirements would receive in seconds the name of a compatible girl who was free that night. The project never panned out, but the computer dating pioneered by Tarr and Dewan was still a major first step in applying a new tool and a new way of thinking to the mating dance, what Justice William Brennan termed the "great and mysterious motive force in human life."

As for Nancy and Gerry, they would marry in 1967. Medical careers would take them from Boston to Syracuse to Denver to Minneapolis, where, in 1977, they would become your correspondent's parents, just as their marriage was careering toward divorce.

The story of how my parents met seems quaint when one compares those clunky old IBMs to the complex algorithms, flashy Web sites, and smart-phone applications employed by dating services today. But it shows that the subject of how technology affects relationships is hardly new.

In the 1920s, Judge Ben Lindsey sat on Denver's Juvenile and Family Court, where he witnessed, firsthand, the chaos of the technologically driven sexual revolution. Judge Lindsey held heart-to-heart meetings with the youngsters who came through his court, during which he gathered stats on teen pregnancy and how teenagers were mating. He condemned adults for their silence in the face of youthful questioning.

Judge Lindsey came to believe that certain modern conveniences had changed mating practices so quickly that Jazz Age youth were left in a kind of cultural lurch: The rules and values they'd been raised with no longer applied. While Lindsey knew that young people had been rebellious in plenty of earlier eras, he argued that Jazz Age youth were different. The youth of past generations didn't have the same economic independence. "Now," he wrote, "it has it. Machinery has made that possible." The "agencies of modern life" to which Lindsey referred in his 1925 book, *The Revolt of Modern Youth*, were ubiquitous:

> Those that immediately present themselves are the automobile (and soon the aeroplane with the kids spooning in the clouds), the telephone, the motion picture, the radio, the jazz dance, jazz music, jazz booze, jazz journalism, "crime wave," the permanent wave, the permanent passing of the chaperone, the parking of the corset, the feminine invasion of the barber shop, growing and changing standards of living, rising wages ... electrical appliances that make women something more than drudges in their homes. . . . The list, you see, includes among other things physical comforts and speeding-up devices of all kinds; and the effect of it all is enormously stimulating.

The social upheaval that Lindsey described began in the early twentieth century, around the time of World War I, when courtship shifted from the privacy of the home to the public sphere of dance halls, movie theaters, and automobiles, giving young people more control over their dating lives and access to a wider social circle. Sound familiar?

Before dating there had been "calling," a system taken from the English upper class, in which a gentleman would visit a woman at her home in the presence of her family. Tea, cakes, doilies, a meddling aunt perched on the couch's arm—these things made a proper setting for the negotiation of love. Calling, by controlling access to a scarce resource, placed control over mating and sexual limits in the hands of women and their families. The idea was that women, through their special virtue, helped men reconcile morality (a devotion to family) with instinct (the sexual urge), while the change a man brought to her life was more tangible, a material rather than spiritual alteration.

The rise of "dating" coincided with the advent of the automobile and the rise of cinema. Unlike the carriage that preceded it, the motorcar had speed, which meant *exploration! adventure! excitement!* Henry Ford and his ilk believed they were marketing something to bring the family together. The car may have achieved that. But it also released youth from the tyranny of parental oversight. Forget tea parties and hay rides. Now every date was a bedroom on wheels. In 1919 the country had seven million registered cars; ten years later that number would have more than tripled. Some cars had front seats that folded back to blend with the backseats. For those who couldn't afford a car with a backseat (the Model T sold for $290, $3,300 in today's money), there was always the back row. Though many in the upper class continued to regard movies—"flickers"—as morally repugnant, working-class society, less restrained by rigid sexual mores, found privacy and romance in the darkness of the cinema. "Oh, oh, that picture show spoon," went a popular jingle, "that's what put kissing on the boon." Marathon sessions of "necking," "heavy petting," and close dancing known as "button shining" replaced the buttoned-up courtship of old. These technologies marginalized old controls by providing islands of privacy to lovers who were suddenly flung out into the public realm, free at last to remake the rules.

But more freedom meant greater uncertainty in courtship, and thus more confusion. When a man came to visit a woman in her family's home, the agenda was clear: an interview couched in a chaperoned social call. But . . . a *date*? What was that about? A date was supposed to end in . . . *something*, yes. But what exactly was the date itself? And more important, what did it imply? Radcliffe College's *Red Book*, which furnished girls with the school's rules of conduct, printed a list of approved restaurants in which they could dine with a young man. Some were acceptable only before 7:30 P.M.; others posed a threat to reputation. The etiquette expert Emily Post wondered why, even though "she may not lunch with him in a restaurant, she is sometimes (not always) allowed to go to a moving picture matinee with him! Why sitting in the dark in a moving picture theater is allowed, and the restaurant is tabu is very mysterious." Miss Manners threw up her arms.

"With the old order of things," wrote Frederick Lewis Allen, a historian of the 1920s, "had gone a set of values which had given richness and meaning to life, and substitute values were not easily found."

For most of the nineteenth century, couples tended to encourage openness with each other, as seen in the letters that flew back and forth prior to the age of the telephone and other innovations, such as the bicycle, that provided connection and proximity. In place of premarital petting, the sharing of confidences defined intimacy. In 1926, *Harper's* magazine reported that, until 1913, "the rule for young couples was conversation in pairs about serious things. There weren't many cars, most movies were not approved of. . . . Couples would spend hours discussing each other." While close dancing and the picture show spoon meant more "contact," emotional openness suffered.

With the birth of broadcast radio and mass advertising in the 1920s, conformity became the new value. "A growing emphasis on personality and physical attractiveness made self-exposure a risky proposition," writes courtship historian Ellen Rothman. To catch a mate you needed to know the right fads, have the right *line*.

Never had standards for behavior undergone such radical change in such a short period of time. The youth that came of age in the 1920s, writes Rothman, "were separated from their parents by as wide a gulf" as had ever separated two American generations. "By 1930, the terrain through which young Americans passed en route to marriage would be almost unrecognizable to their parents." The new code was accompanied by a disillusionment that no amount of fast driving could outrun. Values are primal in their hardwiring. It's difficult to substitute one for another without causing distress. Now, thanks to the widespread acceptance of contraception and a more liberal attitude toward premarital sex, young people faced a new reality: Sex could be divorced from child-bearing. So what was marriage for? Did good sex make for good marriage?

People may have reveled in the new freedom, but that didn't mean they were happy. The trending divorce rate of today began in this post-war decade: In 1910 there were 8.8 divorces for every 100 marriages; by 1928, the rate had doubled—to almost one divorce in every six marriages.

What distinguished the post–World War I generation, wrote journalist Walter Lippmann, was not its rebellion but rather its disillusionment with its rebellion. That "they should distrust the new freedom no less than the old certainties" was "something of a novelty," Lippmann wrote in his 1929 bestseller, *A Preface to Morals*. The wild success of Lippmann's book, which tried to lay the foundation for a new system of belief, suggested that people were tired of tobogganing into mental chaos. "The inexperienced," Lippmann wrote, "must be offered some kind of hypothesis when they are confronted with the necessity of making choices: they cannot be so utterly open-minded that they stand inert until something collides with them."

Lippmann would die in 1974, two decades before the Internet went mainstream. As the pace of technology quickened, his words would gain in resonance for generations to come.

ALEXIS, PART I

$\downarrow$

It's Hard Meeting Men in the City

IT WAS THE SUMMER OF 2005, DURING COLLEGE, WHEN ALEXIS FELL hard for a guy. They had great, memorable dates for several weeks. Then it came out that he had a serious girlfriend who was out of town. "At this point," she remembered, "I was in too deep and stupidly forgave him. He swore to me that he would come clean to her. He did. But she flew home the next day, and he left me for her anyway. Good times."

After college in Colorado, Alexis moved to New York City to attend Parsons, the prestigious fashion and design institute. She'd loved the laid-back vibe of mountain life. But, like her hometown of Chicago, it was too clean, too banal. As an artist, she much preferred the grime and grit of her new Lower East Side neighborhood, where she became addicted to falafel, the Mister Softee ice cream truck, and deli sandwiches with fried eggs and cream cheese. She hummed Lou Reed's "Rock n' Roll," pretending she was the Jenny he sang about, who one fine morning put on a New York station and couldn't believe what she heard at all.

With wit, freckles, a fun sense of humor, and a body toned by frequent yoga, Alexis was confident in her appearance and only a little self-conscious about her jowly cheeks. Men were attracted to her, she knew. She just needed to learn how to avoid the bad ones. But sometimes Alexis got lonely. So she spent time on social-networking sites, where any decent-looking woman could get the attention of at least a dozen guys. "The attention," she said, "revives me."

"I'm twenty-four," she would remind herself when feeling down, "and I'm awesome."

Shortly after moving to New York Alexis began dating Chad, a law student she met at a party. Her father is an attorney. So Chad felt right. He lived across the river in Brooklyn Heights and had a big trust fund. She'd always dreamed of living in a nice house in Kentucky, where she has relatives, and she could see it happening with this guy. They both loved the jam band Phish—an important glue in their relationship—and even though he still had an ex-girlfriend in the picture, when Alexis forced him to choose between them, he chose Alexis.

There was some weirdness, though. He became angry when Alexis wore revealing clothes, such as a tank top with low-cut armholes that showed her bra. "My professors live around here," he would scold her. "Keep that outfit in the Lower East Side!"

"What does he expect?" she thought. "I'm a fashion student."

They also did a lot of drugs, a habit she'd hoped to leave behind in college, when she'd struggled through a relationship with a recovering heroin addict. For her twenty-fourth birthday, Chad took Alexis to a sex shop in Soho called Kiki de Montparnasse, and told her to pick out anything she wanted from among the haute couture whips, leather pony harnesses, and headbands with horse ears. Intimidated, Alexis chose a tamer offering, the Mia vibrator by Lelo, a lipstick-sized travel companion that recharges in any USB port. Then they checked into a fancy hotel, where, on a table, he traced their names, "Chad + Alexis," through a pile of cocaine.

Eventually Chad's insecurity and fawning turned her off, and she left him, feeling a little bad about having been so attracted to his money in the first place. Soon after she began seeing a forty-year-old man she met on a social-networking site for music. He lived just a few blocks away and helped her get an internship at a music label. He was urbane and mature, and this turned her on despite his inconsistent nature. She would wait anxiously in her apartment for his text messages before realizing that, to him, she was nothing more than a plaything. She knew she needed to set boundaries but found it difficult.

"It's hard to meet people in the city," Alexis said. "It seems to be one disaster after the next. They're fine hanging out, talking all the time, and of course fucking. But the second they smell you actually caring about them, they bounce. The ones who are crazy about me, I'm not into. The ones I'd do anything for don't care."

Alexis always thought of online dating as a place for desperate people—until a friend of hers had success on Match.com. For months the friend enjoyed a couple of dinners out a week, with a bunch of different men, and then got engaged to a nice guy. Maybe, Alexis thought, she should give it a shot.

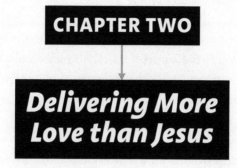

CHAPTER TWO

Delivering More Love than Jesus

HOW ONLINE DATING BECAME MODERN

We are the most important search engine on the Web, not Google. The search for companionship is more important than the search for song lyrics.

—Sam Yagan, chief executive officer, OkCupid

As a youngster in Skokie, Illinois, during the late 1970s, Gary Kremen's future did not seem bright. Half geek, half hoodlum, he recalls getting into the "usual juvenile stuff"—busting windows, breaking into schools, and computer hacking. With his parents' blessing, the police picked Kremen up one day and showed him the inside of a jail cell.

Short, heavyset, and socially awkward, Kremen was accustomed to losing many of life's contests. Making money, he knew, was the one metric on which he might be able to compete, but not if he was locked up.

Although Kremen's high school grades were less than stellar, he managed to talk his way into Northwestern University in an interview by touting his entrepreneurial zeal and technological skills. In 1981, he began a double major in business and electrical engineering. At graduation he turned down several offers from corporate recruiters in favor of a job with a government aerospace contractor, where he was introduced to ARPANET—the Advanced Research Projects Agency Network—the U.S. Defense Department's online network, which eventually became the Internet.

Kremen went on to pick up an MBA from Stanford, and then became one of the Internet's first entrepreneurs. His roommate worked for Sun Microsystems and had a high-speed Internet connection. At night they would download Unix software for free, repackage it, and then sell it. Kremen led the company, Los Altos Technology, until investors replaced him with a new CEO in 1993.

Weeks later, he was taking a shower when the idea struck him: What if I put classified ads online?

Kremen took a $2,500 advance on his credit card and acquired several domain names from the government: Jobs.com, Housing.com, Autos.com, Sex.com, and a fifth domain name that was less literal than the others, Match.com. Match, according to Kremen's vision, would be the personals "vertical" in a larger entity called Electric Classifieds.

"I thought it would be really interesting to use the Internet for relationships, and to do it right," he told *Wired* magazine at the time. The tone of the *Wired* story gives a sense of how Kremen's plan was received: "Cyberlove and chat room couplings are as much a part of online lore as hacker fiends and wild viruses. So, connecting and tracking these millions of plugged-in lonely hearts is a prime business opportunity." Even at a tech magazine, online dating was fodder for derision. But Kremen didn't care. He bought a $750,000 server on credit from Sun Microsystems and, with $1.7 million in venture capital financing, unveiled Match in 1995.

The idea, like Jeff Tarr's idea for Operation Match, was not completely original. Both Tarr and Kremen were second-comers who did it better and with more propitious timing.

Over in France, in the 1980s, Marc Simoncini, who would eventually run Meetic.com, Europe's largest online-dating site, got his start in the computer matching business by hosting services, known as *messageries roses*, or pink chat rooms. These were essentially dating chat rooms, made possible by the Minitel, a text-only computer that hooked into the phone and connected 90 percent of French homes.

The Minitel chat rooms had a precursor in the United States: bulletin board systems, or BBSs, which comprised the online world before the online world went mainstream. The BBS revolution began during Chicago's Great Blizzard of 1978, when Ward Christensen was shut in by the snow. Bored, Christensen, a computer hobbyist and former IBM employee, decided to invent a way to digitize his computer club's message board, a pushpin board on which members posted three-by-five-inch cards with things like "Need ride to next meeting," "Let's get together for a group-purchase of memory chips," "Anyone else have a KIM-1?"

Christensen's creation became the world's first bulletin board system. Early BBSs would be used by clubs and communities to stay in touch and share information. Users needed a computer—such as an IBM XT, an Apple II, a Commodore 64, or Radio Shack's TRS 100—plus a software package; a modem; and a phone line. You accessed a BBS by dialing into the phone number allocated to it. Each BBS was run by a person known as the system operator, or sysop, who was usually the creator of the BBS. It was his phone number that users dialed into.

Nearly everything on BBSs was presented in text, called ASCII, or rendered in low-resolution images called ANSI art. Some BBSs experimented with high-resolution formats, such as remote imaging protocol. Unlike the Web pages of today, BBSs operated as individual systems: They did not converge or connect; information contained on one BBS was not shared with another. The original 110- and 300-baud modems made the first BBSs painfully slow. With the introduction of 1200-baud modems, speed improved dramatically, and so did the popularity of BBSs. The BBS universe would grow to more than sixty thousand boards during the eighties. Geeks could finally unite online. It was their moment. The movie *Weird Science*, a 1985 sci-fi comedy written and directed by John Hughes, portrayed two young geeks who, inspired by the story of Frankenstein, used a computer to create the woman of their dreams by turning on a modem and feeding magazine photographs into a scanner, literally dialing her up.

These movie geeks were close contemporaries of Jon Boede and Scott Smith, two young computer whizzes in Texas. In 1984, Boede and Smith launched the Matchmaker Electronic Pen-Pal Network, known simply as Matchmaker, the first online social network geared toward romance. "We had some awful press coverage," Boede told Andrea Orr for her book about the early years of online dating. "The editors would always turn the story into something like, 'Computer Nerds Need Love Too.' But it was clear to us that we were on to something." In eighty-five, Boede met his girlfriend online.

The Matchmaker network grew into a nationwide chain of fourteen local BBSs spread throughout Texas, California, Florida, Arizona, New York, Illinois, and Virginia. But Boede remained national network administrator, or master sysop. "We call him God," said twenty-seven-year-old Bobby Dominguez. "He's the guy who created it all." Dominguez ran Matchmaker's local BBS for Tampa, Florida. Nonmembers could browse free of charge for three and a half hours. After that, he charged fifty dollars for one hundred hours. Users chose "platonic" or "romantic" mode. A woman whose data showed she was only interested in pen pals would not be introduced to men seeking romance.

In 1992, as BBSs were waning, the *Tampa Bay Times* covered Dominguez's Matchmaker franchise. The paper foreshadowed the imminent demise of BBSs when it noted, at the end of the article, that "Matchmaker also offers a link to the Internet, a worldwide system." Users could soon log in through Matchmaker.com. In a couple of years, when the Internet—along with its most popular application, the World Wide Web—went mainstream, the world of BBSs would try to keep up by becoming more visually appealing. But they could do nothing to offset the appeal of the Web, and eventually faded out.

BBS inventor Ward Christensen saw the usurpation as a good thing. BBS users, he would later say, had been "more elitist, more computer people." Even though early Internet communities seemed to lack the vibrant social energy that had characterized the best BBSs, the Internet meant greater utility, efficiency, and access. Not just for geeks but for everyone.

For online dating, however, the battle was just beginning.

Once computer dating left Harvard in the late 1960s and began to be marketed to the general public, the notion that only the desperate or the criminal would turn to such a scandalous and seemingly scattershot method finally caught up with it. It was one thing for college kids to find each other through a computer-matching system. Quite another for the population at large.

In the early seventies, James Schur, a former advertising executive in Boston, ran a computer-dating company called Phase II. Schur was scheduled to appear on Johnny Carson's *Tonight Show*. But the invitation was rescinded at the eleventh hour when NBC executives became concerned that advertisers would flee.

Even the era's literature reflected societal suspicion. In 1971, an upstart author named Don DeLillo referenced computer dating in his debut novel, *Americana*. The book's opening scene contains a hostile exchange between the protagonist, a philandering television executive named David Bell, and a young woman named Pru.

"Quincy tells me you've got a new boyfriend," David says to Pru. "Quincy tells me you met him through a computer dating system."

Pru replies: "That lying bastard."*

Dating services had a reputation for drawing losers, Phase II's Schur conceded. He also pointed out that there are "losers everywhere."

That's not to say the fledgling industry wasn't producing happy couples. DataMate, a service that cropped up at MIT in 1968, brought together Lawrence Krakauer, a grad student in engineering, with Margret Berman. Forty-five years later, they're still married. "Despite the detailed questionnaire," Krakauer said, "Margret always thought we were matched because we were both short, educated, and Jewish. But, hey, it worked."

Others were less pleased. *Dear Dating Computer*, a book published

---

* I wrote to DeLillo to ask him where, in the late sixties, he'd heard of computer dating. The author replied, somewhat mystified: "I can only speculate that I heard about such a service from someone I knew. Certainly I had no firsthand experience in the matter, and until I saw your letter I would never have guessed that computer dating had somehow sneaked into the novel." There's a decent chance that DeLillo, who in 1964 left his advertising job at Ogilvy & Mather to become a writer, heard of such a service through reports or gossip concerning TACT, New York City's first computer-dating service.

in 1968, compiled letters sent to computer-dating services around the country. The book divided the letters into two sections: The Requirements ("I have studied your questionnaire and frankly I would be most compatible with someone who hates his parents as much as I do") and The Results ("The date was bow-legged, wore glasses, had a faint mustache, and talked with a lisp. I didn't have to pay $6 to find her. If I wanted that kind of a girl I could have gone out with one of my sister's friends").

Given the stigma and the lack of an Internet to spread the word, computer dating remained a small industry. A few video-dating services, like Teledate and Introvision, tried and failed in the early seventies. Finally, one had success. In 1976, Jeffrey Ullman, a handsome young techie and former sixties radical, had been working in broadcasting ever since graduating from the University of California–Berkeley with a journalism degree. Back home in Los Angeles one night, twenty-six and newly married to the first of what would be several wives, Ullman began complaining that he couldn't find a job because it was too hard to meet people in LA. Then he remembered a party he'd videotaped, years earlier, with a camera he got for graduation, a Sony AVC 3400 Porta Pak. When he'd played the tape for a friend who hadn't been at the party, the friend spotted a woman he wanted to meet. Ullman arranged it, and they dated for a year.

The Sony Porta Pak technology, invented in 1967, was archaic. But in the midseventies, several Japanese electronics companies had started backing the new VHS format to compete with Sony's Betamax. Bingo.

Ullman founded Great Expectations, naming his company after the novel by Charles Dickens. The idea was to take old-school matchmaking methods and mix them with modern technology. Members would go to a Great Expectations office, where they would read through three-ring binders of printed profiles. If they liked a profile, they could check out the person's videotape. Ullman would then place personal phone calls to his members with news of a "mutual consent."

It wasn't a bad idea, but there were some problems. For one thing, the tricky logistics—users had to visit a physical place—made it onerous and inefficient. While some people were open to selecting dates based on videos, far fewer were keen on being filmed themselves. The often mannered performances posed difficulties for editors. "I'm a twenty-five-year subscriber to both *Playboy* and the *New Yorker* magazine," emphasized one video dater in a popular montage viewable on YouTube. "Hi Mom," chirped another.

It was just, well, really awkward.

MADtv, the sketch-comedy series that began competing with *Saturday Night Live* in the nineties, ran a regular skit called "Lowered Expectations." In one, a young Shaquille O'Neal dressed in drag posed as "Denise Rodman," the fictional sister of eccentric basketball great Dennis Rodman. In another episode, the company representative of Lowered Expectations pitched the business like this:

> Are you desirably impaired? Do you find yourself serving punch at parties? Would you describe yourself as shy? Old-fashioned? Not on anyone's A-list? Is your ideal date someone in their early twenties with a perfect body and a sparkling personality? Well, unless you win the lottery, you're never going to land that dreamboat. But that doesn't mean you can't find . . . *somebody*. And that's why Lowered Expectations may be for you.

Ullman loved the mockery. It meant his business was becoming relevant. It also helped shape his marketing. Losers, Ullman would argue, are those singles who complain bitterly about the people they're meeting yet do nothing about it. But when Santa Monica Bank advertised that it handles "more zeros than a dating service," Ullman was livid. He organized a demonstration on the bank's doorstep. "Since Santa Monica Bank believes that single people are zeros," he said, "we're asking all people, single and married, to reduce their bank accounts to zero." He handed out bumper stickers that said "I'M NO ZERO." The ploy won him mention in the *Wall Street Journal*. And later, when TV talk-show host Montel Williams asked Ullman if he was preying on lonely people, Ullman shot back: "Yes. Just like restaurants prey on the hungry and doctors prey on the sick and talk-show hosts prey on the people who are too bored to read a book."

Video dating grew in the 1980s and early 1990s, and facilitated many marriages. It also brought in big bucks for Ullman and his partners. At its peak, Great Expectations had forty-nine franchises and grossed $65 million per year, bolstered by a huge direct-mailing campaign. Ullman drove a Cadillac and collected African art. He hired and fired his mother, twice. In the press he derided his sister, who also worked at Great Expectations, for being overweight and a lesbian. "Sometimes he seems to be incredibly proud of being an asshole," his sister told the Los Angeles Times. "Jeffrey would call it tough love. It just gets to a point where you say, 'Do I want to be loved that way?'"

In 1995, as Gary Kremen was launching Match, Great Expectations was sold to a financial-services firm for $18 million. But despite Ullman's business success, video dating never won wide acceptance or overcame its stigma. It would remain a punch line. The matchmaking industry was anxious to see whether its next iteration would break through, go mainstream. "The only people online in the nineties were socially awkward geeks," says OkCupid's Sam Yagan. "So, by definition, they were the bulk of the people doing online dating."

Was that the reason for the stigma? What did membership in a dating service imply that was so bad? For the answer, we must flash back three hundred years, to the beginning of media itself.

In 1690 in Britain, not long after the newspaper was invented, mate seekers began using the "personal advertisement" to find husbands, wives, and "unspecified arrangements"—code for someone seeking a homosexual partner. "Being single past the age of 21 was considered almost shameful in that era," writes H. G. Cocks in Classified: The Secret History of the Personal Column, "and the ads were often a last resort for the men who advertised and the women who read them. If a match resulted, it is unlikely that you boasted the fact to your friends."

Even though matchmaking had been around for centuries, this new form of mate finding—more a searching system than a matching system—garnered harsh criticism. Part of this stigma stemmed from a major ideological shift in how Western culture viewed marriage.

Prior to the eighteenth century marriage was still an arrangement for building a home and a family. And for as long as these arranged marriages existed there had been arrangers: the priest in medieval Catholic society; the rabbi, *yenta*, or *shadchan* in Judaism; the *nokado* in Japan; the *portador* in Mexico; the *kalyn* in Russia. Women were kept inside in Plato's ancient Greece while Athenian men, guys with names like Draco and Heron and Lysander, postponed marriage as long as possible, preferring a public to a domestic life. When the time finally came, female matchmakers, instructed either by the bride's father or husband-to-be, would conduct negotiations. The first known dating agency was run by parish priests in sixteenth-century England, when vicars assembled lists of candidates and paired them based on supposed compatibility.

As spiritual advisers and authority figures, matchmakers were trusted to form wise pairings based on practical considerations such as wealth, politics, and property. The transactions they facilitated could be just as commercially and religiously driven as the relationships sought out on today's more no-nonsense dating sites, such as WealthyMen.com, for men who make at least eighty-five thousand dollars a year and "want to meet interesting and beautiful women," and Jdate.com, which "ensures that Jewish traditions are sustained for generations to come."

It was not until the middle of the eighteenth century, shortly after the personal ad came along, that certain intellectual trends—namely, Romanticism—put a new emphasis on self-expression. The Romantics, according to the *Encyclopedia of Human Relationships*, cast courtship as nothing less than "an individual heroic quest for life meaning, personal identity, and a kind of terrestrial salvation." In a trend that continued from the 1700s to the 1970s, "marriage became redefined from a practical social arrangement . . . to the formal public recognition of a private romantic love."

Classifieds made a comeback in America in the 1960s and 1970s, encouraged by the era's inclination toward individualism and social exhibitionism. "Everybody was letting it all hang out in other ways," said Raymond Shapiro, a business manager for the *New York Review of Books*, "so suddenly it was okay to display oneself in print. It was very important to be 'self-aware.' So you'd get ads like: 'Astrologer, 27, psychology student, desires to establish non-superficial friendship with sensitive, choicelessly aware persons who are non-self-oriented, deep, and wish to unearth real, personness relationships.'"

People got picky. This created some inconsistencies: While the romantic ethos and its emphasis on pickiness reignited the demand for marriage intermediaries, it also made the idea of getting help ideologically unattractive. Romantic love, after all, was "a supernatural force existing outside of conventional social institutions." The use of a commercial intermediary risked profaning "love's sacred essence and was the admission of personal failure." Westerners adopted a view of how two people should meet that went hand in hand with romantic love: Since our relationships are a product of fate, one should leave the problem of finding a soul mate to the universe. This is serendipity: finding good things without seeking them out.

It's been a classic critique of online dating that too little happens online that's not planned out. In 2011, *The New Yorker* observed that the "Internet subverts Kismet," while *GQ* announced, "Technology has trumped serendipity." Technology expands our choices. But it also requires instructions, narrowing inputs: no kids; over five feet eight inches; makes upward of one hundred thousand dollars a year; etc. With all our Googling activities, we no longer "happen upon." Instead, we heat seek via search engine, stuck inside what one author coined the "filter bubble." The thing that was thought to be one of online dating's biggest virtues—the ability to control and direct one's relationship life—was also bothersome.

At the moment, much of society still clings to the idea that two people are "made for each other" even while it conflicts with what we know to be the less romantic reality: Had those two people never met, each would have, most likely, found someone just as unique. And still, we can't resist a good "meet cute"—a Hollywood term describing the most important consideration for the writer of romances: How will the couple *meet*? Regardless of how *un*cute the real-world meeting may actually be—*he bought me a drink at happy hour; she shared her notes in criminal* *law*—it's a story nonetheless, something that can be told and embellished over time, and one that is unique to each couple. The stigma that attached to meeting through an intermediary reinforced how hardwired this idea had become.

So when Gary Kremen came along with Match.com, it remained to be seen whether, given the utility of the Internet, people could be enticed to see serendipity in a new light.

In the early 1990s, Trish McDermott, a recent college graduate, helped market an offline matchmaking service in San Francisco. The service, called the Patricia Moore Group, charged singles anywhere from five thousand to fifty thousand dollars to find "high-end, needle-in-a-haystack matches." One male client demanded to meet only women involved in the arts. Another narrowed it to the ballet.

The job taught McDermott that no amount of career success guarantees someone will find love; wealthy people have the same fundamental problems as everyone else when it comes to relationships. The matchmaking business taught her something else as well: Singles, rich and poor, would pay good money in the pursuit of companionship.

Toward the end of 1994, shortly after Netscape launched its Web browser, McDermott read an article in the *San Francisco Chronicle* about someone out of Stanford Business School who was doing something with the Internet related to dating. When McDermott met him, Gary Kremen oscillated between awkwardness and confidence. After launching Match, he came to his first television interview wearing a tie-dyed shirt and declared that his Web site would "bring more love to the planet than anything since Jesus Christ."

To lure in people who were already using newspaper personals, Kremen experimented with membership fees at or below the cost of the print competition. In early 1996, after building the membership up to sixty thousand users, he turned on pricing, starting at $9.95 per month.

"Today, a dating site that has sixty thousand people would feel like a pretty light community," says McDermott, whom Kremen hired to handle Match's marketing. "But at the time, to be able to find twenty-five people who matched your basic criteria and lived in your area—that was awesome. Some argued that we'd never make money, since everyone thought everything on the Internet was supposed to be free. But coming from my old job, where I saw people pay fifty thousand dollars to find someone, I knew that dating was a unique service."

In the days of newspaper and magazine personals, mate searchers were advised to place their ads in the publications they read, suggesting that mutual allegiance to a print product might be a proxy for compatibility. In this way, personals provided a measure of search capability but not the matching service that online dating offered. With Kremen's simple idea of putting the personals online, search and match had finally been merged, and the introductions business took a giant step in the direction of user control.

It was this control that separated online dating, and the Internet in general, from all other media that came before. The Internet, writes communications historian Tim Wu in *The Master Switch: The Rise and Fall of Information Empires*, "defies every expectation one has developed from experience of other media industries, which are all predicated on control of the customer, whereas the Internet abdicates control to the individual; that is its special allure, its power to be endlessly surprising."

In the mid-1990s, the online community was still quite small. About 5 percent of Americans had Internet access, and the majority of people online were men. So Kremen got every woman he knew to post a profile on his site. Even though he was in a relationship, he signed up for Match and asked his girlfriend to do so as well. When membership reached critical mass, Kremen discovered that his success, like that of David Dewan thirty years earlier, would come at his own expense: Kremen's girlfriend met someone else through Match and left him. Oh well. At least he knew the site worked.

The problem, however, was that the site's most satisfied customers were unlikely to spread the word. Meeting your mate online was like getting a nose job—you'd just as soon not tell anyone about it. "In those first few years at Match," McDermott says, "people who met their partner or spouse on the site would lie about it. At one wedding, I watched a couple who met on Match stand up before their friends, relatives, and church community and lie about how they met. They felt it would cast a shadow over their marriage." When successful Match users called the company with requests to have hard copies of their profiles mailed to them for posterity, they'd often request that the profiles be sent in blank envelopes, without the Match emblem, so the mailman wouldn't see. "Here people were, meeting the love of their life and feeling like they'd done something wrong!"

But the stigma they felt was real. Lois Smith Brady, the journalist who began writing the Vows column for the *New York Times* in the early nineties, remembers hearing about a couple who met online. She was reluctant to cover the wedding: "It seemed so risky and dangerous. What if other people followed?" The stigma was also felt by Match's financial backers. Kremen's venture capitalists never fully embraced the online-dating industry, even as success stories abounded: more than two hundred marriages reported; a dozen babies; and countless dates. As membership grew by as much as 10 percent a week, Kremen clashed with the board over issues like whether to include gays on the site. The board removed Kremen but failed to find a CEO replacement, and decided to wash their hands of online dating. In 1997, Match was sold to a consumer-services company for $7 million, of which Kremen walked away with a small fraction—and no girlfriend.

"It's really a bummer," he told the *San Francisco Chronicle* at the time. "I've helped a lot of people, but it just hasn't helped me."

Copycats followed. Jdate, the site for Jewish singles, and Lavalife, based in Canada, entered the market. Nerve Personals, the personals portion of an online magazine for "literate smut," was a hit with the kinds of intellectual, edgy urbanites found on OkCupid today. Gradually, the industry gained ground. Matchmaker.com, born in the BBS era, built a loyal following, with about four million registered daters. In 2000, it sold to Lycos for $44.5 million.

Customer patronage and societal acceptance were different things, however, and the lingering stigma meant that the online-dating industry was largely ignored during the Internet boom of the late nineties—with one exception.

Having dropped out of UCLA after one semester, Barry Diller found himself working in the mailroom of the William Morris Agency during the 1960s. Following an improbable rise through the ranks of ABC's television unit, he became the head of Paramount Pictures at age thirty-one, created the Fox Broadcasting Company in the eighties, and built up USA Network in the nineties. In 1999, Diller bought Match for $50 million. The dating site would become the crown jewel in Diller's Internet empire, IAC (Inter-ActiveCorp), joining the travel Web sites Expedia.com and Hotels.com, the search engine Ask.com, the borrowing site LendingTree.com, and the news site TheDailyBeast.com.

While Diller enjoyed the bragging rights that came with being a leading aggregator of Internet brands, he had no specific interest in on-line dating. What drew Diller to Match, and to the Web in general, was a vision he had about the future of media convergence, what he called "interactivity at scale." The vision for IAC had come to him many years earlier, in the early nineties, while standing on the selling floor of QVC, the home teleshopping network in which he owned a $25 million stake. Born in 1942, Diller was accustomed to thinking of media in its distinct forms: There was print, broadcast, and film, and they didn't mix. But QVC's business combined telephones, televisions, and computers. Diller saw them all work together in a kind of primitive convergence. When phone calls came in from home shoppers, he watched their orders regis-ter on a computer screen, with the digital bars rising and receding in waves. He thought, "This is going to change things."

Diller probably didn't realize the full extent of what convergence would mean for dating. But his thinking put him ahead of his time. The matching of computer dating, the searching of personal ads, the virtual reality of video, and eventually, the pinpointing capability of GPS—they could all one day converge on one screen. Over the next decade, his IAC would come to own more than two dozen dating sites, including Eu-rope's Meetic and OkCupid, the industry darling.

"I wish I could say it was all planned," says Greg Blatt, the young

lawyer who helped take Martha Stewart's company public before de-
camping to Diller's Web empire, where he became CEO of Match and
then of IAC. "But back in those days the company was simply buying up
a bunch of Internet businesses. Dating just happened to be something
that worked out, so we stuck with it."

Back in the sixties, when the average marriage age was twenty-three for
men and twenty for women, students turned to computer dating because they were sick of coming home empty-handed from college mixers. But during the first decade of the new millennium, with the average
marriage age creeping toward thirty (twenty-eight for men; twenty-six
for women), singles faced a new set of efficiency problems. Bars fell out
of favor after the postcollege years. The primacy of work left less and
less time for mate searching. Women's biological clocks were already
ticking away by the time they got serious about settling down. And as
people remained single for longer, they grew to be more discerning daters, pickier about what they wanted and what they'd settle for.

"I prefer younger guys," said Miriam, a thirty-three-year-old speech
pathologist from Maryland who joined the secular community after living
as an orthodox Jew for twenty-five years. "Because I date online I can go
with whoever I want." An easily accessible, rationalized marketplace of
relationships: This was the big, game-changing difference between online
dating and the other forms of relationship intermediation that came before. The online-dating industry sold choice and control at a time when
choice and control were exactly what many people wanted and needed.

By 2011, the eighteen-to-twenty-nine demographic accounted for 44
percent of the online-dating market; people aged thirty to forty-nine
comprised 35 percent.

"I believe it all came down to *You've Got Mail*," says Trish McDermott, referring to Nora Ephron's 1998 hit romantic comedy about a couple of book lovers played by Meg Ryan and Tom Hanks. The movie wasn't
about an online-dating site, but the two met in an AOL chat room. "A
lightbulb went off for single people. Suddenly it was seen as possible to
meet someone who's smart and interesting online."

Surely many societal trends overwhelmed the online-dating stigma. Major pop-culture events like *You've Got Mail* may have helped. But most industry execs interviewed for this book believe it came down to one thing: access. This theory is also supported by findings from social science. Researchers say that attitudes toward online dating become more positive as social milieus provide less access to partners. Over time people lack the social capital to afford a stigma.

Up the age ladder, baby boomers divorced in droves: In 2010, nearly 33 percent of people between forty-six and sixty-four were divorced, separated, or had never been married, compared with just 13 percent in 1970. Being single later in life no longer carried the stigma it once did— and neither did online dating. For Match, eHarmony, and Plenty of Fish, three of the largest dating sites in North America, the fifty-and-over crowd became one of their most reliable demographics, accounting for 21 percent of the market, a valuable 21 percent because these were the people who were (a) likely to have money and (b) unlikely to believe that everything online should be free. Match launched a new site, OurTime .com, for singles fifty and up. The press release cited corporate research that singles over fifty are "considerably happier than their younger counterparts." With the pressures of child rearing and career lifted, the over-fifties "experience less stress about their personal lives." They also have fewer options.

Throughout the first decade of the 2000s, the stigma gradually reversed itself. Match employees got invited to weddings, where they were asked to give toasts. Happy couples, proud to have met online, put Match-branded matchbooks on the wedding tables as gifts. Groomsmen wore Match baseball hats. One bride even designed her wedding cake to look like the Match homepage. "Now," McDermott recalls, "it was as if people wanted to say, 'I'm tech-savvy. I was there at the beginning of the online-dating movement!'"

After fifteen years the online-dating industry reached a tipping point. The U.S. industry had become saturated, with over fourteen hundred dating sites making $2 billion per year. The top ten players—led by Match and Plenty of Fish—owned 60 percent of the U.S. market's approximately thirty million customers. A widely parroted 2010 finding estimated that one in five committed relationships originated online. The ratio was expected to climb dramatically in the coming decade.

Dan Winchester runs a free dating site in the United Kingdom. Like many of his colleagues, Winchester is an online-dating evangelist. Given this amazing tool, he wonders, why would anyone leave the most important decision of their life to chance? He predicts that the prospects of access and control will, in time, turn every adult into an online dater; and that the vast selection of online dating—expanding one's pool by hundreds or thousands of people—will mean a future of smarter mate selection and better relationships.

"When I meet someone," says Winchester, "I always ask where they met their boyfriend or girlfriend, or wife or husband. If they say, 'In a bar,' which they often do, I ask, 'How did you know what his interests were, or whether he had that same problem that you had with your last six relationships? How do you know you're not just making the same mistake over and over?'"

Just how much *do* daters control when they go looking online?

ALEXIS, PART II

↓

Go Ask Phantasy Tour

AS AN ART STUDENT, ALEXIS SHOWCASED HER WORK ON A PER-
sonal Web site. As an intern at a music label, she marketed content online. As an aspiring set designer for film and television, she networked
for jobs on social-media sites like Facebook and Twitter. As a music enthusiast, she posted regularly, sometimes obsessively, on a fan forum
devoted to her favorite jam band, Phish.

The forum, called Phantasy Tour, is less about music per se than
bringing Phish fans together in a place where they can sound off on relationships and sex, posing questions and seeking advice. Whatever
Phantasy Tour may have been intended for originally, it functions as a
place for young adults of a similar cultural bent to crowd-source feedback on common coming-of-age conundrums in their personal lives.

Unlike, say, the vast connectedness of Facebook, the PT community
is limited, specific, and isolated. Because Phantasy Tour members,
known as PTers, or "bears," post under anonymous screen names, their
conversations tend to be characterized by heavy disclosure, blunt honesty, braggadocio, and lots of off-color humor. It works like this: A PTer
poses a conversation topic, or thread: "Can you be friends with an ex?"
"Tell me about your worst breakup!" "Sex on the first date?" Conversations then unfold over hours, days, or months, reading like raw, often

R-rated streams-of-Millennial-generation-consciousness. Typical fodder ranges from the normative—whether, after a first date, one owes the other an official "I don't want to see you again"—to the prescriptive: "Don't date girls who won't admit to mastying [masturbating]. They will never let you hit it from behind, touch your balls, give frequent Bjs, have sex with the lights on, or SIIHB [stick it in her butt]." The Web site operator caps conversations at seventeen pages, a limit that is often reached.

In the winter of 2010, Alexis initiated a thread entitled "Match.com." As the so-called original poster, or OP, she asked: "So, who's done it? Weird experiences? Horror stories? I'm just curious if it's essentially a bunch of dudes looking to date/fuck multiple girls as sport."

Comments flowed: a mixture of encouragement ("If you can trudge through that initial awkwardness, it might be a fit"); caution ("It's the electronic version of the bargain bin at Filene's"); and leavening perspective ("I find it truly comical that people in this thread are poo pooing online dating. We're all message-board dorks! Online is where it's at!").

"Okay," Alexis wrote after several hundred comments had been posted. "I will just enjoy some random dinners, see what happens, and let you all know, of course. Side note: facepalm [head in hands]."

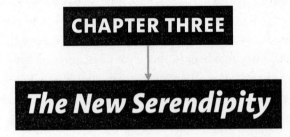

CHAPTER THREE

The New Serendipity

HOW A BUNCH OF GEEKS REENGINEERED ROMANCE

It's all about hooking people up and being as fast and efficient as possible.

—Markus Frind, founder of Plenty of Fish

A couple of years before Carrie and her husband moved from Salt Lake City to New York, when their son was new and their marriage was still healthy, they filled out OkCupid profiles and answered some questions on the site. It was just for fun, to see if they were good for each other, and, according to the algorithm, they were: a 96 percent match.

The OkCupid site had a soft blue background with writing in blue and pink. "I liked the whole tone," Carrie recalls. "Nerdy and coy. There was this strong sexual edge to the questions they asked, but they were nice about it, like friends asking you incredibly intimate things but without judgment. It was all in the name of efficiency."

Carrie, thirty-four, was born in England and raised in Iowa. She met her husband during college at the University of Illinois, while getting a degree in industrial engineering. She loves her son and enjoys talking about him. She thinks of herself as a highly rational person. She calls herself an "atheist and borderline antitheist," and says religion is "a force for evil in the world."

So after the move to New York, when Carrie's husband announced he was unhappy and wanted to split up, these two criteria—antireligion, prochildren—were foremost in her thinking about a new partner. "I haven't dated since college," she says, "when all you do is get drunk and see what happens."

When I meet her, Carrie is seated among children's toys in the living room of a one-bedroom apartment in downtown Manhattan. Her ex moved out recently. At the moment she's trying, without success, to remove iced-tea stains from an expensive wool carpet. "I knew OkCupid from their blog, which is about patterns and trends in data," she says. "As someone who knows statistics, I like their matching process, the way they do it with questions and a weighting system rather than just have you define yourself by ticking off a bunch of boxes."

Doing things better based on data—that's what Carrie's job at a credit card company is about. A devotee of corporate America, she believes human greed is too strong to regulate, and that transparency is the only antidote to Wall Street corruption. Her friends call her the Plutocrat.

Carrie tried Match but didn't like it. "On Match the guys can sort profiles by what body shape they want," she explains, "which pisses me off." If Carrie were a petite woman, her red mop of hair would look devilish, almost too cute. But size gives her aspect a certain seriousness. "I wouldn't qualify as 'curvy,'" she says, "not like Kim Kardashian. I'm definitely bigger than that. But I'm not quite 'big and beautiful' either. So out of the five options on Match I picked 'full figured.' But I'm pretty sure that most of the guys on there, even if they're chubby, check off 'skinny' or 'average' as their requirements for women. Give me a break! We all prefer to go out with someone insanely sexy. But be realistic about it! *You* get to stay skinny after kids, but I don't. In any case, I don't think Match picks up on the fact that I'm passing over all these guys because of their weight requirements. But OkCupid can because it allows me to rate the importance of guys' answers to their weight questions."

Carrie logs onto OkCupid. The homepage greets her: "The Internet rejoices in your return!" says a message from the OkCupid staff. There's nothing written in her profile, but the site still has her basic stats from when she and her ex tested their compatibility.

Ethnicity: White. Height: 5' 4". Body Type: Full figured. Diet: Mostly anything. Smokes: No. Drinks: Socially. Drugs: Never. Sign: Capricorn, but it doesn't matter. Religion: Atheism, and very serious about it. Education: Graduated from masters program. Job: Executive/Management. Income: $150,000–$250,000.

Carrie adds her age, zip code, and a screen name: VociferousInNYC.

Immediately she receives a message from Chris Coyne, an OkCupid cofounder, who writes: "If you want the best people to contact you, you should share interesting facts about yourself on your profile page. . . . Around the site you'll encounter match questions. When you see them, you can answer them in three parts. First, you'll give your own answer. Second, your ideal match's answer. And finally, you'll tell us how important (if at all) that question is to you. In this way OkCupid lets you—and only you—control how matches are sorted. The more you answer, the better your matches."

Users can answer thousands of questions, or none at all. Carrie goes to the lifestyle and dating tabs, where she answers questions about the topics that are most important to her: Are you Christian? "No," she replies. "I much prefer Aesop's fables." Should evolution and creationism be taught side-by-side in schools? "No, and it's very important that my partner agrees." If you made a bright orange bowel movement that had glowing purple polka dots, would you tell your partner about it? "Yes." How much can intelligence turn you on? "A lot!" Do you believe that men must be the heads of their households? "No." Do you have a child? "Yes, and it's very important that my partner be okay with that." Is your ideal match well-off financially? "I don't think I want to be a sugar mama," she writes, "but I'm not too picky." Do you think boys should be circumcised? "No! Keep your knife away from my son's penis!" Do you Google someone before a first date? "Yes. Knowledge is power!"

Carrie then answers questions in the sex category, marking many of them "irrelevant" in terms of how important they are to her relationships:

Orgasms are clearly the most important part of sex. "I agree." Do you prefer to achieve orgasm by intercourse, oral sex, masturbation, or pure force of will? "Masturbation." Would you date someone just for the sex? "Not very likely but maybe." Do you usually feel the need to shower or bathe after having sex? "No." Have you ever tasted your own sexual fluids? "Yes." Is there such a thing as having had too many sexual partners? "No." Under the right circumstances would you allow your partner to lick your anus? "Yes." Would you find shaving your partner's pubic hair exciting? "No. (I wouldn't like brushing his teeth either. It should be done beforehand.)" Would you consider inviting someone to bed with you for clearly stated nonsexual purposes on a first date? "Yes. (I did. It was nice!)" Have you ever had sex in a place where there was a high risk of getting caught? "No." If your partner asks you to have sex in a sex-shop booth with others watching, would you? "Yes." Would you rather be tied up during sex, do the tying, or avoid bondage altogether? "Be tied up." Would you play out a rape fantasy with a partner who asked you to? "No." Would you do a striptease for your mate? "Yes." Have you ever had sex with a person within the first hour of meeting them? "No." Can you remember the names of everyone you've ever had sex with? "Yes." Would you ever consider cutting a partner in sexual play who asked for it? "No." Do you have a hidden stash of pornography? "Yes." Would you be okay with your significant other thinking about someone else while having sex with you? "Maybe. It would depend who they're thinking about." Do you own sex toys? "Yes. Who doesn't these days?"

The next step is photos. Carrie uploads five pictures: two of her in a black evening dress, sitting down; another of her typing on her Black-Berry; a fourth "strategic photo" of her holding her son; and a fifth of her doing yoga. She presses a button labeled "My Best Face." The site tells her which photos are most attractive, so she can order them accordingly. She decides to remove the yoga picture, because it shows too much cleavage. In the about section she writes a few paragraphs. She says she is "warm and fun" but has a "cynical side." She's "enthusiastic" and has "been trying to do more things out and about in the city," like "biking, seeing plays and taking yoga classes." She says she has a son who lives with her part-time.

Days go by: Carrie receives no messages from eligible candidates, nor does she get many responses to the messages she sends. After browsing profiles she realizes that her own is, well, pretty boring. It doesn't sound much different from the profiles of those guys who say "I like to work hard and play hard." She takes another stab, beginning with a joke from her sister:

> An atom walks into a bar and says, "I've lost an electron." Bartender says, "Are you sure?" Atom says, "I'm positive."
>
> I grew up in Iowa but have been in NYC for 9 years. I like to think that I'm nice like a classic Midwesterner but can keep up with life in New York. My undergraduate degree is in engineering but I turned to the dark side, business, soon after I graduated. I have a 5-year-old son who lives with me part-time (read: my biological clock has gone off once and is now on snooze). I love raising him in the city and he inspires me to broaden my horizons.
>
> I have a weak spot for people who are intelligent and a little geeky but with a touch of sophistication. Perhaps someone who has seen a few Woody Allen movies but won't judge me when I sing along to Adele. Someone who is generally optimistic but can get annoyed by politicians or people who block the doors on the subway.

Under "The most private thing I'm willing to admit," Carries writes: "I had a C-section, didn't breastfeed (read: everything is still as it was!), and dropped my son on his head when he was 6 months old."

Messages begin rolling in. The atom joke proves to be a good conversation starter. About half of her suitors reference it or come with a joke of their own. Carrie goes on ten dates in the next two months. The main criteria she uses are kids, atheism, and education—the guy needs at least a college degree.

Many of the dates go well. But "the kid thing" seems to get in the way. "Many men without kids seem to like kids and say they want kids of their own," Carrie says. "But the fact is, if you don't have kids, then you only think kids are entertaining for a while. Eventually you want to move on to other conversations, about going out at night and skiing in the Alps and things that parents don't have the time for. I'm like, yeah, I did that stuff—eight years ago."

When Carrie's son becomes a sticking point on yet another date with an otherwise promising twenty-nine-year-old guy with a graduate degree and a good job, Carrie comes home, opens her laptop, and does an "advanced search" on OkCupid using just two criteria: He must have kids and he must be an atheist. "My money is taken care of," Carrie says. "I don't need money. I need the rest of it." She leaves the education, job, and income fields blank.

While Barry Diller was buying Match and other Web sites in the nineties, the math geeks of Generation X—those born in the late 1970s who had dial-up connections in high school—were also trying to capitalize on the Internet. Back at Harvard, a math geek from Maine named Chris Coyne saw eBay.com, the auction site, go public and sell for insane multiples. He began brainstorming ideas for his own Web site.

Coyne is a waifish six feet five inches with spiky blond hair and steely eyes. He looks like a male model conflated with a basketball prospect—not your typical geek. In the spring of 1998, as Coyne approached the end of his junior year at Harvard, he heard about the Last Chance Dance. Seniors listed up to fifteen secret crushes and were then told which of the fifteen liked them back. Coyne wondered why someone hadn't put this on the Web. Seemed like it would spread really fast.

He asked a friend to build a Web site called Pimpin' Cupid. They listed some people who they thought were hot. Then those people would get an e-mail asking them to list the people *they* thought were hot. There were no profiles, no photos, no searching. The site just matched people who said they liked each other. It quickly spread around Harvard and other universities for a few weeks and then crashed, but it was the start of something.

Coyne's math buddies from Kirkland House, Max Krohn and Sam Yagan, shared Coyne's ambition—however ambiguous it was—and joined him.

The goal wasn't to build a dating site; certainly the idea of online classifieds never occurred to them. "There was an Internet boom happening," Coyne recalls. "People our age who were building things online didn't necessarily think of their creations as specific businesses. We talked about making sites that would 'grab eyeballs.' I thought of a Web site as a portal into something engaging or entertaining or interesting that would keep users coming back." Coyne, Yagan, Krohn, and a fourth geek—a double math and English major named Christian Rudder—kept testing ideas. The next project to catch fire was a humor blog called TheSpark, much of which was written by Rudder.

"When spring rolled around," recalls Yagan, "I was in Chris's dorm room with a bunch of guys, saying, 'You know, being funny every day is going to be really hard. We need to make something that will have lasting value.'"

Krohn suggested putting their own version of *CliffsNotes* online; he recommended hiring students to write their own study guides for Shakespeare and other subjects.

Two years after they launched SparkNotes, *CliffsNotes*, publisher of the iconic yellow and black study guides founded in 1958 by Nebraskan Cliff Hillegass, had had its monopoly disrupted. In 2001, SparkNotes was bought by iTurf, and then shortly thereafter Barnes & Noble bought SparkNotes from iTurf for $3.5 million. By then the site had published over six hundred free online study guides on topics such as literature, history, economics, math, and chemistry. Barnes & Noble turned SparkNotes into one of the leading education brands in the world.

After selling SparkNotes, the guys disbanded for a year. At the end of 2002, Coyne was stumbling drunk around Manhattan's East Village when he called Yagan with an idea.

"We should make a site that has a big blind-date button on it!" he said. "You just push the button and you get a blind date. We'll send people to bars to meet each other. The site will be free. The bars will subsidize us."

"Okay," replied Yagan. "Call me back when you're sober."

Coyne's idea, which would eventually launch, fail, and launch again, was called CrazyBlindDate.

"But OkCupid was the launchpad," says Max Krohn, who graduated summa cum laude from Harvard with a degree in computer science, and now also has a PhD in computer science from MIT. "We thought from the beginning we could only launch CBD once we had a sufficiently successful dating site."

Shortly before the acquisition of SparkNotes the team had been working on a dating site called SparkMatch. SparkMatch offered a personality test, called the Purity Test, that was based on the Myers-Briggs Type Indicator. It classified people on four dimensions: independent/dependent; good/evil; love/sex; taker/provider. This resulted in sixteen personality types, each of which Rudder, who had a knack for funny writing, named: a man who qualified as a Furry Dildo (dependent, evil, sex, provider) might do well with the female character Battleaxe (dependent, evil, love, taker) but should avoid the Mermaid (independent, good, love, provider).

"Chris and Christian always believed that consumer Web products should have a personality, an attitude, that they should be fun to use," says Yagan. "If you look at the SparkNotes and OkC brands, they really share an irreverence and a (sometimes not-so) subtle sense of humor."

SparkNotes had become a success by 1) being better than its incumbent competitor and 2) being free. SparkNotes relied on advertising rather than subscriptions to make money. What other industries could Coyne & Co. disrupt with this two-point business plan? It needed to be an industry in which the user gives something in return for the free service—something that would appeal to the advertisers the site would need to court in order to make money. Online dating, with all its potential for massive data collection, could be a good one. But they would need to ask their users to do more than just push a button.

In 2004, the reorganized company launched under a new name, OkCupid, and was now prepared to tackle online dating full time. Krohn wrote the OK Web Server (OKWS), Coyne worked on the matching system, and Rudder cultivated a voice.

Early on the site featured a version of the Purity Test. A man might learn that he's a Billy Goat, a Backrubber, a Vapor Trail, a Poolboy, or the Last Man on Earth. The Hornivore ("roaming, sexual, subhuman") might want to consider the female type Genghis Khunt ("master of man, bringer of pain") and avoid the Sonnet ("romantic, hopeful, composed"). To figure out what you were you had to answer questions about yourself, some of which were written and submitted by users. Over time, the questions multiplied.

At OkCupid's headquarters—a no-frills loft office in Midtown Manhattan—Coyne explains how his matching system works today. "The objective," he says, "is to figure out what you want. To accomplish that we play a giant question-and-answer session with everyone on the site at once."

The prototypical user, let's call him John Dater, is not required to answer any questions. But OkCupid is premised on the idea that the more questions John D. answers, the better the site works for him. Questions range from the abstract (Would you prefer that good things happened, or interesting things?) to the specific (How often do you feel the need to get really drunk?); from penal policy (Which of the following is the more appropriate penalty for rape: death, castration, prison, or community service?) to trust (Would you be okay with your significant other spending a lot of time with his/her ex?); from the forward looking (Does finding a long-term partner give you license to "let yourself go"?) to the practical (Ideally, how often would you have sex?) to the downright intimate (How do you feel about kissing your partner after he/she goes down on you?).

For each question, John provides three answers: 1) his own answer, 2) the answer(s) he's willing to accept from a match, and 3) the level of importance he attaches to the question: irrelevant, a little important, somewhat important, very important, or mandatory.

When John clicks on a new profile he's shown a "match percentage" that accounts for all the questions that he and the potential match have *both* answered. If they've both answered the same one thousand questions, for instance, then OkCupid's algorithm generates a match percentage based on six thousand answers: the product of one thousand questions times three answers per question times two daters. Beyond that, John is welcome to go "behind the numbers," so to speak, to see how his potential mate has answered any given question, provided she's chosen to make her answer public.

The innovation of OkCupid—and what distinguishes it from other "matching" sites, such as eHarmony—lies in its pliability. Coyne believes he can give members the power to sort through matches online the same way they would offline, assuming a world of perfect information. "Suppose," he explains, "that your buddy tells you he has a girl he wants to set you up with. No matter how much you trust him, you're not going to say yes without asking questions first. In your mind, you have a filtering process that's built in, which is different from another guy's filtering process. eHarmony would say they know everyone's filtering process. We say we don't. But we can give you the tools to express your filter. We can show you how everyone stacks up against your filter, and how you stack up against theirs. Then you're on your own."

Offline, when you're on your own, you're not relying on such detailed data. The most obvious difference between meeting someone in real life and meeting someone online is, of course, what you see first. Instead of assessing and greeting a physical person, you assess and greet an avatar, some combination of text, photographs, and match percentages flashing in the corner of the screen. Biological attraction gets replaced with something far less sexy, "computer-mediated communication," or CMC.

In broad strokes, the science of human attraction is something we all grasp, intuitively, even if we've never thought much about it. In a 1991 study, for example, researchers observed 109 "attraction tactics" in a singles bar, including sucking seductively on a straw, offering to buy someone a drink, puffing out one's chest, and staring. Women say the most effective tactics for attracting them are displaying good manners and acting sympathetic. Men, meanwhile, favor signals that are more easily quantified: accentuated curves; a strut in her step; a sexualized appearance that might include tight clothes, short skirts, and low-cut tops that slip off the shoulder. On a seven-point scale, men placed a woman's act of rubbing her chest or pelvis against him at 6.07, the second most effective tactic. Only an explicit agreement to have sex beats the chest/pelvis rub.

Women experience strong physical reactions too, though they tend to place more importance on scent. Pheromones—from the Greek words *pherein* (to carry) and *hormon* (to stimulate)—are secreted by apocrine glands in the skin, mouth, feet, and vagina. In *The Evolution of Desire*, David Buss defines pheromones as "chemical messengers secreted by one person's body that produce physiological and behavioral changes in another person." Women are attracted to men with symmetrical faces. We think of symmetry as a visual quality, not an olfactory one. Scientists report, however, that symmetry has its own natural perfume: Women have evolved an ability to *smell* it. In one famous study, T-shirts worn by symmetrical men smelled more pleasant to ovulating women than the dirty T-shirts of less symmetrical men.

Ovulation sends its own signals: Her voice becomes sexier; her skin color becomes lighter and vascularized—she glows. During the fourteen days approaching ovulation, called the follicular phase, she emits more copulins—vaginal fatty acids—than she does during the luteal phase, the next fourteen days. In another dirty T-shirt contest, men found odors emitted during the follicular phase to smell more pleasant than odors emitted during the luteal phase.

When computers began talking to each other in the 1970s and 1980s, scientists believed that because nonverbal cues—the hair flip, the straw, the copulin—were filtered out of the process, CMC felt too unreal to facilitate social bonding. In the 1990s this perspective was debunked: Given an unlimited time frame to correspond, as well as "richer" online media—photographs, more text, interactive questions—studies found that even without a physical presence, people will use whatever communication tools they have at their disposal to connect. A mood becomes an emoticon. A fast e-mail response communicates warmth.

That people can bond online doesn't come as a huge surprise. People have been meeting through personal ads and bonding through letters for centuries. What's different about online dating is not necessarily that you're selecting mates through a digital representation of a person but rather that you're doing it through an interactive medium, entering loads of detailed information into a Web site that runs that information against the information of others. Of course you can't smell the person you're looking at—until later—but meanwhile, the computer is crunching more information than you could ever gather in a glance across the bar, or a chest/pelvis rub.

The online-dating industry has experimented with different ways of imitating real-world attraction online, making self-presentation more authentic and communication more effective. How best to let someone express who they are and what they want? How to let them search? What kinds of information should be prioritized? At the moment the industry is heading in the direction of greater user control, with different ideas about how to achieve that. The goal, however, is always the same: Within any given pool, matching up potential mates should be as efficient as possible, getting you what you say you want, or what the site observes that you seem to actually want.

"You can ask people surface stuff or more psychologically penetrating questions," says Gavin Potter, a retired business consultant with a degree in psychology. "But either way, in the past it's always depended on the person filling out a questionnaire. I'm not interested in that."

Potter made his name in 2007, when Netflix ran a competition offering a million dollars to whomever could create a movie-recommender algorithm 10 percent better than its own. Math geeks and scientists teamed up to compete for the prize. Early on, Potter emerged as the dark horse. He worked alone in his London home, using an old computer to run math formulas on data sets. Rather than going with the purely mathematical approach favored by other contestants, Potter based his Netflix algorithm on human psychology. What does this mean? It gets abstract. But basically Potter designed an algorithm that takes account of, and corrects, psychic concepts like "ratings inertia," whereby a Netflix user who has recently given a lot of above-average ratings to movies is likely to continue to do so, out of habit. Potter's approach has been compared with the field of behavioral economics, which incorporates into traditional economics those features of human life that are lost when you think of a person as a rational machine, or as a list of numbers representing cinematic taste, or taste in people.

Potter lost the Netflix competition. But it would lead him to a new line of business. Through a company called IntroAnalytics, he now sells a matching algorithm that prioritizes implicit preferences over explicit. "Why would I trust a woman to tell me whether or not she likes facial hair when I can simply monitor her browsing behavior and get a definitive answer?" Potter explains. "Even assuming people are good judges of what they want, which they aren't, there are so many options. I help people discover what they want and then recommend people who will want them in return." By letting users design their own filter, Potter does something similar to OkCupid. The difference is that they design the filter without answering questions. He calls the approach "revealed preferences," and a version of it is being used increasingly at dating sites, including Match.

"In any mating pool, you have a supply and a demand," says Amarnath Thombre, the chief of algorithms at Match. "It's a numbers game. Our job is to match people up within the pool we have, keeping in mind that people are not great at describing themselves or what they want."

Match's headquarters in Dallas is located on the top two floors of an office building in Highland Park, one of the wealthiest suburban neighborhoods in the world. When Thombre arrives each day he passes fresh orchids and a wall of digital clocks announcing the time in London, Tokyo, Beijing, Madrid, Munich, Paris, and Stockholm. A coffee table displays clay pots of wheatgrass and paperback copies of *The Cheat Sheet: A Clue-by-Clue Guide to Finding Out If He's Unfaithful*, *The Breakup Bible: The Smart Woman's Guide to Healing From a Breakup or Divorce*, and *Love for No Reason: 7 Steps to Creating a Life of Unconditional Love*. The lobby, with its velvet-covered chaise longue and Boho-chic couches, feels as though someone dimmed the lights on the furniture section at Anthropologie. Affixed to the wall is a porcelain sculpture entitled "Penrose Tilting." The piece, according to its description, consists of repeating kite and dart shapes that "connect to create patterns but will never form the same area of pattern twice—no matter how large the piece gets."

Lining the elegant staircase that Thombre climbs to get to his office are three flat-screen TVs looping real Match.com first dates and real Match.com success stories. A sign at the top of the stairs reminds employees of their mandate: POSITION MATCH AS A PLACE WHERE REAL PEOPLE MEET AND FALL IN LOVE; DISPEL CUSTOMER CONCERNS, GIVE THEM A REASON TO BELIEVE US; SHARE OTHER CUSTOMER SUCCESSES PROMINENTLY AND OFTEN.

Conference rooms are labeled "Chapel of Love," "Dirty Dancing," and "Casanova Executive Office."

With a degree from the Indian Institute of Technology in Bombay, and an advanced degree in chemical engineering from the University of Arizona, Thombre's qualifications as head of analytics—the algorithm guy—go unquestioned. He, along with the head of product, a serene and precise Indian woman named Sharmistha Dubey, were recruited to Match by the current CEO, Mandy Ginsberg, a spunky, dimpled Jewish woman in her early forties who looks like she could still be captain of the high school soccer team. Ginsberg, Dubey, and Thombre all came to Match from i2 Technologies, a supply-chain management company where they found ways to move products around the country with ever greater efficiency.

Before Thombre arrived at Match, in 2008, the site's searching and matching functions reflected an earlier state of the art. "Originally," explains Thombre, "it was very simple. The site created a bunch of dimensions on which you could define yourself and what you want in someone else. The technology was a basic evolution from personal ads: Your dimensions or parameters would be matched up against those of others, and when you looked at another's profile you'd get a visual representation"—the matching green bubbles that RedPepper referred to—"of how your specifications lined up with theirs. This was the original Match. Over the first decade of online dating, systems grew, in the sense that they added more users and more parameters, but the basic technology stayed the same."

Thombre continues: "Eventually we realized that not all parameters are equal. You may say you like people with red hair and a college degree. But education is a much more important parameter. So if she has a college degree but no red hair, that doesn't mean it's only a 50 percent match. Education should count for more. Things like age, height, political preferences, smoking versus nonsmoking, wants kids versus doesn't want kids—these are the really defining parameters. So it's possible for people to match on only seven of fifteen parameters and still be a 90 percent match."

The algorithms got smarter at defining what mattered and what didn't, but they were still based on what people said they wanted.

That began to change in 2008, shortly after Thombre arrived. "I wanted to understand why, when the algorithm says two people are a 100 percent match, it can still lead to a bad match," says Thombre. "When we dug further into the data, we began to see how frequently people break their own rules. When you watch their browsing habits—their actual behavior on the site—you see them go way outside of what they say they want. We realized that people were creating a much more holistic idea of what a person really is. The mind makes a very complex judgment that can't really be defined, beforehand. This is when the whole idea of dissonance came into focus."

Dissonance, a popular concept in social psychology, is the difference between what you say you want and what you'll actually go for. Think of it in terms of movies. Just because you can tell Netflix why you like a movie, and perhaps even describe features of movies you tend to like, doesn't mean you can describe all the characteristics a movie must have in order for you to like it. The hard-core horror guy can still be pleasantly surprised by a well-done romantic comedy. The right plot twist, joke, or character flaw can pull him in, appeal to an unrecognized side of himself.

After an early divorce, CEO Ginsberg tried out Jdate. But being a single mother made dating hard. She was surprised, eventually, to find herself married to an engineer she met offline, at i2 Technologies. "If I had laid out criteria for what I was looking for, it would not have been a guy from south India," she says. "People are complex. You're constantly like the same women that you like also tend to like this other woman over here.'"

From Tom's perspective, Kelly's profile showed a fit blonde with green eyes and a big smile. One photo showed her strolling along the beach in a turquoise summer dress. In another she looked away from the camera, model-like, as the wind blew back her hair. In a third photo, taken at a party, she sat atop a guy's shoulders while pumping her fist.

Kelly had been on Match for six months, the average "lifetime" of a Match user. Tom, a newbie, had been on for two weeks and had not yet subscribed. He was still a free user, meaning he could send winks but not messages until he paid. He sent her a wink. She replied with a message. He subscribed in order to correspond. Tom suggested a date at the Georgia Aquarium and Kelly agreed.

"I saw her on the site," recalls Tom, "and said to myself, 'Okay, she looks *really* attractive. Is that how she actually looks?'"

Yes, it was. "I guess it was my looks that attracted him on Match," Kelly says, "though I doubt that's maintained his interest for over a year."

At first Kelly wasn't crazy about Tom. "It took a while," she says, "because he was nice, and I wasn't used to nice guys. It didn't start out intimate. I was just open to seeing where it would go. The whole thing about being on Match in the first place was that I felt more open to trying new things and not being tied so much to some image of who I should be with."

Tom learned how to play the guitar. She was impressed. "He told me, 'I don't want to be your friend. I want to be more than that. I'll treat you better than anybody will ever treat you.' I've been told a lot of things by a lot of guys," Kelly says, "but I believed him because he's so honest and upfront."

"She said on her profile that she smoked occasionally," Tom says. "When I found out that she actually smokes *daily*, I was like, holy shit! I would usually never go out with anyone who smokes. But at that point I liked her so much—her high energy level, how she treats me, that she's always smiling—that the smoking didn't mean anything. The biggest difference from past relationships is that she's really low maintenance. I don't have to spend much money on her, and if I do, she tells me I don't

making trade-offs about who's too tall, too short, too smart, a
dumb. People come in and tell us a bit about what they're looki
But what you say and what you do can be different." A woman
tell Match she wants a nice Catholic guy between thirty and
who's never been married, Ginsberg says, by way of example. But
weeks on Match she might get an e-mail from a guy who has kids
accept that.

When he signed up for Match, Tom, twenty-eight, a nice Catl
guy who'd recently moved to Atlanta and didn't know anyone, wa
search of a nice girl. A world traveler, Tom had once been engaged
Chinese woman he met while working in Hong Kong. Socially reser
and buttoned-up, he is an accountant who enjoys movies, Garth Broc
and sleeping in. He lives for Italian food, hates salad, and struggles w
asthma. Smokers were out, no exceptions.

On paper, Kelly, twenty-three, was horrible for Tom: an extrove
who tends to gravitate to "dramatic, indie-type guitar players" and ca
sit still for long periods. Kelly loves salad, hates Italian, and pops out
bed in the morning. She had no experience with long-term relationship
nor had she traveled outside the country. And the ultimate deal breaker
She smoked. Intellectual incongruities aside, Tom should've been physi
cally revolted.

But Kelly showed up in Tom's "Daily 5"—the five matches that Match
sends its users each day—for other reasons: The matching algorithm determined that neither Kelly nor Tom had married, and they both wanted
to meet someone who'd never been married; both have college degrees;
both are social drinkers; and both want children (Kelly: "definitely";
Tom: "someday"). The behavioral algorithm took account of Tom's likelihood of getting in touch—he had sent winks to some smokers, despite
his no-smoking rule—as well as Kelly's probability of responding.

Lastly, Thombre's "triangulation" algorithm considered the messaging habits of other men who tended to like the same women that Tom
liked: Of the women Tom had winked at, other men who also liked those
women had contacted Kelly as well. "The triangulation algorithm helps
determine someone's type," explains Thombre. "It says, 'The men who

need to and suggests free things. She's a lot more into spending time than spending money. I was used to a girlfriend being a big investment."

Now they're living together in a new city, Las Vegas, where Tom works as an accountant for casinos, and Kelly is looking for work. Is it a great match? Time will tell. Tom was alone, now he's with a beautiful woman. Kelly had never been with a nice guy, now she is. Both say they've found the love of their life. Neither, when filling out their Match profiles, imagined the other as an ideal partner.

Back in Manhattan, Carrie also found someone she'd never imagined, but with the help of a different algorithm.

"It was like he'd been pulled out of the pile especially for me," she recalls. "His username was AteoBoricua, and the first line of his profile said something like, 'My main focus is trying to raise my children right.' And I was like, yes!"

She sent a message:

> AteoBoricua—Puerto Rican atheist. I'm probably the last person in the US who doesn't speak Spanish so I have to admit I googled that!
>
> I have to head to bed but I wanted to drop you a note so I don't lose track of a nice person among all the "hey sexy lady" messages (groan).
>
> Hope to hear back from you!
>
> - Carrie

He responded saying he'd just returned from the Poconos, where he'd been on vacation with his kids. But for Carrie the thing that nailed it was their mutual response to OkCupid's question about whether women should keep their legs shaved: Both said shaving was "preferred but not required."

"Any guy who can tolerate that I don't wax my legs in the winter," she says, "is good for me."

AteoBoricua doesn't have a college degree, which had been one of Carrie's main criteria. As a computer technician he makes a fraction of what she makes in her management job. She comes from an upper-middle-class family. He was raised by high school dropouts. "It creates some interesting gender-role issues," she says, "because he's used to being the provider." AteoBoricua wanted to pick up the check on their first date, but Carrie insisted on splitting it. "That first night turned out to be a great test case for how things are now," she says. "He was gracious, and I was bold, and it worked."

Socioeconomic status is thought to be a fundamental aspect of compatibility, but between them there are enough similarities and good things to override its importance. They're both divorced, and they both live for their children. He's three years older—thirty-seven to her thirty-four—and is attracted to how opinionated she is. "We both work for big companies," she says, "so there's that. I think I was rude the first time we discussed moving jobs offshore, but I'm better at this now. At work I have direct reports and he doesn't, which was awkward at first. But he's really good at his job, and takes it seriously, and that's what matters. It would be an issue if he didn't think our work lives were important. Maybe he hasn't read as many books as I have, but we've got plenty to talk about."

On their first date he told her about moving back to Puerto Rico as a kid and not speaking Spanish. She told him about working in Asia. Even though their backgrounds are different, their politics align on some key issues. "We bonded over the fact that we both support universal health care," she says. "He influenced my views on minimum wage, and I think I influenced his."

They share a love of pubs and good barbecue. Most important, Carrie's son met AteoBoricua on a Fourth of July weekend, and they hit it off.

"We still bump into each other when we go to pay the check," Carrie says, "but he always takes my hand when I step down a curb in high heels, and that kind of thoughtfulness is what's really important to me. Our differences are less of an issue because we aren't twenty-two-year-olds looking to weave our entire lives together and define ourselves by our relationship. I don't care how he decorates his apartment, because I have my own. He doesn't care how often I do the dishes, because he doesn't have to see them every day. It's fantastic!"

"If you're geeky and you get excited about everything and have a clear idea of what you want, then OkCupid's algorithm is going to work better for you," says Match's Thombre. "If you want to put in less effort but still learn what might work for you, then I think Match is better. OkCupid goes deeply into hundreds of questions. We're focused more on behavior."

Match, OkCupid, and eHarmony represent different parts of an industry spectrum between "search" and "match." Match, despite its name, is more of a searching site. Even though it asks some questions, the filters are minimal. On the other end of the spectrum is eHarmony, a matchmaking site with a fixed filter. In the middle somewhere is OkCupid, a matching site that lets users design their own filters.

But despite their differences, they all combine written profiles, photos, and some kind of matching algorithm based on responses to questions. These sites—along with the many that resemble them—represent Phase I of the online-dating industry's evolution.

Phase II occurred between 2007 and 2011, when the rise of smartphones allowed online dating to go mobile. In 2003, a service called Proxidating used Bluetooth technology to alert users when a person with a matching profile was within fifty feet. Match also introduced a mobile version that year. But these apps were ahead of their time. It wasn't until the 2007 introduction of Apple's Web-friendly iPhone that people could easily access a new world of mobile-ready sites on-the-fly.

For online-dating entrepreneurs, this was a no-brainer. Three of the biggest complaints about the medium in its traditional form, say dating execs, are the problems of distance (becoming attached to someone online only to find out they live too far away); "funnel time," the days or weeks that lapse between the initial online introduction and the first in-person meeting (known in the industry as "asynchronicity"); and a lack of transparency, the idea that, online, a man can't see how "surrounded" a woman is by other men, which results in inefficiencies because women get overloaded with messages while guys get ignored.

"When I walk down the street," said Google CEO Eric Schmidt, "I want my smartphone to be doing searches constantly." Schmidt's utopia can be described as search-without-search, a world in which your phone knows to search for what you want before you do and can help you find the people and things you don't yet know but might like to get to know, right around you.

In Europe, Latin America, and, more recently, the United States, a "social-discovery" app called Badoo facilitates meeting on-the-fly, based on little more than a photograph, an age, and an interest or two. Badoo was invented in 2006 by a young Russian, Andrey Andreev, while he was living in Spain, a country where people tend to be more gregarious in public places.

"It's no coincidence that Badoo was built in Spain," says Badoo's chief of marketing, Jessica Powell. "When I was living in New York, you'd go out with your friends but you wouldn't talk to the people next to you. When you're out in a place like Rio or Madrid, it's just much easier to start conversations. There's more natural social lubrication in those cultures." Meeting people is the basis of evolution, says Powell. And unlike with dating, with meeting there's no pressure, no unnecessary work up to something that may not go anywhere. On Badoo, dating becomes a less distinct activity, one integrated with the rest of life's activities. By 2012, it claimed 35 million active users, with another 120 million registered.

"If we were a normal dating site," explains Powell, "we'd have a matching algorithm and long user profiles that don't tell you anything. We view interests as just an icebreaker. The most successful conversations don't start with 'Hi' or 'I like your profile.' They start when you say something that's interesting to the other person. After all, when a woman sees a guy on the street, there's no voice on her shoulder saying, 'He's thirty-six, works on behalf of animal rights, and likes the same cereal you do.' No, she sees a person who looks good. She experiences something, and sends a signal."

In 2013, IAC had wild success with Tinder, a Badoo-like product that IAC financed. Users sign in to the Tinder app with their Facebook IDs. This gies Tinder the user's name, age, photos, and sexual orientation. Users are immediately shown the face of a person of their preferred sex and can swipe right if they like what they see or swipe left if they don't. Another face appears for appraisal, then another. When both people like each other, a chat box appears. *Bloomberg Businessweek* called Tinder "pathologically addictive," and described the dismay of a woman who, out at a bar, returned from the bathroom to find the guy she'd been chatting up staring at Tinder. "I was like, 'Are you kidding?!' And he was like, 'No, I mean, someone matched me, and I'm checking it!' I was like, 'OK, dude.'"

Generation Y, the people born in the eighties and nineties, have grown up on things being very visual, says Lloyd Price, another marketing executive at Badoo. "There's not a lot of text, not a lot of substance. It's about appearance. And everything's very quick. 'Show me your photo, tell me how old you are, then let's connect.' Badoo just makes the world work faster. Do you want to meet people in your neighborhood? Do you want to do this quickly and in a noncommittal way? The key reason for Badoo's success is that Badoo reflects society. It's all about you."

Badoo and its competitors, such as Skout, another popular meeting app, are part of a growing universe of smartphone apps specializing in social discovery with a dating bent. "Any site that can be used for flirting will be," says Paul Davison, who founded Highlight, another location-based dating app. "But this is much bigger than that. You'll be able to walk into a room, look around you, and know everyone's name and everything about them. It can make profound, new things happen." The field of social-discovery apps includes others with names like Intro, Qrious, Mingle, Sonar, Kismet, and Glancee, which was bought by Facebook in 2012.

Traditional online-dating sites are hoping to keep up. "We are thinking more about ourselves as simply a dating site rather than an online dating site," said Sam Yagan in 2012. "We want the focus to be getting people to meet in person, actually going on dates." Earlier that year, at iDate Miami (where Yagan was finally allowed to speak), he told a conference room: "Now we're seeing a lot of sites that are starting off as dating sites, and then trying to do things to move into social, like taking the pink hearts off the homepage. Because think about the offline world: In a bar, you don't announce you're there to meet women. So sites like Zimride"—a social-discovery site geared toward carpooling—"are finding that you don't have to be explicitly for dating in order to generate datinglike behavior."

Just as important as the change in technology—going from Web site to mobile—is the subtle shift in branding. Savvy entrepreneurs hope to beat the lingering taboo and draw in more users by offering social discovery (a sunny-sounding product that only a philistine or hermit would reject) rather than online dating (an icky redoubt of the desperate). In 2012, Sean Parker, the former Facebook president, teamed up with his old Napster cofounder, Shawn Fanning, to build Airtime, a social-discovery site in video format that works in conjunction with Facebook. Airtime, Parker told CNN, "allows me to use my interests, and all the other information I've built up about myself on Facebook, to match with people who I haven't met, people I might like to get to know." The word "dating" appeared nowhere in the company's press materials nor in the media's massive coverage of Airtime's launch.

Could any heavily trafficked Web site be a potential dating site? What about other sites that operate on matching algorithms? In 2012, Spotify, a music-streaming app similar to Pandora, integrated with a dating site for music lovers called Tastebuds.fm. Tastebuds scans your most frequently played music on Spotify, shows you people nearby who have similar tastes, lets you browse their playlists, listen to their music, and send them messages.

Dating through Badoo or Tastebuds versus dating through OkCupid or Match changes how we meet people, as well as how we think about what we want. But whether online or off, we ultimately select mates based on a small handful of key attributes: age, looks, income, education, ethnicity, children, and marital history. Men and women weigh these attributes differently. But any pool, small or large, online or off, tends to sort itself out automatically, as if by magic.

A 2010 study coauthored by Duke University's Dan Ariely, a leading scholar of online-dating behavior, found that the "natural equilibrium mechanism" by which people pair off in any online-dating pool generates "sorting patterns that are qualitatively similar to those observed offline." The study found, in other words, that dating online is different from dating offline largely—and perhaps only—because it turbocharges that equilibrium mechanism, creating what Ariely calls "an efficient, frictionless market environment."

Had it not been for Match, Tom may never have wound up with a smoker. But given the opportunity to browse and meet hundreds of women offline, he may have. This, then, is the new serendipity. Yes, Tom and Kelly were both on Match and therefore both looking for a partner. But technology helped them stumble on something good that they might never have discovered on their own.

"The question for us," says Match's Thombre, "is always the same: Who's the best person we have to show you today?"

Relationship success, on the other hand, is another issue. It's one thing to put a pretty, low-maintenance smoker in front of Tom and watch him bite, or serve Carrie up the child-friendly divorcee she requested. Whether they're "made for each other" is a much tougher question. Still, many dating sites claim they can predict compatibility, and, in some cases, they may be telling the truth.

ALEXIS, PART III

|

What's the Etiquette Here?

DESPITE HER PROMISE TO SHARE HER ONLINE-DATING ADVENTURES with a large community of people she's never met, Alexis is serious about finding a boyfriend. In her Match profile, she writes:

> I'm a passionate person with a big personality, I suppose not for the faint of heart. Always trying to live healthier, learn more, read more, see more, do more.
>
> My Kentucky-raised mother says I am "very loving and loyal but not one of those nice girls." Thanks mom. She's referring to my sarcasm and my at-times inappropriate sense of humor, but I get more from my Southern upbringing than she thinks. I mean, I keep my nails perfect and wear lots of dresses. I was raised in ballet to be graceful. When I drink it's always Kentucky bourbon on the rocks. I have a charming, diplomatic demeanor and love entertaining. I'm very traditional in the sense that I love cooking for friends and loves . . . but I must warn you I can be a control freak about it, and unless you have verified skills you can best help me by sitting on the couch and enjoying your beer.
>
> Looking for a guy who takes pride in being good to his friends and family. Who's looking for something serious. Who dances at

shows, who can take a joke and tell a story. Who is happy having a quiet night in sometimes, but can play hard as well. Who is good to his body and challenges himself. Who perhaps likes Phish and The Grateful Dead but does not live in a van down by the river.

Immediately, in the first few days, Alexis is inundated with messages from people she calls "icky folk." For laughs, she posts one on Phantasy Tour: "Love, Do you want to go clubbing? Me and my friend are going this Friday. It's not the best place to get to know someone but the music is bitching. Bring friends if you want. I'll pay for you but not your friends."

"Tell me," she asks Phantasy Tour, "do you actually send the 'not interested' automated thing? Or should I just ignore people? What's the etiquette here?"

"There is nothing more infuriating," replies a PTer, "than spending several hours carefully crafting a letter to someone with whom you think you'd have a connection only to be ignored. I make it a point to politely thank writers for their interest, but say I'm not sure it's a match. I feel better treating people the way I'd like to be treated, even when it's awkward to do so."

"My suggestion, from the girls I know, is to be pro-active," writes another. "Don't just wait for guys to message you, or you'll be inundated with creep-shows. Search for people with common interests, and say what's up to them."

Alexis agrees there's no reason that the offline tradition of men initiating a relationship should apply online. The point, after all, is control. So she takes matters into her own hands, searching the Match database for exactly what she wants—a college-educated professional in his early thirties who doesn't post annoying pictures and has written a funny, sex-free profile. Must love music.

"I prefer older guys," she tells Phantasy Tour. "My peers can be annoying. Plus I like to see how a guy shakes out as a man. I don't need some jobless wook [a hippie without ambition] I have to pay for. I don't have an income listed for my match," she writes, "but I work really hard and don't want to be the one pulling the weight, and they need to be able to support my potential babies. I come from a long line of lawyers, so they get a plus one." Her comments set off a Phantasy Tour debate over modern gender roles.

"Holy shit," writes a PTer, "what a trixie [prostitute]."

"Let me point out that men and women live in two entirely different universes," writes another PTer. "What you ladies have to do is consent. That is all. What men have to do is . . . everything. We have to charm you, prove our worth, be indifferent, be cool, have an attractive career, be talented and sexy, buy you stuff, go in for the kiss, fuck you (but not cum too soon!)."

But Alexis believes men of her Millennial generation suffer from a kind of schizophrenia: On one hand, they decry feminism and women who think they can have it all, children and a career; on the other, they resent traditional women who expect men to be breadwinners. Men her age, it seems, want stay-at-home Stepford wives but also think it's a crime for them to have expectations. "A woman giving up a career to raise your babies and wash your balls with a warm wet rag deserves a payoff of security without resentment," she writes.

Some male PTers defend themselves, but Alexis continues: "Fantasy football, video games, shaving hairs left all over the sink, treating women like trash, reading Tucker Max books and *Maxim* magazine (aka men's *Cosmo*)—you all have your own annoying issues. ESPN is just as gossipy as E!. And women who dress slutty or act ditzy do it because they're taught it's what you want. Maybe if you reinforced that you actually want a woman of character, instead of idolizing *Playboy* sluts, you could change the culture."

CHAPTER FOUR

It Knows My Anal Preferences?

AMAZING REVELATIONS FROM
THE SCIENCE OF DATING

No one knows what chemistry is at work when two people fall in love, least of all a computer. The claim that some scientific match has been made is obviously misleading.

—Dr. Igor Aleksander, British scientist, 1973

In his 2010 novel, *Super Sad True Love Story*, satirist Gary Shteyngart imagines a future of perfect information transparency. Every character carries an "äppärät," an iPhone-like device that can access every piece of information imaginable, including, for instance, the financial and property holdings of a prospective date's father.

In an early scene, the novel's bumbling hero, Lenny Abramov, meets his friends at a Staten Island nightclub called Cervix. Inside the club, Lenny's friend Vishnu tells him to take out his äppärät and set the "Community Parameters" at "Immediate Space 360," then to look at a woman he likes—any woman—and press the äppärät to his heart.

Lenny narrates:

The girl across the bar laughed immediately without even turning my way. A bunch of figures appeared on my screen: "FUCKABILITY 780/800, PERSONALITY 800/800, ANAL/ORAL/ VAGINAL PREFERENCE 1/3/2 . . ."

"But I don't even know her personality," I said. "And how does it know my anal preferences?"

"The personality score depends on how 'extro' she is," Vishnu explained. "Check it out. This girl done got three-thousand-plus Images, eight hundred streams, and a long multimedia thing on how her father abused her. Your äppärät runs that against the stuff you've downloaded about yourself and then it comes up with a score. Like, you've dated a lot of abused girls, so it knows you're into that shit."

As I write this, just two years after the novel was published, Shteyngart's hi-tech fantasy world isn't really much of a fantasy. Much of the dating technology he describes in *Super Sad True Love Story* already exists in some form. As for the transparency Shteyngart imagines, it's easier to speculate about what information about us will be accessible online in the future than to guess what *won't* be. Facebook founder Mark Zuckerberg predicts, not without self-interest, that over the next decade a thousand times more information about each individual could flow through Facebook. "People are going to have to have a device with them at all times that's [automatically] sharing," he told David Kirkpatrick for *The Facebook Effect: The Inside Story of the Company That Is Connecting the World.*

Four decades after Jeff Tarr had the idea to install hundreds of special typewriters around Harvard so that a boy could type his requirements and immediately receive the name of a girl who was free that night, location-based dating services—GPS applications that show you every eligible dater within, say, five hundred feet of your Immediate Space 360—are becoming all the rage. Grindr, the premiere mobile-dating application for gay men, was so successful that it released a heterosexual version, Blendr. HowAboutWe.com, the popular dating site based on first-date ideas ("How about we grab brunch and tackle the Sunday crossword puzzle?"), has a location-based app. eHarmony released a "location conscious" app called Jazzed. Match has Crowded Room. Ok-Cupid has Locals. Now many dating sites, or social-discovery platforms, launch primarily, or even solely, as mobile applications.

"OkCupid Locals merges a Twitter-like broadcast feature, Foursquare's location database, and insights on OkCupid's 8-million person membership to give you nearby connection opportunities," wrote Sam Yagan in an e-mail to users notifying them about the launch of Locals.

Notice how Yagan chooses his words carefully. He doesn't use terms like "personality profiling" or "compatibility." Instead, he says that OkCupid generates "insights" on its users, the implication being that the system can glean a little more about you than you can and then use that knowledge to provide you not with soul mates or matches but with "connection opportunities."

What's the difference?

Even in the early days of Jeff Tarr's computer dating, people assumed, or hoped, that the fact of technology-as-mediator would mean not just *more* dates but *better* dates. The Great God Computer must know something we don't, the thinking went. It just *must*. Even while academics doubted that something as complex as compatibility between two people who've never met could be predicted, the notion that it could became a wonderful marketing tool, and red meat for the media. "Every journalist just assumed we were making better matches," Tarr recalls of the Operation Match era, "and we were happy to perpetuate that thinking."

From the company's perspective, claiming a superior "scientific matching system" or "personality profiling test" could distinguish you from the field. The truth, Tarr and Dewan knew, was something else. "Any date was a good date," Tarr recalls. "The idea that we were matching based on compatibility was purely a marketing thing. It was always more art than science."

Dewan agrees: "There was a lot of randomness to it. 'Do you like pizza?' 'Me too!' 'What kind of movies do you like?' 'Romantic comedies?' 'Me too!' Then you go meet her, and most of the time you put your head in your hands because she was so ugly—and she was thinking the same about you. Everyone lied about their looks. We found that 96 percent of women and 92 percent of men said they were above average in terms of looks. On the other hand, the matching worked when it came down to the basics. The big hang-up was appearance. But we were dealing with computers that had twelve kilobytes of memory. We couldn't do pictures."*

Digitally intermediated introductions have evolved quite a bit from the days of Contact and Operation Match. Back then, two companies battled for domination over a market that extended to thousands of students in the United States. Today thousands of sites are going after *tens of millions* of mate searchers around the world. It's not enough for these companies to say, as Dewan did, that their questionnaire is more sophisticated. The pitch must be more elaborate, more official sounding. The computer must know something we don't.

The first five years of the online-dating industry evolved in two stages. First there were sites like Match and its progeny, which were basically searchable personal ads. Whether on a general site like Match or a site that targeted a specific niche, such as Jdate, you answered some questions about yourself and about your ideal partner, and then the search was left to you. This changed in 2000, when Neil Clark Warren introduced a new online-dating model—or marketing gimmick, depending on one's point of view.

Born in 1934, Warren was by far the oldest of the online-dating pioneers—three decades older than Gary Kremen. Warren's interest in compatibility developed early, during his childhood in rural Iowa. His parents' marriage may've lasted seventy years, but Warren's childhood was spent with two people who never talked. "They had a nice marriage," he said, "but they were not a very well-matched couple. . . . My dad was just so stinking bright, and my mom was so sweet, but she was two standard deviations below him in intelligence." Warren's father, who owned a Chevrolet dealership, a John Deere outfit, and a grocery

---

* On a modern computer, five kilobytes of memory are allocated just to display the cursor on the screen.

store, wanted to talk about things like "Why do you think the Jews and Arabs are continuing to fight over the earth?" while his mother, Warren said, "didn't know there was a Middle East."

When Warren's father ran for office in Polk County, his mother voted for another candidate, because she thought politics was a dirty business. Warren remembers being bored to death growing up.

After receiving an undergraduate degree from Pepperdine University, a Christian liberal arts college in California, Warren got a master's in divinity from Princeton Theological Seminary and a PhD in psychology from the University of Chicago. For fifteen years, between 1967 and 1982, he served as a professor and then as dean of Fuller Theological Seminary's Graduate School of Psychology while maintaining a private practice as a psychologist.

Warren considered his own longtime marriage to his wife, Marilyn, to be a lucky success. Many of their friends suffered "the excruciating pain of divorce," Warren said, while he and Marilyn wound up having broad-based compatibility without knowing it. Warren refused to let his three daughters rely on luck alone, however, because it would be, he said, like sending them out to skate on thin ice. Warren focused his practice on marriage compatibility, counseling couples, and performing "divorce autopsies" on failed marriages. In 1975, he published a pamphlet entitled "Selecting a Marriage Partner," and then went on to write ten books, including *Learning to Live With the Love of Your Life*, *Loving the Life You Live: 3 Secrets to Feeling Good—Deep Down in Your Soul*, and *Date . . . or Soul Mate? How to Know If Someone Is Worth Pursuing in Two Dates or Less*. Warren curated an image of grandfatherly affability: square glasses, elegant sport coats, and a well-manicured white coiffure that matched his teeth. There was something distinctly welcoming about his pillowy lips. His soft blue eyes beamed trust and understanding.

In 1993, Warren published *Finding the Love of Your Life*, a "primer on all the qualities that two people should consider before committing to marriage." Two years later, he and his son-in-law, a former real estate developer named Greg Forgatch, started Neil Clark Warren & Associates. The company, which offered seminars and teaching tools based on the book, quickly moved online. "We came to the conclusion that single people in America do not want more education about relationships," Warren said. "They're sick of that. They want somebody."

In early 2000, Warren and Forgatch redesigned the site as a matchmaking service called eHarmony. The goal, however, wouldn't be creating great first dates. It would be creating great marriages. "Not every marriage made at eHarmony is going to last," Forgatch said. "But the purpose of being here is to lower the divorce rate. That's Neil's vision—literally to change the world."

Warren's matchmaking process on eHarmony began with the user filling out a 436-question personality profiling test. The user then received a list of other users on the site with whom he or she was most compatible. In order to correspond with others, they were required to subscribe. There followed a "Guided Communication" process through which the site regulated interaction.

Rather than a big searchable database of singles based on the idea of newspaper personals, eHarmony was about science, algorithms, and a secret sauce. The system determined matches and predicted compatibility based on "29 Dimensions of Compatibility." These dimensions were divided into "Core Traits" ("defining aspects of who you are that remain largely unchanged") and "Vital Attributes" ("based on learning and experience and are more likely to change based on life events and decisions you make as an adult"). The "scientific precision at the core of eHarmony's matching methodology" was, according to corporate literature, "proven to predict the success of long-term relationships." Warren's system focused on similarity—rather than difference—and was based on research he conducted with five thousand married couples.

Further elaboration was vague. But some hard-and-fast rules did apply. The system would not match women with men who were shorter than them. Nor would it match people who were already married—a group that, eHarmony claimed, accounted for nearly one third of the million users it rejected. A thirty-year-old woman would be matched with men between twenty-seven and forty, while a thirty-year-old man would be matched with women between twenty-three and thirty-three. People who had been married four or more times were rejected, as were gays and lesbians, as were people whose responses to the questionnaire failed eHarmony's "dysthymia scale," indicating depression.

eHarmony's paternalism felt reassuring, both to those who entered the date-o-sphere with trepidation and to those who felt like they needed help with their search. A huge TV marketing campaign fueled eHarmony's growth. Within three years it had more than two million registered users. The site claimed to have a 20 percent "conversion rate" of free users to paying subscribers. That was four times the industry average.

Success, however, became a problem. Much of eHarmony's initial popularity was due to Warren's relationship with James Dobson, founder of Focus on the Family, the nonprofit evangelical organization aimed at "nurturing and defending the God-ordained institution of the family and promoting biblical truths worldwide." It had been through Dobson's radio show that eHarmony attracted users. Around 2005, Warren realized that for eHarmony—a for-profit enterprise—worldwide influence would require a more secular vision.

"I think there is something very incredible about Jesus," Warren said. "I don't back away from that. At the same time . . . the public we want to serve is the world."

Warren bought back the rights to three of his books that Focus on the Family had published. He said the public recognizes Focus on the Family as occupying "a very precise" political and spiritual position and to have its name on the top of his books would be a killer for the company. eHarmony grew to be less exclusive, accepting gays and lesbians after a lawsuit forced its hand. Not long after its break from Focus on the Family, the site claimed to have fourteen million registered users from more than two hundred countries.

The story of eHarmony showed that the market for "scientific matching" was strong. Naturally, competitors arrived and quickly tried to differentiate themselves. Duane Dahl, the CEO of PerfectMatch.com, which was founded in 2003, referred derogatorily to eHarmony's approach as "marriage in a box." Dahl said his members are looking for a genuine person "who can respect them for who they are, what they are about, before getting married."

Really, though, there were more similarities than differences. Just as Warren mugged for eHarmony, the copycats would also put professionals on the homepage, people with official titles who claimed to have cracked the code of human compatibility: Relationship Scientist; Sexual Anthropologist. These sponsors tend to hold doctoral degrees and write self-help books. In labs, they reproduce the conditions of relationships, study interactions, and generate conclusions. People of type A are compatible with people of type B. Here's why they worked. Here's why they failed. Here, read this new book.

Dr. Pepper Schwartz, coauthor of *Love Test* and author of *Getaway Guide to the Great Sex Weekend, Everything You Know About Love and Sex Is Wrong*, and much, much more, is one such promoter. Dr. Schwartz is a professor of sociology at the University of Washington in Seattle, and in her spare time she poses for PerfectMatch, with whom she helped develop The Duet® Total Compatibility System. A pocket-sized woman with a calming smile, Schwartz says the system is based on the Myers-Briggs Type Indicator, a questionnaire designed to measure how people perceive the world and make decisions. You can read about The Duet® Total Compatibility System in her book, *Finding Your Perfect Match: 8 Keys to Finding Lasting Love Through True Compatibility*.

GenePartner.com took scientific matching to the cellular level. For $249 users receive a kit with which to swab the inside of their mouth Then they send the swab back to the company and receive a Gene Partner ID. For an extra fee they can hunt for their genetic soul mate on the site.

The media eats it up, often parroting the claims of scientific matching sites as hard news. When ABC's *Good Morning America* covered Gene-Partner, it introduced the segment in awed tones, reporting: "Now, hard science is making it easier to find true love. A new matchmaking system uses DNA to help you find your dream date, and it's redefining what it means to be compatible. . . . Making that first match has always been an inexact science, kissing a few frogs, unavoidable. Until now. With the use of DNA technology, the science of dating has become a whole lot less inexact."

The academic community called bullshit. In 2012, a team of five psychology professors, led by Eli Finkel at Northwestern University, published a withering rebuttal to what sites like eHarmony, PerfectMatch, and GenePartner claimed to do. It is "virtually impossible," the authors argued, "to succeed at the task many matching sites have set for themselves"—specifically, "their promise to identify potential mates who are uniquely compatible with their users."

Finkel and his coauthors laid out their argument in a paper published in *Psychological Science in the Public Interest.* According to the paper, the most dubious claim made by scientific matchmaking sites is that the likelihood of any two people having a successful relationship is knowable *in advance* of their meeting. It is one thing to look at a couple that's already together and predict the likelihood of their success. Indeed, it's been practiced for nearly thirty years by John Gottman, a psychologist at the University of Washington who was made famous in *Blink: The Power of Thinking Without Thinking,* Malcolm Gladwell's 2005 book. By measuring certain emotions and reactions that a couple might express during a conversation—for instance, contempt, defensiveness, stonewalling—Gottman can predict, with 95 percent accuracy, whether a couple will still be married in fifteen years. Other research teams have reported similarly high levels of accuracy in predicting marital outcomes for couples who are already together.

This line of research has been taken as encouragement for matching sites that claim to predict compatibility between strangers. But Team Finkel argues that the success of Gottman's technique means nothing for matching sites. Why? Because the Gottman marriage prediction studies don't actually predict anything. They merely: 1) assess a couple on many variables; 2) follow the couple to see if they divorce; and then 3) use a computer to identify the combination of variables that best accounts for the outcome. This is not *prediction.* It is *postdiction.* The Gottman studies can identify things like "contempt" as a relationship killer, a strong determinant of a certain outcome. But that is all. In a way, Gottman's ability is the same one that Warren, as a marriage therapist, claimed to bring to eHarmony. He had diagnosed problems in *existing* couples. Did that mean he could predict compatibility between strangers?

No, Team Finkel says, because prior to meeting the most important elements of relationship success are unknown and, therefore, excluded from the matching process. Granted, there are some concrete factors, such as geography and socioeconomic status, which are important to relationship success, and they can be measured easily in a questionnaire and plugged into an algorithm. These concrete factors are meaningful. Whether someone dates online or off, he or she tends to look for people who live nearby and share a background. But these factors don't narrow the pool much. Meanwhile, far more relevant factors are unknowable in advance, such as the way a couple will experience and handle stress, particularly stress arising from things outside the couple's control— unemployment, career unhappiness, infertility, and illness.

Team Finkel then takes aim at the matching models themselves. Sites that claim to offer scientific matching generally adopt one of two perspectives: the "relationship aptitude perspective" or the "compatibility perspective." The relationship aptitude perspective is more simplistic; it functions on the premise that some people are more likely to succeed at relationships than others. You can spot these people by asking about certain traits, preferences, and aspects of their personal history, such as whether they had positive relationships with childhood caregivers. As the term "aptitude" suggests, this perspective considers relationship ability to be a sort of talent, a quality that, though it can be nurtured and improved over time, remains relatively stable. Team Finkel concedes that the effects of these personality differences on relationships are well supported by research but argues that they leave "most of the variance in adult romantic relationships unexplained."

The compatibility perspective, on the other hand, assumes not that some people are bound to fail in relationships and others succeed, but rather that there is someone for everyone. The most frequently cited basis for compatibility is similarity—as eHarmony believes. But similarity, Team Finkel says, is difficult to measure: The perception of similarity between two people can have as much to do with relationship satisfaction as with actual similarity. Second, there's no clear consensus on what kinds of similarity matter. Again, concrete things like religion, wealth, and education have been associated with relationship happiness. But scientific matching sites aren't claiming to match on these concrete variables. They focus, rather, on psychological variables such as personality, the idea being that two people will succeed romantically if they interact with and view the world in similar ways. In any case, Team Finkel argues, similarity, whether actual or perceived, accounts for only a tiny variance in overall relationship satisfaction. Besides, matching on negative personality traits, such as neuroticism, is unlikely to yield relationship bliss.

At eHarmony, Gian Gonzaga, the relationship scientist who took over for Neil Clark Warren, sees it differently: "A very anxious person," Gonzaga says, "will be better off with someone who has experienced anxiety, even in just one area of their lives, because that person will be empathetic."

On Valentine's Day 2012, WBEZ, a Chicago affiliate of National Public Radio, invited two locals, Eli Finkel and Sam Yagan, to debate the issue of just how much dating sites can deliver on their matching claims. OkCupid, to be clear, does not pitch itself as a scientific matching site. But it does collect as much information from its users as any dating site and feeds that information through an algorithm to generate match suggestions.

"It *is* the case," began Finkel, "that people in same-race marriages are less likely to divorce than people in interracial marriages. But it's not like these matching algorithm sites are saying, 'Hey, you're white. I can introduce you to someone who's also white.' No, they're claiming that they match you to someone who's similar to you based on psychological dimensions, like personality or values. And the evidence [from eighty years of relationship scholarship] is just very weak that that actually predicts long-term relationship well-being."

Yagan didn't address Finkel's point directly. Instead, he argued that OkCupid can narrow down large pools of people and suggest the ones you're likely to like: "But Eli . . . wouldn't [your critique] apply equally to Google? Online dating is a search for a person. Google is a search for anything. When you type something into Google, it takes all the billions of pages on the Web and says, 'Here are the ten that we think are the best *options* for you.'"

Yet the position of Team Finkel, if taken to its logical extreme—that predictive matching on psychological variables is a false promise—would deny Yagan's claim. If anything, their NPR debate highlights a fundamental incompatibility between a social psychologist and a math guy, a professor and a salesman.

In fact, Team Finkel's argument came as no surprise to the dating industry. For a decade the people at Match had disbelieved scientific matching. "When eHarmony took so much market share in the early 2000s, we hired the best science people," recalls Brian Bowman, who at the time was Match's vice president of product strategy. "It was clear that there was absolutely no validity to personality profiling. But eHarmony was doing a huge marketing push. The good white-haired doctor was the big presence on TV. So we had to offer what he was offering."

Match considered buying eHarmony. Instead, it spun off a competing site called Chemistry.com in 2006 and paid anthropologist Helen Fisher (*Why Him? Why Her?: Finding Real Love by Understanding Your Personality Type*) to put her face on the homepage. Dr. Fisher developed a matching system built around four personality types: Explorer (adventurous, creative, energetic); Builder (calm, cautious, conventional); Director (dominant, analytical, decisive); and Negotiator (empathetic, idealistic, emotionally expressive). Fisher's questionnaire asks Chemistry's daters about the length of their index finger compared to the length of their ring finger. The differential, she claims, is associated with the level of testosterone, which in turn corresponds to one of the four personality types, which in turn determines who you are scientifically compatible with.

Chemistry ran competing TV ads that differentiated it from—and bashed—eHarmony. "I mean, I *am* a good person, right?" asks an actress in one of the Chemistry spots, just as a giant red "Rejected by eHarmony" graphic slams onto the screen, followed by a note that eHarmony has denied more than a million mate seekers. eHarmony tried to punch back. Lanny Davis, eHarmony's crisis management lawyer who served as special counsel to Bill Clinton during the Monica Lewinsky affair, asked NBC and *People* magazine to stop running the Chemistry ads. But to no avail. Chemistry soon ranked among the top twenty dating sites in the United States, not far behind eHarmony.

The online matchmaking space was heating up. Between 2007 and 2010, personality-profiling sites—which were defined as those sites that require users to fill out lengthy questionnaires—grew steadily, coming to account for a quarter of the market. Plenty of Fish spun off its own matchmaking site, eVow.com, which advertised "an innovative compatibility matching system" for long-term relationships. "No more browsing online dating profiles wondering if that person is actually serious about finding someone! In fact, we reject more than 10% of people who we know aren't serious."

To Brian Bowman's mind, the concept of scientific matching is no different than any other dating niche. "As a marketing hook," he says, "it works great. Because consumers are eager to latch onto this idea that you hit a button and your soul mate pops up. That's why the industry is obsessed with relationship success metrics."

Bowman calls this obsession pedantic. "What you have to remember about the dating industry—and this is one reason why even top dating sites rarely sell for more than $100 million—is that the products are largely undifferentiated. In any undifferentiated market, you're left to fight a branding battle with the guy who's spending the most to go on TV. In the dating business, that's meant that the message to the customer must be: 'We're asking you to invest in something that has unique value, i.e., high marriage rates.' Meanwhile, everyone knows that all personality profiling is bullshit. Statistically, you can't put people into categories and say, 'Here's a formula.' If dating sites were being fully honest, they'd stick to one success metric: 'Did you have a good first date?'"

The great algorithm debate is unlikely to be resolved. The academics who do not work for dating sites will continue to be skeptical. Sites will continue to guard their secret matching formulas while producing studies that support whatever conclusions benefit their bottom line. A 2013 study, sponsored by eHarmony, concludes that over a third of marriages now start online and that meeting your spouse online is associated with a lower rate of marital breakup (and a higher rate of marital satisfaction) than meeting your spouse offline. The study's lead author, John Cacioppo, is a University of Chicago researcher who also sits on eHarmony's advisory board. When the study was published, Cacioppo defended his potential conflict of interest: "There has been very little government funding for research about love, marriage, and relationships in the last several decades," he said. "It's easy to make fun of, but it's really important for us to understand because we aren't doing it very well." Cacioppo said the online-dating industry might be the relationship scientist's only partner.

At the moment, the consensus for how far technology can go in predicting compatibility seems to fall somewhere between Finkel, on the one hand, and Bowman and Yagan on the other: *We can show you the people you are mostly likely to connect with on a first date. After that, we make no guarantees.*

But the story doesn't end there.

The industry's obsession with predicting compatibility overlooks one of the more intriguing implications of the Internet's rising dominance as a matchmaker. On personality profiling sites, and even on sites that don't ask any questions, online daters provide an incredible amount of information. Not only when they fill out a questionnaire, but every time they post a photo, send a message (or ignore a message), leave a site (or return to one). What are sites doing with all this data? Does it exclusively benefit their business, or does the Internet's novel ability to monitor and document the many details of social interaction help us arrive at a better understanding of what we really want, how to go about getting it, and what those people we like want from us?

Let's take Shteyngart's scene in the Cervix nightclub a step further. Curious about the brunette, Lenny approaches her at the bar. Thanks to his äppärät, he knows they align on certain metrics. But he's still nervous. What does he say? Hmmm. Well, he sees she's Asian and drinking a beer. Do these facts mean anything for how he should comport himself? Has he learned anything useful from past encounters that he could apply to this one? Will he learn anything useful from this encounter that he can apply to the next?

Suppose there was a robot following Lenny around, cataloging his every move, her reaction to his every move, and providing a feedback loop of information advising him on how to enhance his likelihood of success, cluing him in to the mistakes other guys were making and setting him straight on the disconnect between what he says he wants and what he actually seems to want, with every interaction saved, broken down, and analyzed? Lenny is closing in now. He hears the brunette talking to her friends about a horror movie. Lenny likes horror films too! He can see that she has a curvy figure, is eating a salad, and has a crooked tooth. What does it all mean?

The study of how we behave on online-dating sites is a kind of sister science to the studies of mating and sex that began around the turn of the twentieth century. It was then that two pioneering sex surveys—one by Katherine B. Davis, the other by Dr. Clelia Mosher—penetrated the shame surrounding America's hush-hush sexual culture. They reported, among other things, high rates of contraceptive use, high sex drives, and regular masturbation among married women. A majority of the women polled confessed to believing that pleasure was a legitimate purpose of conjugal relations. More studies followed. At midcentury, Alfred Kinsey's investigation of male and female sexual behavior represented the first prominent coupling of science and sex. *Look* magazine predicted that Kinsey's studies could "have a tremendous effect on the future social history of mankind. For they are presenting facts. They are revealing not what *should* be, but what *is*. For the first time data on human sex behavior is entirely separated from questions of philosophy, moral values, and social customs."

The dispassionate format of science became its own kind of religion. In 1966, William Masters and Virginia Johnson, the other pioneers of sex research, published *Human Sexual Response*, their write-up of a ten-year study of sexual physiology. Among other conclusions, they reported: 1) as female climax is reached, the clitoris, counterintuitively, becomes too sensitive for direct contact and therefore retracts shortly prior to the moment of truth, becoming a potential source of confusion for her partner; and 2) the head of the penis, or glans, becomes oversensitive after ejaculation, and therefore a woman should not resent a man for pulling out before she's done.

Kinsey, Masters, and Johnson believed there were social values to be obtained by the spread of such knowledge—about sexual physiology, sure, but also about what your neighbor thought about sex, or how your neighbor was doing it better, or differently, or the same. Fast-forward four decades: The math geeks and data wonks behind online dating own gobs of raw data, the quantity and quality of which would turn Kinsey, Masters, and Johnson green with envy. "We can't even say what the learning curve looks like," says Markus Frind, referring to the amount of data Plenty of Fish accumulates. "Because every day we climb the slope of new information and learning, and every day it gets steeper." The date-o-sphere begged for a Masters and Johnson.

In 1999, Christian Rudder was a senior English major at Harvard when he decided to add a math concentration. In addition to becoming an indie film actor* and rock-band guitarist, Rudder became a partner in OkCupid. In 2009, when OkCupid became popular, Rudder began playing around in the site's data trove as if it were his own personal sandbox. He started writing a corporate blog called OkTrends. Its mission: No truth, no matter how ugly, would be spared. In an early post about racism in dating, Rudder wrote:

> Welcome back, dorks. We've processed the messaging habits of over a million people and are about to basically prove that, despite what you might've heard from the Obama campaign and organic cereal commercials, racism is alive and well. It would be awesome if the other major online-dating players would go out on a limb and release their own race data, too. I can't imagine they will: multi–million dollar enterprises rarely like to admit that the people paying them those millions act like turds. But being poor gives us a certain freedom to alienate our users. So there.

Alienating users became integral to Rudder's aesthetic: "The basic currency of the Internet is human ignorance," he wrote, "and, frankly, our database holds a strong cash position!" While his style incorporated

---

* Rudder appeared in Andrew Bujalski's *Funny Ha Ha*, for which Rudder's band, Bishop Allen, supplied music. The movie, which was named to a 2005 Top 10 list by *New York Times* film critic A. O. Scott, is said to have invented the "mumblecore" genre.

elements of shock and humor, Rudder set himself a rather serious course: to present empirical proof that many perceptions and assumptions about modern mating were out of sync with reality. Like his progenitors, Rudder wanted to get down to what was really real. Able to monitor and catalog the behavior of millions of people who didn't know (or, because of the anonymity accorded by the site, didn't care) that they were being watched, Rudder embarked on a social scientist's dream, becoming something of an industry oracle. Here's a smattering of lessons he taught the online-dating community:

Even though white men get the most responses to their messages, they write back 20 percent less often than other men; they do tend to reply often to Middle Eastern women. Black women reply to messages at the greatest rate, yet get by far the fewest replies to their messages, including those sent to other blacks.

White women—even though they have above average compatibility with almost every group—prefer white men, to the exclusion of everyone else. Asian and Hispanic women prefer white men even more exclusively.

Jewish and agnostic men, on the whole, get along with people much better than Hindu and Muslim men, and Jewish men match Muslim women better than Muslim men match Muslim women, *not* meaning that Muslim men are bad people, just that they're harder to please.

When categorized by religion and gender, Jewish women are the most likely to claim they've never masturbated.

The ideal length of a first message is two hundred characters, and you should never use text-speak, except for those phrases that denote humor, keeping in mind that "haha" beats the slightly evil-sounding "hehe."

You should compliment anything *except* looks. Guys should be self-effacing but women should not.

Vegetarian women are twice as likely as nonveggies to enjoy giving oral sex (for those intrigued: VeggieDate.com).

A woman's desirability, measured in messages received, peaks at age twenty-one. At age forty-eight, men are nearly twice as sought after as women.

Women are harsher judges of physical beauty than are men.

As men get older they're more likely to develop a yen for rough sex, whereas the rate of women who like it rough, which was never very high in the first place, descends with age.

As women get older they are more reluctant to emphasize their bodies in profile photos, opting instead to show themselves in nonsexual contexts, such as being outdoors, despite the fact that striking sexual poses is a very good strategy for achieving increased message voume. Photos showing the woman doing something interesting, however, such as playing the guitar or scuba diving or walking through a desert, are more likely to lead to actual conversations, Rudder points out, rather than just "Hey, nice rack," which is unlikely to get a reply.

Women prefer photos in which men are looking away from the camera (hypothesis: less intimidating), and men prefer the opposite (they want a woman's full attention). Profile photos should be taken with a Panasonic, a low f number, and no flash.

iPhone users report having more sex than BlackBerry and Android users.

If you're a twentysomething guy with a nice body, you should take off your shirt, but if you're over thirty, you should not.*

---

* As one twenty-seven-year-old OkCupid-ite put it: "You should message me if you enjoy shirts, and wearing them in photos." Older male online daters I spoke to agreed that candid shirtless shots are more successful than posed shirtless shots, implying some kind of link between shirtlessness and maturity: As men age they are expected to do useful things, or at least active things, rather than just pose naked with pectorals and six-pack flexed—a strategy that remains successful for younger guys. However, if older men happen to be photographed shirtless while doing useful/ active things, then the resulting image may be an asset in mate acquisition. Whereas women should just be naked all the time.

The average thirty-year-old man spends as much time messaging eighteen- and nineteen-year-olds as he does messaging women his own age.

Men who chase teenagers sacrifice more than just their souls because:

→ 75 percent of thirty-nine-year-old women rank sex as one of their favorite activities versus only 25 percent of eighteen-year-old women;

→ 81 percent of thirty-year-old women enjoy giving oral sex versus only 63 percent of nineteen-year-old women;

→ 40 percent of thirty-five-year-old women would be interested in a threesome with another woman versus 29 percent of twenty-four-year-old women; and

→ (as if more evidence is needed) younger men tend to want to be dominated in bed, and it just so happens that older women are interested in doing precisely that.

White men like Tom Clancy and *Ghostbusters* while white women prefer Jodi Picoult and *When Harry Met Sally*. The top preferences of white women—bonfires, boating, horseback riding, thunderstorms—demonstrate what Rudder calls "a rural self-mythology," while the preferences of white men amount to the "frat house" stereotype. It's unclear whether one begot the other.

Among gay people, 2 percent have 23 percent of the total reported gay sex, despite the image of gay people and promiscuity. But other stereotypes of gay men hold entirely true. To wit, their top preferences: *The Devil Wears Prada*, Britney Spears, *Mean Girls*, and Kelly Clarkson. Online daters are, on average, two inches shorter and 20 percent poorer than their profiles claim.

Based on their browsing history, 80 percent of users who claim to be bisexual are in fact interested in only one gender.

One in every seven straight men and two in every seven straight women would like their partner to put a strap-on dildo inside them.

The more men, as a group, disagree about a woman's looks, the more they end up liking her, and having some men think she's ugly actually works in her favor. To simplify: If *some* men think a woman is ugly, then other men (who don't think she's ugly) are *more* likely to message her. Whereas if *some* men think she's cute, then other men (who think she's more than cute) become *less* interested. "Suppose you're a man who's really into someone," Rudder writes, attempting to unpack this better-to-be-ugly-to-some-guys-than-to-be-cute-to-some-guys paradox. "If you suspect other men are *uninterested*, it means less competition. You might start thinking: maybe she's lonely; maybe she's just waiting to find a guy who appreciates her; at least I won't get lost in the crowd. Maybe these small thoughts, plus the fact that you really think she's hot, prod you to action. You send her the perfectly crafted opening message: 'sup.'"

By contrast, says Rudder, someone who's "conventionally cute, but not totally hot" might appear to be more in demand than she actually is: the curse of cute. This is mathematical evidence that minimizing your flaws is the *opposite* of what you should do: "If you're a little chubby, play it up. If you have a big nose, play it up. If you have a weird snaggletooth, play it up: Statistically, the guys who don't like it can only *help you*, and the ones who *do like it* will be all the more excited."

Women who do not like to exercise report twice the orgasm problems of women who do.

When it comes to self-confidence, curvy women pass skinny women at age twenty-nine, and curvy women consistently have the highest sex drive among body-type groups that include skinny, thin, average, full-figured, a little extra, and overweight.

Tall people have more sex.

Black men like soul food more than anything else, and black women like soul food even more than that. Latino men like merengue and *bachata* more than anything else, and Latino women like merengue and *bachata* even more than that.

Asian men and Asian women tend to describe themselves, above all, as "simple."

To determine whether you and your date have potential, see if you align on three questions: 1) Do you like horror movies? 2) Have you ever traveled around another country alone? 3) Wouldn't it be fun to chuck it all and go live on a boat? One third of the couples that meet via OkCupid agree on all three questions, which, Rudder calculates, is 3.7 times the rate of simple coincidence.

Cutting to the chase: If you want to know whether your date will have sex with you on the first date, you should ask whether he or she likes the taste of beer. Because of all OkCupid's casual questions—the questions users answer that are not specifically about sex—whether someone likes the taste of beer is the single best predictor of whether he or she has sex on the first date, suggesting there is something empirically true in the image of beer drinkers as practical, unfussy, free of pretension.*

---

* On this issue of first-date sex—who's likely to go for it, who's not—more data exists. A free dating site in the UK, FreeDating.co.uk, correlated certain physical and non-physical attributes with a willingness to knock mops on night one. As it turns out, women who are overweight and/or over five feet nine inches—obese and/or tall—are prime candidates for first-date sex. (Whether a man is overweight has no effect on first-date sex. Although men with athletic builds are most likely to be open to it.) Bizarrely, an interest in cars predicts a *decreased* likelihood of first-date sex in men, while in women the reverse is true. Meanwhile, women under twenty-five are most open to first-date sex, and their willingness *decreases* with age. Whereas the opposite is true for men: A man in his thirties is more open to first-date sex than a man in his early twenties. As for education, a man's propensity for first-date sex increases with his education level, whereas the opposite is true for women. Reducing these principles to their core meaning, Free Dating advises: "The youngest, largest, most drunken woman is about as open to first-date sex as an average sixty-year-old guy."

OkTrends underscored a crucial feature of online interaction: It leaves a trace. "Vast digital trails of social interaction," writes Jon Kleinberg, a data scientist at Cornell University, "allow us to begin investigating questions that have been the subject of theoretical inquiry and small-scale analysis for a century or more—a reflection of the broader principle that science moves forward whenever we can take something that was once invisible and make it visible."

Technology and time separated Rudder's work from that of his predecessors. Whereas Rudder used a computer to run mathematical processes on data sets, Masters and Johnson relied on somewhat cruder instruments; e.g., a thrusting mechanical penis-camera that could have sex with a woman and *film it from the inside.* Whereas Kinsey led a team of men on fact-finding missions, zigzagging the country in planes, trains, and automobiles, rounding up interview subjects in restaurants, libraries, and bars, Rudder sat in a Manhattan office, shoeless and sipping tea while the data rolled across his screen.

The mainstream print media jumped all over Rudder's dispatches. In 2010, the OkTrends blog served as fodder for at least half a dozen *New York Times* articles and blog posts. "The PR that was generated from the blog was transformational for our brand," says Yagan, who appeared on CNN and elsewhere to discuss some of the OkTrends findings. "We were able to take dating into the workplace. Because we can tell where people are reading it. Whether it was an investment bank or a consulting firm, people would read this stuff at work and share it around with colleagues."

Social scientists descended like vultures, purchasing OkCupid's raw data for five-figure amounts in order to study topics such as how political opinions factor into choosing social partners. In 2012, the rights to Rudder's forthcoming book about how the profusion of data is changing our understanding of everything from humor to history fetched a seven-figure advance.

Rudder's findings attracted attention because he was not interviewing online daters or chronicling his own experiences or bringing his own biases to bear. He was aggressively analyzing data on how OkCupid's membership used the site, which, like a bar, is an enormous laboratory of human behavior.

There are differences, of course, between a bar and a dating site. In a bar the interactions and behavior are *un*structured. Nothing is documented and little is remembered. On a dating site the preferences and histories and tendencies become highly structured, saved, and analyzed. A dating site owns what online marketers call the "structured version of your preferences." The next step for dating technology, then, is to capture real-world behavior by gathering data on how daters actually date, IRL. At OkCupid, Yagan continues to believe in the power of data to improve relationships, or at least first dates.

"When people talk about the impact of mobile dating," he says, "everyone focuses on real-time meeting—this idea that my pocket will vibrate every time a hot girl walks by. That's important. But it's not transformative. The thing that's underdiscussed in mobile is the ability it will give us to understand how people are actually behaving in the real world. Historically, the only way we could measure success on OkCupid was by asking, 'Did an online conversation occur between these two people?'" (OkCupid defines "conversation" as a message, a response, and a reply to the response; they call it a three-way.) "But with mobile," Yagan continues, "we're going to be able to verify who actually went on a date. That alone is huge, but then we can also ask, 'How'd the date go?' Whether Foursquare or Facebook, people are feeding their phone information constantly. So this won't require any huge shift in consumer behavior. Being able to put that data back into our matching algorithm will just make it that much richer."

Even Eli Finkel, the industry scold, agrees that data on real-world behavior could mean major advancements in what we know about attraction and compatibility. "I think it's possible that really smart people working with loads of data could increase the chances of predicting initial attraction, and perhaps by a significant amount," Finkel says. "I hedge only because this ability has never been proven. But the promises get a lot more plausible once you stop talking about soul mates and start talking about increasing the likelihood of hitting it off on a first date. That, to me, is entirely reasonable."

ALEXIS, PART IV

↓

It's Good to Say You Want a Real Relationship

THANKS TO ALEXIS, HER FELLOW PTERS FLOCKED TO ONLINE-dating sites—Match, eHarmony, Plenty of Fish, OkCupid.

"This is the power of PT!" one rejoices.

"I hope my height and lack of funds appeal to women who like short broke men," writes another.

"I Googled 'best first message,'" reports another. "Found one that someone had put max effort into, and then mailed it to the 6 hottest girls on Plenty of Fish. No responses. But I was contacted by a chick that looks like Snookie and has a kid. LOL."

Another online-dating initiate shares the introductory message he's sending to women on Match: "Hey, I know of this great little Italian place. Their salad and breadsticks are to die for. It's called the Olive Garden. You may have seen their commercials on the cable TV. I would love to take you there some time. If things go well, maybe I can hide your engagement ring in the breadsticks. Hope to hear from you soon!"

"Sarcasm," advises a female PTer, "is hard to read online. I wouldn't respond to that in a million years. Just saying."

"I don't like that OkCupid tells you exactly who is viewing your profile and WHEN," writes another. "On Facebook the whole point is that you can view people's profiles without them knowing, which is essential for stalking people. I don't want a chick to know I was checking her out at 10pm on a Saturday (loser) or 3:30 am on a Tuesday (crackhead)."

"If y'all like creepin' online," writes another, "I have a way to find girls' Facebook pages. Often they'll use the same picture for their dating profile as they use for their profiles on LinkedIn or Facebook. So just drag and drop their photo into the search bar on Google Image. It can be helpful. I have three mutual friends with a girl I'm going on a date with from OkCupid."

"I can't believe how many women say they're bi on OkCupid."

"I hate when they write on their profile that they find online dating bizarre. Do they really expect me to be impressed that they're above this shit, when their method of telling me was their fucking online-dating profile?"

"These are girls that are obviously tired of getting stuffed by dudes they met at bars, or just got out of a shitty relationship with a dude like that," offers another. "Spin this to your advantage. Also, have a reason to be on there, i.e. work doesn't give you time and shit like that. Being a pussy who can't talk to girls is pretty easy to spot."

"I think that when a chick gets a message, she immediately starts to look for things not to like about the guy's profile. And if I'm being honest, I do the same thing. Online dating is making us far too judgmental and dismissive of each other."

For the benefit of the guys, Alexis posts her own advice manual on online dating:

⇒ Have your primary pic be one where you can actually see you. You can keep the Halloween pic in your secondary album to show some personality, but as the default pic, I would probably assume you were immature and annoying at first glance.

⇒ It's good to say you truly want a real relationship. Don't talk, infer, or gesture about sex on your profile.

⇒ Take the time to write a short, lighthearted paragraph about what kind of girl is ideal for you. The checklist approach comes off a little douchey. This is a harder thing to accomplish, but if in your "about me" paragraph you can show who you are without explicitly say-ing you are funny, smart, caring, whatever, then that is better than just listing qualities. Everyone says the exact same shit. They like to party but stay in sometimes. They live to travel. How fascinating. Instead, tell an anecdote that exhibits who you are and the way you interact with people.

→ Lastly, put some pictures up of you with family, pets, guy friends. Having 5 pictures of you with hot girls does not impress hot girls. It makes it seem like you are insecure and needing to show off all your bitches.

On Match, she comes across a thirty-three-year-old lawyer who seems to fit the bill. His main photo is a picture of him smiling at a party and look-ing off screen. Other photos show him being active outside—in a kayak, on a road trip. In his profile he pokes fun at the online-dating process:

I don't require much from a lady, except that she be perfect in every respect. I want a bookish girl who can throw down when it's time to party. I want Type-A competitiveness sometimes, a devil-may-care attitude others. I want blue eyes. But I also want green eyes. I require a woman who can effortlessly manage the sched-ules of three teenagers, rake in a six-figure salary, and be attentive to my every need—while also taking responsibility for maintain-ing passion in the relationship . . .

"Your profile," she writes to him, "WINS."

His name is Ben, and in his response he mentions that he's seen Phish in concert, a big plus for Alexis. She responds. He asks her out for a drink.

Back on Phantasy Tour, Alexis posts an update: "I've been e-mailing this guy. He is hilarious and eloquent. I have my first online-date on Fri-day! I think this is the preliminary meeting when they see if you have all your fingers and toes and didn't post pictures of yourself 30 pounds ago. Right?"

"Is Poundtown a possible post-date destination?" asks a PTer.

"No Poundtown till the 5th date," she replies. "I plan to put off sleeping with any of these online dudes for as long as possible." She's trying not to have high hopes, she writes, because for all she knows this Ben may be "banging biddies all over town." In past relationships she's been too open to sex too early, and it never goes well.

Alexis's first love, she tells Phantasy Tour, "began with a first date bone. But we were young, 18. Now that I'm a bit older I can't just bone everyone I'm attracted to who wants me. My numbers would be sky high and every new relationship would have high emotional stakes. I just feel like it's wise to have discussed what you're looking for in a relationship before you bone. Once you do, there are usually feelings at stake, most likely for the girl. So if the dude doesn't want a relationship it burns, eventually. And it drags on longer than it should because the dude stays in it just for sex. It's a good sign if sex is tempting on the first date. But I'd rather know their intentions and their character before sex. Personality can shine on a first date, but character takes time to reveal. If you both just want to fuck, go for it. If you want real feelings, it's always better to wait."

CHAPTER FIVE

Better Relationships but More Divorce

WHAT TECHNOLOGY MEANS FOR COMMITMENT

Fast Company: If you were standing in front of a group of business school students who were trying to decide what industry to go into, what would you tell them about online dating?

Greg Blatt: First . . . you can ask them how many people in their own lives they know who are single who complain that they're not meeting the right people, and yet they're not using online dating. That creates a huge market opportunity. . . . Second, this is going to sound a little cheesy: If you go into retail, and you successfully sell someone a coat, you've sold someone a coat. But you really change people's lives with Match.com and other services.

—interview with *Fast Company* magazine

Back home in Oregon, after college on the East Coast and a few years bouncing around, Jacob was surprised at how difficult it was to meet women. He was used to small, ready-made social scenes. In Portland most of his friends were dating people they met in college, pursuing careers, and discussing marriage. When Jacob wasn't coaching youth football and basketball, he liked to watch sports on TV. He also took an academic interest in the city's microbrew scene, frequented concerts, and enjoyed the occasional poker game. Past girlfriends found Jacob's pursuits tiresome. He'd been called lazy, aimless, and irresponsible with money.

Following a long period of singleness, Jacob met a slightly older woman—thirty to his twenty-six—who seemed independent and low maintenance. She moved in, but soon demanded more than just brunch on Saturdays. "I've never been able to make a girl feel like she was the most important thing in my life," he says. "It's always 'I wish I was as important as the basketball game or the concert.'" An only child, Jacob tended to make plans by negotiation: She would watch the game with him, he would go hiking with her. He was passive in their arguments, hoping to avoid confrontation. Whatever their relationship amounted to, he told himself, it was better than being single in Portland again.

After five years, she left.

In 2009, at thirty-one, Jacob felt he had no idea how to make a relationship work. Was compatibility something you learned? Would permanence simply happen, or would he have to choose it? Just meeting people seemed hard enough. It was around this time that he signed up for two dating sites: Match, because he'd seen the ads; and Plenty of Fish, because word of the site had spread down to Portland from its Vancouver headquarters.

"It was fairly incredible," he remembers. "I'm an average-looking guy. I wasn't used to picking and choosing that way. All of a sudden I was going out with one or two very pretty, ambitious women a week. At first I just thought it was some kind of weird lucky streak."

After six weeks Jacob met a twenty-two-year-old secretary named Rachel through Match. Her youth and looks reinvigorated Jacob's outlook. His friends were jealous. Was this the one? They dated for a few months and then she moved in.

Markus Frind did not go to Stanford or Harvard or MIT. To say that his roots are small-town doesn't quite describe the obscurity of his upbringing. He was raised in Hudson's Hope, British Columbia. Closer to the

Yukon Territory than to the United States, Hudson's Hope, a logging town of one thousand people, is near the start of the Alaskan Highway. Frind's parents, German farmers, emigrated there after his fourth birthday. They bought a twelve-hundred-acre plot, where they lived in a trailer without electricity, phones, or running water. It was lonely and desolate. The boy played a lot of chess, struggled to learn English, and didn't have many friends.

At eighteen, Frind drove fourteen hours south to Vancouver and enrolled in a technical school. In 1999, just as the tech bubble was preparing to burst, he graduated with a two-year degree in computer programming.

"Every six months I got a new job," he said a decade later. "It'd start with thirty people, and then five months later there'd be five. It was brutal."

But Frind was learning how to simplify complex code and make computers run faster. By early 2003—as Sam Yagan and Chris Coyne were getting their Harvard buddies back together on the opposite coast—the technology economy in Vancouver continued to struggle. Facing the possibility of another layoff, Frind devoted a couple of weeks to learning about Microsoft's new tool for building Web sites, ASP.net. He decided he would teach himself by building the hardest kind of site he could think of, an elaborate network of user-designed avatars that gawked at, winked at, and spoke to one another.

The idea came to Frind when he looked at Lavalife, Canada's then-largest dating site. "I thought it was ridiculous," he said. "It was this rinky-dink little site charging money for something anyone could make. I was like, I can beat these guys."

The task, however, was not to build a better dating site than Lavalife or Match. The challenge, rather, would be how to make a free site profitable, relying exclusively on advertising instead of subscriptions to make money. For users, the value proposition would be great. The challenge would be finding them. On a per-user basis, paid sites could afford to spend one hundred times more on their advertising budget. Match, with its thirty dollars to forty dollars per month subscription, could spend at least that much, if not several times more, to acquire a single user. A free site could spend maybe forty cents.

Back East, Yagan and Coyne set out to make OkCupid not only free but *better* than the competition. Frind set his sights lower: simple functionality. The key would be dispensing with all frills. No customer service, no employees, no user feedback taken into account. With its drab light-blue background, it looked as though it had been built by a retiree selling used auto parts out of an attic, circa 1995. The site's hallmark was its distorted profile photos, squished or elongated, that required users to click through in order to get a sense of what a user actually looks like. This resulted in more page views and, consequently, more advertising revenue.

In the summer of 2003, Google introduced AdSense, a tool that allowed small businesses to automatically sell advertising space on their sites. By the end of the year Frind was making more than thirty-three hundred dollars a month, largely by selling ad space to paid dating sites that hoped to persuade Frind's free users to trade up. By mistake or design, Frind had built a place for paid sites to spend those enormous marketing budgets. If he could serve as a gateway for the rest of the industry, he wouldn't need Madison Avenue or a huge sales force to make a go of free dating. When the tech community doubted Frind's claims that he was making ten thousand dollars a day through Google AdSense in 2006, he posted a picture of a check from Google for nearly a million Canadian dollars, representing two months' worth of revenue and implying that his site was making nearly $5 million a year.

"The thing that amazes me is that I'm becoming some sort of icon in Canada," Frind wrote on his corporate blog. "There are no counterparts to Bill Gates, Facebook founder, Myspace founders, Amazon, etc. I assume the conversations go something like this. He makes how much??? That is the ugliest site ever."

As Plenty of Fish membership hit the roof, becoming the most heavily trafficked dating site in the world, Frind found it necessary to keep the site free not only of scammers—people trying to con his legitimate users out of money—but also of those whose searching and messaging behavior indicated they were in pursuit of sex, even if their profile stated otherwise. The women who date him on the premise that he's looking for a relationship come away with, as Frind put it, a bad experience. A bad experience for a Plenty of Fish user is bad news for business. He needed to organize people according to *intent*.

"It's easy to spot them," says Frind, when asked how something as cerebral as intent can be monitored. "Suppose a guy says he's looking for a long-term relationship but then messages people in the Intimate Encounter section, or uses sexual language in his profile or his messages. The program will pick up on that and stop showing him women who are interested in a relationship. I don't care what the user says he wants. Most guys, regardless of what they're really looking for, will say they're looking for a long-term relationship. Why? Because they think they need to say that in order to meet women online—and they may be right. But I know whether he's telling the truth. I can see everything he does."

In ordering his site, Frind can make money at the same time by bombarding sex searchers with ads for Fling and Adult Friend Finder, which function like steam valves for Plenty of Fish. These sites are part of the adult date-o-sphere, which also includes Online Booty Call and XXX-Cupid, where daters often forego headshots in favor of genitalia close-ups, selecting mates based on vasculature and labial presentation, cutting through deception at least on these dimensions.

By 2011, Plenty of Fish was drawing 2.8 billion page-views and a little over six million unique visitors per month. With so many people providing so much personal information, all kinds of advertisers, from book publishers to tobacco-addiction remedies, loved the opportunity for targeted marketing. For just a few dollars you could have one thousand lonely smokers see your ad for nicotine chewing gum or the latest self-help book.

Frind wrote on his blog:

> I figured I should go back to the basics and see what dating is all about.... This weekend I'm taking my girlfriend and 4 of her really hot girlfriends for a week-long trip to Mexico in a 5-star all-inclusive

resort in Cancun. I'm going to sit on my big plush bed under a ca-
bana with a steady stream of drinks supplied to one hand by my
girls, while holding my laptop with the other hand. Being that it is
spring break, I can watch how people behave—people in Mexico
are similar to those who go online and date because they all behave like no one is watching, and nothing matters. . . .

In between the time it takes you to read this and my next drink
arrives I'll have made your weekly salary. Now that is either going
to make you angry, or it's going to inspire you to go create something. The choice is yours.

"I feel like I underwent a fairly radical change thanks to online dating,"
Jacob says. "I went from being someone who thought of finding someone
as this monumental challenge to being much more relaxed and confident about it. Rachel was young and beautiful, and I'd found her after
signing up on a couple dating sites and dating just a few people."

We all know what a dreadful relationship looks like, how it unfolds
from day to embattled day in tremors, each party's misery redounding
to and justifying the other's. Hell-bent on the correctness of your
choice—or merely resigned—you adapt to a life in which obscene stores
of energy are frittered away in the effort it takes to live with someone
you secretly hold in contempt, or just don't really enjoy that much. Why?
Because it would take even more energy to start over, and no one wants
to run the risk of being alone. It could be years until another suitable
mate comes along. Whatever it is, it's better than being single in Portland
again.

It's what the behavioral scientists call "learned helplessness" and
what everyone else calls "settling"—relegating yourself to your current
situation on the assumption or belief that no escape route exists, that
you have no control. Evolution drives this. It's thought that the "brain
pain" of lost love—the extreme anxiety one feels at the prospect of relationship failure—evolved as a physical alarm to alert us to the dangers
of social isolation, not unlike the alarm system that keeps our hands
away from hot stoves and makes us look both ways at an intersection.

The relative difficulty of moving on heightens the intensity of this alarm system; it can skewer our standards for happiness and keep us in sub-prime relationships.

There were good things about Jacob's relationship with Rachel. She didn't mind his sports addiction and enjoyed going to concerts with him. But there were issues too. She was from a blue-collar military background. He came from doctors. She placed a high value on things he didn't think much about: a solid credit score; a forty-hour workweek. But Jacob was thirty-four now. He felt pressure. His parents were getting anxious to see him paired up. While a younger girlfriend bought him some time, biologically speaking, it also alienated him from his friends, who could understand the physical attraction but couldn't really relate.

In the past Jacob had always been the kind of guy who didn't break up well. His relationships tended to drag on. His desire to be with someone, to not have to go looking again, had always trumped whatever doubts he'd had about the people he'd been with. But now, after having met Rachel so easily online, he felt differently. He felt like he could assess the situation and acknowledge their problems with a clearer mind. He felt no need to pretend to be sure of something he wasn't sure of.

"I'm about 95 percent certain," he says, "that if I'd met Rachel offline, and if I'd never done online dating, I would've married her. At that point in my life I would've overlooked everything else and done whatever it took to make things work. Did online dating change my perception of permanence? No doubt. When I sensed the breakup coming, I was okay with it. It didn't seem like there was going to be much of a mourning period, where you stare at your wall thinking you're destined to be alone and all that. I was eager to see what else was out there."

The day Rachel informed Jacob she was moving out, he logged on to Match. His old profile was still up. A few messages had even come in from people who couldn't tell he was no longer active on the site.* The site had improved in the two years he'd been away. It was sleeker, faster,

---

* When you stop paying for Match, the company leaves your profile up. Many Match users I interviewed reported having to call customer service to have it taken down.

more efficient. The population of online daters in Portland seemed to have tripled. He never imagined there were so many single people. Now he could see them all.

We live in an age of customization. Homes, cars, vacations, college degrees, even children—they can all be specialized and designed to suit every need, fad, desire, and whim. Love and relationships have also become customizable things, defined in a boardroom, built to fit, and pushed out by sites like eHarmony and Chemistry, or offered up by Ok-Cupid and Match as one choice among many, as a box that can be checked along with other boxes, such as long-term dating, short-term dating, new friends, casual sex, activity partners, long-distance pen pals, have children, (definitely) want children (someday), not sure about children, do not want children but it's okay if my partner already has children, etc.

Or consider the Gaggle, a theory of relationship customization that looks a lot like segmentation, an industrial term for gaining efficiencies by dividing up and isolating the means of production. The Gaggle is a multimedia franchise—a Web site, a book, a movie—invented by two women in their twenties named Jessica Massa and Rebecca Wiegand. A term they coined to describe the romantic arrangement adopted by their peers in the face of "hook-up culture," the Gaggle lays out the new relation-scape of a postdating society: Instead of dating individual men consecutively, just long enough to be disappointed by one before seeking out the next, the Gaggle philosophy encourages young women to maintain relationships with a gaggle of men, each of whom fulfills a specific role: the Accessory; the Boyfriend Prospect; the Ex-Boyfriend Who's Still Around; the Hot Sex Prospect; the Career Booster; the Unavailable Guy; the Ego Booster. It's important for women to understand how they fit into each man's gaggle. If he's her Career Booster, for example, then she might be his Work Wife. Perhaps she sees him as the Hot Sex Prospect, and he sees her as the Last Resort. ("He is not seeing you as the cool girl that you are.") Of course it's bad if her Boyfriend Prospect considers her to be his Short-Term Investment. ("He is asking you to hang out, but not in supermeaningful settings" or "He starts pulling the slow fade. . . . And then you become a bitter, paranoid woman.")

On their Web site, "WTF is Up With My Love Life?!" Massa and Wiegand explain:

> Looking at the guys in your Gaggle, you might be explicitly romantically involved with some of them. But many of them are just "friends"—co-workers, teammates, bandmates, neighbors, etc.—who play different roles in your life and allow you to explore your romantic desires and needs, in a time when traditional dating relationships can't be expected. We've found a way to get all the perks of dating, without actually having to sit around and wait to be asked out to dinner . . . to figure out who you are, what you want, and where you're going to be hanging out on Saturday night. It's about living an awesome life and having guys be a part of it.

Even assuming young women feel that traditional dating relationships can't be expected, many may still seek out long-term monogamy. But that's not really the point. The Gaggle is less a solution-oriented scheme than it is a theory of how to perceive the world around you. Recall what Walter Lippmann wrote in 1929, after technological innovation helped foment the twentieth century's first sexual revolution, unmooring the young from an earlier value system: "The inexperienced must be offered some kind of hypothesis when they are confronted with the necessity of making choices: they cannot be so utterly open-minded that they stand inert until something collides with them."

Once again, aspects of modern life—remoteness, access to all manner of relationships through social networks and online-dating sites—have elevated efficiency and convenience but also deepened the confusion when it comes to romance, especially for the first generation of people to have been born and raised in the postprivacy (and perhaps postdating) era of the Internet. Massa and Wiegand, by expanding choice and offering a broader view, are trying to impose a working structure on modern norms. The Gaggle, with its go-girl undertone, is about options. Don't settle. Don't sit at home waiting. Instead, adapt. This is their hypothesis.

Relationship advice-givers have been trying to define America's new relation-scape since the 1960s, when the old marital ethos founded on a good job and a neat home entered decline, buffeted by a wave of anti-institutionalism. Abraham Maslow's Human Potential Movement mocked the idea that human growth culminated with a singular peak accomplishment, marriage. Life was fuller than that. It was an adventure marked by an ascending sequence of growth experiences, including, but not confined to, the loss of a job, divorce, and even, eventually, dying as a growth experience. Maslow's fervent individualism was, in a sense, the inexorable capstone of a movement that had begun two hundred years earlier, when romanticism put a new emphasis on self-expression and turned courtship into that heroic quest for life meaning, personal identity, and terrestrial salvation.

Dr. Albert Ellis, a Maslow contemporary, tried to chart this new world of permissiveness in a string of books, including *The Case for Sexual Liberty* and (with Edward Sagarin) *Nymphomania: A Study of the Over-Sexed Woman*. In his writing, Dr. Ellis came across as a sex-crazed quack, though an assiduous and practical one. "Without experience and practice at heterosexual relations," he wrote in *Sex and the Single Man* (a response to Helen Gurley Brown's *Sex and the Single Girl*), "there is a very low probability that you will succeed with them." In a chapter devoted to picking up women, Ellis concluded: "*How* to meet suitable girlfriends is a more difficult question.... The general answer in this regard is clear: stop defining yourself as a no-goodnik whenever you fail, and keep trying, trying, trying."

What's different about today's revolution, of course, is its covertness. We can't see young people frolicking for the first time in movie theaters and steaming up car windows. We can't turn on the evening news and see baby boomers dancing naked in the mud at Woodstock. Instead, for information we turn to opinionistas like Massa and Wiegand, data-wonks like Christian Rudder, and bloggers like Chiara Atik and Scott Alden.

Alden and Atik are the male-female blogging duo at How About We, the dating site based on first-date ideas. Alden was fed up with the overly simplistic distinction between "casual" and "serious" relationships. There are actually ten varieties of casual-but-emotional-sex, he says, including intense orgasm sex ("And there you are. Feeling more vulnerable than you intended to."); rough sex ("It doesn't matter if you met that night and never intend to see each other again—if you're beating the heck out of each other, it's not casual."); I hate you sex ("Being pissed at someone doesn't mean you don't feel anything for them, especially if you're expressing it sexually."); accidental pregnancy sex ("Maybe you *thought* it was casual, but if the stick turns pink, it's definitely not casual anymore."); anal sex ("Unless you're one of those people who just finds butt sex super easy to pull off [and bless you if you are], you're going to need to deal with lube, possibly toys and a lot of trust to make it work. Again, you *can* have anal sex with someone you don't know very well, but it's never 'whatevs.'").

There are degrees of disinterestedness. And any variety of deceptively noncasual sex could be a stepping-stone toward (or away from) any one of nine "pre-exclusive relationships," or PXRs, of which Alden compiles a litany, including OGBC (ongoing booty call: "You've probably never seen your OGBC before midnight"); FWB (friends with benefits: "The most infamous of all PXRs. . . . we keep acting like we're emotionally invincible until we ruin a perfectly good friendship"); SEO (seeing each other: "You're not necessarily exclusive, but you're interested in the *possibility*"); XWSEX (ex with sex: "There were probably a lot of reasons that you and your ex called it quits. But maybe the sex wasn't one of them"); PMX (pretty much exclusive: "The PMX period is a time when you're basically obligated to take advantage of any and all uncomplicated sex that comes your way—because it won't last long"); and, perhaps the most perplexing of all PXRs, the SF (significant frother: "You're not dating them. You're not sleeping with them. But whoever you are dating or sleeping with will probably get inexplicably jealous of them. Your SF is your 'When-the-hell-are-you-two-just-going-to-get-married?!' friend").

There's a biological basis for our obsession with choice: The experience of choice—confronting, say, forty-five versions of peanut butter at

Whole Foods or a dozen styles of tattered cuffs at The Gap—elevates activity in brain regions associated with motivation and reward. The perception that one has options instills feelings of autonomy, which in turn contributes to psychological and physical health.

At the same time, however, the notion that too many options makes us miserable is a well-documented phenomenon in late-capitalist America. Acquisitions of things that used to be viewed as utilitarian and standardized, such as cars or blue jeans, can now cause a gnawing distress, a suspicion that you chose nonoptimally. As early as 1970—thirty-five years before Barry Schwartz published *The Paradox of Choice*—Philip Slater (no relation) wrote *The Pursuit of Loneliness*, in which he argued that "the major problem for Americans is that of choice: Americans are forced into making more choices per day, with fewer 'givens,' more ambiguous criteria, less environmental stability, and less social structural support, than any people in history."

In online dating, choice influences mate seekers in at least two ways. First, there's the choice one confronts at the selection phase. Second, there's the mere existence of online dating as an easy, discreet mate-finding channel *after* selection has occurred. At selection, researchers have seen that as choice sets grow larger, mate seekers are liable to become "cognitively overwhelmed." They deal with the choice overload by adopting lazy comparison strategies and examining fewer cues. After selection, researchers say three ingredients determine the strength of relationship commitment: 1) satisfaction level (one's subjective evaluation of the relationship); 2) investment size (such as time and effort, shared experiences and emotions, and the importance that the relationship holds for one's identity); and 3) quality of alternatives.

Both satisfaction level and quality of alternatives could be directly affected by a larger mating pool. No studies in the romantic realm have looked at how choice affects satisfaction.* But when it comes to quality

---

* Research elsewhere has found that people are less satisfied when choosing from a larger group: Those who selected their chocolate from an array of six think it tastes better than those who select the same chocolate from an array of thirty.

of alternatives, evidence shows that the perception of appealing alternatives to a current romantic partner is a strong predictor of low commitment to that partner and eventual breakup. The opposite situation—the perception of *diminished* choice—supports the same conclusion: People exhibit stronger positive illusions about a partner when they believe that access to alternative partners is scarce.

"You can say three things," says Northwestern's Eli Finkel, of Team Finkel fame. "First, the best marriages are probably unaffected. Happy couples won't be hanging out on dating sites. Second, people who are in marriages that are either bad or average might be at increased risk of divorce because of increased access to new partners. Third, it's unknown whether that's good or bad for society. On one hand, it's good if fewer people feel like they're stuck in relationships. On the other, evidence is pretty solid that having a stable romantic partner means all kinds of health and wellness benefits."

If online dating can blunt the emotional pain of separation, if adults can afford to be increasingly demanding about what they want from a relationship, including when and how they want it, the effect of online dating seems positive. The bar for what we consider a good relationship will be raised. But what if it's also the case that the prospect of finding an ever more compatible mate with the click of a mouse means a future of relationship instability, a paradox of choice that keeps us chasing the illusive bunny around the dating track? Does it matter that the latter—serial online daters returning to the date-o-sphere—is what the industry is hoping for?

Despite their competing business interests, a majority of the dating execs interviewed for this book agreed with what research appears to suggest: The rise of online dating will mean an overall decrease in commitment.

"The future," says Dan Winchester, "will see better relationships but more divorce. The older you get as a man, the more experienced you get. You know what to do with women, how to treat them and talk to them. I often wonder whether matching you up with great people is getting so efficient, and the process so enjoyable, that marriage will become obsolete."*

"Historically," says Greg Blatt, CEO of Match's parent company, "relationships have been billed as 'hard' because, historically, commitment has been the goal. You could say online dating is simply changing people's ideas about whether commitment itself is a life value." A forty-something bachelor in Manhattan, Blatt underscores the role that mate scarcity plays in people's relationship decisions, including his own: "Look, if I lived in Iowa I'd be married with four children by now. That's just how it is."

Another online-dating exec hypothesized an inverse correlation between commitment and the efficiency of technology. "I think divorce rates will increase as life in general becomes more real-time," said Nic Formai, the head of social-media marketing at Badoo. "Think about the evolution of other kinds of content on the Web. Stock quotes, news. The goal has always been to make it faster. The same thing will happen with meeting. It's exhilarating to connect with new people, not to mention beneficial for reasons having nothing to do with romance. You network for a job. You find a flatmate. Over time you'll expect that constant flow. People always said that the need for stability would keep commitment alive. But that thinking was based on a world in which you didn't meet that many people."

"Societal values always lose out," says Noel Biderman, the founder of Ashley Madison, which bills itself as "the world's leading married dating service for discreet encounters," i.e., cheating. "Premarital sex used to be taboo," explains Biderman. "So women would become miserable in marriages, because they wouldn't know any better. But today more peo-

---

* U.S. Census data from 2010 showed that 39 percent of all Americans believe marriage is becoming obsolete. Yet 47 percent of the unmarried adults who believe marriage is becoming obsolete say they would like to marry someday. This suggests that a huge chunk of the population, despite disbelieving in marriage, has not discovered a satisfactory alternative. At the moment, the marriage void is being filled partly by an increase in cohabitation, indicating that a wish for some kind of stability remains a driving force in the absence of legal commitment.

ple have had failed relationships, recovered, moved on, and found happiness. They realize that that happiness, in many ways, depends on having had the failures. As we become more secure and confident in our ability to find someone else, usually someone better, monogamy and the old thinking about commitment will be challenged very harshly."

Even at eHarmony, where marriage and commitment are billed as the only acceptable goals of dating, Dr. Gian Gonzaga, the relationship psychologist who replaced Dr. Warren, acknowledges that technology is at odds with commitment. "You could say online dating allows people to get into relationships, learn things, and ultimately make a better selection," says Gonzaga, who wrote *eHarmony Guide to Dating the Second Time Around: Finding Love That Lasts.* "But you could also easily see a world in which online dating leads to people leaving relationships the moment they're not working, an overall weakening of commitment."

In 2011, Mark Brooks, a consultant to the online-dating industry, published the results of an industrywide survey entitled, "How Has Internet Dating Changed Society?" From the survey responses of thirty-nine executives, here are some conclusions:

- ➡ "Internet dating has made people more disposable."
- ➡ "Internet dating may be partly responsible for a rise in divorce rates."
- ➡ "Low quality, unhappy, and unsatisfying marriages are being destroyed as people drift to Internet dating sites."
- ➡ "The market is hugely more efficient. People expect to—and this will increasingly be the case over time—access people anywhere based on complex search requests. Such a feeling of access affects our pursuit of love. Increasingly, the whole world (versus the city we live in) feels like the market for our partners. Our pickiness will probably increase."
- ➡ "Above all, Internet dating has helped people of all ages realize that there's no need to settle for a mediocre relationship."

Alex Mehr, a cofounder of the dating site Zoosk, is the only executive interviewed for this book who disagrees with the prevailing view. "Online dating does nothing more than remove a barrier to meeting," says Mehr. "Online dating doesn't change my taste, or how I behave on a first date, or whether I'm going to be a good partner. It only changes the process of discovery. As for whether you're the type of person who wants to commit to a long-term monogamous relationship or the type of person who wants to play the field, online dating has nothing to do with that. That's a personality thing."*

Some psychologists argue that online dating enhances commitment: since the Internet offers so much information about potential dates, your decision about whom to date is likely to be more deliberate, more informed. That assumes, of course, that information online is accurate. It also assumes that more informed decisions about dating lead to more commitment. Others who doubt that online dating erodes commitment point to census data showing that divorce rates are finally declining after decades of increase. Fair enough. But census data also shows that the marriage *rate* is at a historic low—the lowest it's been in over a century—and continues to decline precipitously. Many aspects of modern life, including online dating, are influencing that trend.

Meanwhile, online connections might be playing a bigger role in divorce. "I've seen a dramatic increase in cases where something on the computer triggered the breakup," says Gilbert Feibleman, a divorce attorney and member of the American Academy of Matrimonial Lawyers. "People are more likely to leave relationships"—particularly ones that aren't going well—"because they're emboldened by the knowledge that it's no longer as hard as it was to meet new people. But whether it's dating

---

* Fidelity might be a genetically programmed trait. "As far as researchers know," writes Louann Brizendine in *The Female Brain*, "human males represent behaviors on a spectrum from totally polygamist to totally monogamous." Brizendine, a neuropsychiatrist, speculates that there's a link between the length of a man's vasopressin gene and his likelihood of being unfaithful—the longer the vasopressin gene, the less likely he is to stray. "So the current joke among women scientists is that we should care more about the length of the vasopressin gene in our mates than about the length of anything else."

sites, social media, e-mail, it's all related to the fact that the Internet has made it possible for people to communicate and connect, anywhere in the world, in ways that have never before been seen."

Single again, Jacob cut his hair close and started working on his paunch. "Ever since college I've been a little loose in the cage," he says. "But I'm doing this DVD program called P90X, Tony Horton's extreme home fitness. It didn't seem to be working at first, but now women are telling me how athletic I look. It's amazing how much of a difference that stuff can make, even if just for confidence."

Back online, Jacob is meeting all kinds of women. Some like going to basketball games and concerts with him. Others enjoy bar hopping. Jacob's favorite football team is the Green Bay Packers, and he has success using Packers fandom as search criteria on OkCupid, the latest site he's trying out.

Many of these relationships become physical very early, sometimes before the date happens. Prior to a first date with a zookeeper from Ok-Cupid, she sends him a text message: "Do you want to just meet at my place?"

Jacob is seeing a paralegal and a lawyer who work at the same law firm; a naturopath; a pharmacist; and a chef. Three of them he slept with on the first or second date. The others are headed toward intimacy. The chef says she has hips like handlebars and encourages him to grab them. The naturopath wants to wait until she gets waxed, but emphasizes how much she enjoys threesomes. He likes the pharmacist most. She's a girlfriend prospect. The problem is that she wants to take things slow. This worries Jacob. If need be, he knows he'll just get it somewhere else. There's always a pepperoni pizza in the trunk, is how Jacob thinks of it. A publicist who enters the picture via Plenty of Fish requests to be choked during sex.

"Some of these women are sort of losers," Jacob says, "but they supplement my life while I pursue the long-term prospects." In addition to the pharmacist, Jacob envisions long-term potential with a fellow fly-fishing enthusiast after they exchange twenty-two messages on OkCupid. But shortly after the first date the relationship morphs into a sex-only situation.

On Match one day, he comes across a twenty-five-year-old. "Curiously obsessed," she writes in her profile, "with random things like cleaning out my iTunes, always having a pen on me, and pointing out inefficiencies. I have an amazing life but am frustrated with the lack of assertive men in this town."

"I've been hearing this a lot lately," he writes to her, "and I have to agree with you. I think it's a ton of factors, starting with Portland's laid-back lifestyle. There are also a lot of niche interests here to take up our time. I'm sure there's more to it."

She responds, seeming interested, but he doesn't ask her out. She strikes him as too demanding.

One night the paralegal tells Jacob a workplace anecdote that references the lawyer whom Jacob is also seeing. The paralegal then confides in him: Her prior relationships haven't gone well, she says. But he gives her hope. All she needs in a relationship is honesty, she says, and Jacob thinks, "Oh my God." He wants to be a nice guy, he says, but Jacob knows that sooner or later he's going to start coming across as a serious asshole. While out with one woman he has to silence text messages coming in from others. He must start paring down "the clubhouse."

He tries calling the naturopath. She doesn't answer, so he sends a text message: "Hey, I wanted to talk to you about what's been on my mind. I started online dating thinking that I just wanted to see what was out there and not jump into something with one person again too soon. In other words, I want to date other people right now and not be exclusive. I am uncomfortable that we haven't spoken about this yet and wanted to tell you because it's the honest thing to do."

"You are making a huge mistake," she replies. "I will be your biggest regret in life. Lose my number."

Women seeking commitment have evolved strategies to detect deception and guard against it. They might withhold sex in order to assess his intentions and/or whether there's competition or prior commitments. Theoretically, her withholding sends him a message: I'm not that kind of girl. Theoretically, his willingness to wait sends a message back: I'm interested in more than sex.

But the pace of technology is upending these rules and assumptions. Relationships that begin online, Jacob finds, move quickly. He chalks this up to a few things. First, familiarity is established during the messaging process, which also often involves a phone call. By the time they meet face-to-face there's already a level of intimacy, which often feels particularly strong because they connected online, without physical chemistry. Second, if she's on a dating site there's a good chance she's eager to connect. But for Jacob, the most crucial difference between the date-o-sphere and offline meeting is the sense of urgency. Occasionally, he has an acquaintance in common with the women he meets. But by and large they come from different social pools. "It's not like we're just going to run into each other again," he says. "So you can't afford to be too casual. It's either, 'Let's explore this' or 'See you later.'"

Social scientists say that all sexual strategies carry costs, whether risk to reputation (promiscuity) or foreclosed alternatives (commitment). As online dating becomes increasingly pervasive, the old adaptive problems of a short-term mating strategy will give way to a new set of problems. Jacob, for instance, notices he's seeing his friends less often. Their wives get tired of befriending his latest girlfriend only to see her go. Also, he finds himself unable to dismiss certain women even when he's seeing someone, or several people, he likes better. Research shows that people will often overinvest to keep an inferior option open, even when doing so means underinvesting in the superior option. Some say a desire for flexibility drives this tendency. Others chalk it up to an aversion to loss, that we're not pursuing the pleasure of utility but rather avoiding the pain of disutility.

Historically, men pursuing a short-term strategy have faced at least three constraints: 1) the problem of partner number, or variety; 2) the problem of identifying which women are "sexually accessible"; and 3) the problem of minimizing commitment and investment. Whether by accident or design, online-dating technology innovated around all three of these constraints, known in social-psychology literature as "adaptive problems."

Any new medium originates, often, as a solution to a problem—*I need to communicate in real time with people who live in other places; I can't find a date*—and in solving the problem it creates a new irritant: *I can talk to everyone all the time; I can go on a date every night.* Communication mediums, argued media guru Marshall McLuhan, change us by changing our perception of the world, of reality, of what is possible.

Jacob has mixed feelings about his altered perception. "Each relationship is its own little education," he says, "you learn more about what works and what doesn't, what you really need and what you can go without. That feels like a useful process. I'm not jumping into something with the wrong person, or committing to something too early, as I've done in the past." But he does wonder: When does it end? At what point does learning become an excuse for not doing what it takes to make something last? "Maybe I have the confidence now to go after the person I really want," he says. "But I'm worried that I'm making it so I can't fall in love."

Over time Jacob feels less excitement over each new date. "Is that about getting older," he wonders, "or about dating online?" How much of the enchantment associated with the experience of romantic love had to do with scarcity? *This person is exclusively for me.* How will romantic love hold up in a marketplace of abundance? *This person could be exclusively for me, but so could the other two people I'm meeting this week.*

Using OkCupid's new Locals app, Jacob can broadcast his location and desired activity and then meet people on the fly. Out alone for a beer one night, he responds to the broadcast of a woman who's at the bar across the street, looking for a karaoke partner. He joins her. They spend the evening together, and never speak again. When Jacob wants to be taken off the grid, he hits a button on his iPhone. When he wants back in, he hits another button. The choice between dating and not dating: It's hardly a choice at all.

ALEXIS, PART V

↓

Sometimes Things Do Work Out

HER FIRST DATE WITH BEN, OVER A DRINK, GOES WELL. THEY MEET the next day for dinner and music.

Alexis likes the way he looks, likes that he's affectionate and laid-back but takes control when appropriate. That she met Ben online and doesn't know much about him makes her nervous. But she Googles him obsessively, finding out everything she can, and he seems legit. "I am pretty much smitten," she writes on Phantasy Tour. "I want to wait on the sexy time front though because I really am looking for an actual boy-friend and don't want him to think I'm a sloot [slut]." Then she asks: "Is it really kosher though to go home with someone and not get it on? I would hope there would at least be some cab make out sessions or something in the meantime. . . . The no sex sleepover seems a bit cruel."

"I don't mind no sex sleepovers if I like the girl," replies a male PTer. "It's a great way to get quality time in."

"I think it's rather presumptuous to think you're going to sleep with someone the first time you sleep over," writes another. "So I wouldn't expect the declaration. If that bothers someone, they're clearly not quality."

Meanwhile, the chatter turns to other relationship issues. "I came home from work and I could tell she was pissed about something," writes a PTer. "Then she said she found a tissue and wanted me to say, honestly, if it was from me jerking off. I just said, 'Yeah,' and laughed. But I guess she figured since we live together now that I don't need to do that anymore? I got through my teenage years without getting busted. Now it's finally happened and I'm 26 years old."

"She should be telling you to jerk off on to her," Alexis offers. "Get a new girlfriend."

"Having a solo session is not a big deal," someone else replies. "Just because you're living together doesn't mean you have to share every moment of your lives. People need their space and private thoughts."

"If I was the OP," writes another, "I would David Blaine her and keep on walking."

"'David Blaine her'?"

"A David Blaine is when you're fucking somebody from the back, and, goddamn, you let your friend slide in without her knowing, and then you run around and bang on the window and wave at her ass. That's called a David Blaine."

A week later Alexis updates the PT community on Ben: "Date #3 tonight," she writes. "If your prophecies are correct, and I wind up in the East River, know that I have always loved you Internet." But Alexis is enamored with online dating: "The people you meet might live a mile away from you, but you'd never run into them IRL," she writes. "Plus, the online profile screens for red flags. If you're serious about meeting someone with long term potential, there's no need to waste time on 3 dates only to find out homeboy still lives with his mom and failed out of junior college. It's still exciting and scary and new to get to know someone you meet online, and a bit magical as it starts to work out."

"Oh gimme a break," writes a PTer. "You know what's going to happen? This guy, who is probably pretty good looking if you're going to bang him a week after meeting—this dude is going to walk man. Twenty-to-one he walks after 5 bangs. I know like 35 dudes in NYC who just mack it up on Match. Most have 2 restaurants they take the girls to. One that's darker if they're ugly and one that's a little brighter."

Others agree that Alexis should proceed with caution.

"I will tread lightly," she writes. "But it's kind of depressing that everyone's response to this is just some warning about how he is probably ill-intentioned and has no real interest in being any good to me. Blah. Thanks for the concern PT. But sometimes things do work out, mmmkay?"

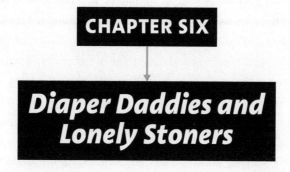

CHAPTER SIX

Diaper Daddies and Lonely Stoners

NICHE DATING AND THE ULTRAREFINED SEARCH

Laura Brashier's diagnosis amounted to a mixed blessing: Stage IV cervical cancer was rare in a woman of thirty-seven, but her youth opened a greater range of treatment options, a full menu of chemotherapy along with extensive radiation ranging from below her breasts to the top of her legs. In the surgery to scrape metastasized cancer cells from her groin, thirty-three lymph nodes were removed, leaving her with a permanently swelled right leg that would need a stocking. During radiation, the omentum, a sheet of tissue that covers the organs around the stomach, melted. The doctors had to cut it away and tack it back on. The colon was irreparably damaged, maiming her digestive system. At the cancer site, radiation turned her vagina to scar tissue; it nearly closed completely. The doctors advised her to keep having sex.

"A cancer liability with a scarred vagina," Brashier recalls. "No one was going to sign up for that."

Brashier, an attractive California blonde who works as a hairdresser in Orange County, was given a dilating device to help keep her vaginal canal open. They told her to use it for ten minutes per day. But scar tissue doesn't expand like normal tissue. The burning pain was unbearable.

She bore the ordeal patiently, with little remonstration, and then the difficult part began. Three months after the diagnosis, she was cancer-free. She was also postmenopausal, having lost her ovaries before her thirty-eighth birthday. She figured she was just going to live alone. She felt reclusive and quiet, especially these days, with so much of everything revolving around sex and discussion of sex. It didn't matter whom Brashier met, or how she met them. The likelihood of hitting it off on a first date was nil. There was something about her that she couldn't talk about. "We live in our brains anyway," she says. "So you're trying to date and just talk about life and substance, and meanwhile you have this heavy thing on your mind. Do you tell them, straight up, that you can't have intercourse? Or do you wait?"

Brashier began dating someone she met at a party who lived an hour away. She liked him. There was chemistry. But then he lost his job and said he couldn't afford to court her anymore. "It was for the best," she thought. At least she wouldn't have to tell him the secret.

During the 1980s, personal ads enjoyed a resurgence in the United States. Americans could advertise in a number of publications geared toward their needs. In New York City, at least fifteen publications carried personals, including *Chocolate Singles*, a bimonthly magazine for blacks, and the *Mensa Bulletin*, for the high-IQ set. Elderly singles met through *Sweet 'n' Sexy Seniors*.

The modern mail-order bride industry originated in these pre-Internet personal ads. American men unhappy with the women's lib movement at home could shop for submissive Asian wives in a catalog published by Cherry Blossoms, one of the oldest mail-order bride agencies, founded in 1974 by John Broussard. A Harvard graduate and former hippie, Broussard had been importing Oriental bowls and vases when he decided to diversify his business to include Philippine women. By 1986, one hundred mail-order bride agencies had blossomed in North America. The Philippines exported twenty thousand mail-order brides per year. At the time, Alfredo Perdon, the director of the Philippine government's Commission on Filipinos Overseas, told Reuters that his country had "become a real shopping market for the foreigner in search of a wife." In 1992, after the fall of the Soviet Union, one hundred more agencies would surface to meet the new demand for Russian and Ukrainian brides.

Gay people mingle in gay bars. Bikers congregate in biker bars. Significant minorities—religions, political interest groups, sports fans—often enjoy some real-life venue in which to mix and date. But what about the thousands of other disparate, marginal, or downright deviant interests that lack nonvirtual meeting places? And what about people like Laura Brashier, who face "thin markets" for partners?

The nichification of personal ads coincided with the rise of cable television, another niche media product. Many later blamed cable, as they would blame the Internet, for dividing Americans and degrading their tastes with "down-market" content. Highbrow or low, there was no question that these innovations changed the way people lived. "There is a difference," writes Tim Wu in *The Master Switch*, "between a nation in which on any given night conservatives are watching Fox News, sports fans are tuned to ESPN, and teenagers are glued to MTV, as compared to the America of television's yesteryear, where the nuclear family would watch *I Love Lucy* and the *CBS Evening News* together, whether they would have preferred to or not." By targeting one demographic, other demographics were, as a matter of course, turned away or excluded. "The alienation was, in a way, the message, and the product," writes Wu, invoking the aphoristic language of an earlier media theorist, Marshall McLuhan, who famously said, "The medium is the message."

After Barry Diller's IAC bought Match in 1999, it moved the dating company from California to Texas. Trish McDermott, in charge of marketing, was one of the only original execs to stay on. Shortly after the move, she recalls, the option to list yourself as bisexual suddenly disappeared from the site. McDermott, a lesbian, was annoyed by this. So she brought it up in a meeting. Management explained that since Match was building a brand about monogamy, about finding your special someone, it couldn't allow bisexuals, because if you were bisexual, you'd always be looking for something else. If you were a bisexual man who found a great woman, you'd still always be looking for a man. "Huh?" McDermott protested. "I'm pretty sure bisexual people still have monogamous relationships."

McDermott won that round. Bisexuality was restored as an option. But it was the beginning of what she calls Match's identity crisis. Internally, the company wanted to be everything to everyone. Tim Sullivan, Match's CEO at the time, called it the bookend theory: The Match brand must speak to all the "books" on the shelf, everything from "just messing around" to "serious about marriage," from fat to skinny, black to white, religious to non, gay to straight. The bookend theory meant excluding no one in particular. It also meant speaking to no one in particular. In 2001, McDermott was instructed not to use the word "single" in press releases. Match's research showed that "single" had a negative connotation; it was a temporary status that people wanted to shed. Later she was told not to use "marriage." Match didn't want to discourage those who weren't looking to get hitched.

When Dr. Warren's eHarmony, the marriage-minded site, began accumulating a big membership in the early 2000s, Match considered buying it. But Match's leadership was concerned that the eHarmony brand defined "appropriate" too narrowly.

But to many at Match, it was bad business to remain general, to try to be CBS in an MTV world. By catering to more niches you removed a big barrier to meeting for the people who were interested in the niches. Because Match refused to be specific, it opened the door for others to be specific. Match had more Jews than JDate, but JDate marketed to them and Match refused to.

Frank Mastronuzzi, a young gay man, wanted to change this. As Match's head of business development, it was his job to strike up partnerships with other Web sites in order to drive traffic to Match. He urged the company to spin off separate dating sites—for gays and lesbians, for Asians, African Americans, Latinos, and Christians. He urged Match to purchase People Media, one of the industry's first niche dating companies. Leadership wasn't interested. Instead, the company continued to pursue partnerships with general media sites, like AOL, MSN, and Village Voice Media. Eventually Mastronuzzi did an advertising deal with Black Entertainment Television. BET put a banner ad for Match on its Web site, showing a black couple laughing. When BET's customers clicked on the ad, however, they were taken to Match's homepage, where they got bombarded with white people.

"Match," Mastronuzzi recalls, "just wasn't relevant for tons of communities. Take gays. We have our own unique concerns. Are you a top or a bottom? What's your HIV status? A general dating site can't get at that stuff."

During the first decade of online dating—between roughly 1995 and 2005—many in the industry thought the best site was the site with the most people on it. You'll recall that in the early days of Match, Gary Kremen envisioned an electronic version of a personals column, a giant, undifferentiated arena of mate seekers. But as the date-o-sphere grew and choice expanded, efficiency problems arose: Women got deluged with messages from guys they weren't interested in; men got ignored. The best site, went the new thinking, was not the one with the most people on it but the one with the most people on it for *you*. Through the questions asked in the sign-up process and the content posted on its site, a niche site like JDate could make itself feel culturally relevant to Jews (JDateTV, JMag, Jblog) in a way that Match's one-size-fits-all approach could not.

When Greg Blatt took over as CEO of Match in 2009, he saw niche dating as a sensible branding play and decided to buy People Media for $85 million. "People's decisions about what they do are a lot more random than they think," Blatt says. "Someone joins a dating site because they happen to see the advertising for that site, which frankly is the reason people do most of what they do. If it works for them, helps them get whatever they're looking for, they use it again. Most of our users are return customers." The People Media empire includes about thirty communities, such as Black People Meet, Senior People Meet, Single Parent Meet, Little People Meet, and BB People Meet ("Meet big and beautiful singles today!").

By 2011, niche dating sites had taken nearly a third of the market, or roughly ten to fifteen million online daters in North America. But across the pond, a young innovator had beaten Match to the punch.

In 2002, after moving back in with his parents, Ross Williams, a twenty-four-year-old Brit, started a company that designed Web sites. At night he dabbled in online dating. In the UK then there were two big dating sites, Match and Dating Direct. In Europe there was another online-dating company called Dating Central that allowed affiliates to build their own dating sites, which then tapped into Dating Central's main user database. Williams tried building his own site within Dating Central, but it didn't work very well, because traffic was hard to come by. But the idea of partnering with affiliates, he thought, was solid.

Building traffic on a new dating site can cost millions. Williams couldn't afford to buy and market new sites like Match could. And even if he could, how would a Brit know what kind of dating site would work in a far-flung place like, say, South Africa? Or how best to market that site to South Africans? Even more tricky would be developing sites that accommodated niche interests with which Williams was unfamiliar. Tattoo enthusiasts, swingers, fetishists—the list was mind-boggling.

So he borrowed a marketing concept that had worked in other industries: white labeling. A white-label business model is often used for mass-produced, undifferentiated products, such as electronics or food. The white-label product—say, cornflakes—is made by one entity and marketed by another, or by several others. A second entity brands the cardboard box, a third entity brands the store in which the box of cornflakes is sold.

After building up a small membership base through a generic dating site called Singles365, Williams began partnering with affiliates who wanted to operate their own niche sites that would then tap into Williams's mother database. To create an optimal dating site for South Africa, Williams would partner with a South African and let that person design and market the site locally. This would also solve the traffic problem: The local affiliates—the "storefronts"—funneled business to the "manufacturer," and vice versa. The affiliate gets a cut of money for each subscriber he pulls into the network through his white-label site. Williams called his company White Label Dating, and its parent company Global Personals.

Rather than market to users with the promise of raw size, he would claim to offer endless choice on the assumption that someone joins a dating site because they happen to see advertising for that site. Someone who wants to date a redhead can visit a virtual redhead bar, such as Date Ginger: "If you have the good taste to know that red is best, if you want to linger with a ginger, if you like pale and interesting, fiery personalities and partners that look fabulous in green. . . ." While another person who wants to be collared during sex can visit a virtual bar full of people who enjoy doing just that, at CollarMe.

But niche dating wasn't just about creating culturally relevant dating communities for specific interests. It was also about branding interests and fetishes that might not be socially acceptable to acknowledge publicly, creating judgment-free zones where the like-minded can mingle freely and furtively through a friendly flashing portal that screams: *See how many people are just like you?*

See, for example, goth dating;* pet-lovers dating;† sites for military widows;‡ nerd dating;§ plus-size dating;¶ a large subset of dating sites for rich guys and the women who love them; sites for prisoners;** a site for

---

* GothDating, GothicMatch, GothScene. (GS member Sara says: "Music rapes my life. Some of my favorite bands are The Birthday Massacre, Cradle of Filth, and Psyclon Nine. I'm a really sweet person. I have a one-eyed black cat, a ferret, and a pretty cool snake.")

† DateMyPet ("Date Me. Date My Pet.")

‡ MilitaryCupid, USMilitarySingles, MilitaryDatingOnline.

§ NerdPassions, SweetonGeeks, Gk2Gk.

¶ LargeFriends, LargeandLovely, Fat Singles, FatDatingService. FDS explains: "You'll find big fat women, proper fat chicks, college fat girls, fat black singles, fat white babes, the working class fat guy, cute fat females, old fat lovers, beautiful fat strippers, reserved fat Christians, fat Indian men, fat moms, bi fat people, hot fat Japanese singles, or even the ever popular skinny fat man. . . . Tired of hanging out at the night clubs for fat people with no results? Let us be your fat cupid."

** Meet-An-Inmate, ConjugalHarmony, WomenBehindBars. WBB advertises thusly:

Are you tired of wondering if she's cheating on you? Do you love to leave the toilet seat up? Want to enjoy freedom on the weekend and watch a little football with your buddies, rather than work on your "honey do" list? Well, now you don't have to worry about any of that with the latest craze in adult dating, dating and marrying inmates for conjugal visits. With a conjugal marriage, you will finally have a wife with the perfect amount of freedoms and rights, and more importantly, you will finally start enjoying your own.

people who look alike;* a site for Star Trek fans;† sites for cowboys;‡ a site for sea captains;§ sites for the fitness obsessed.¶ Some of these sites appear to have rather vibrant communities, and some of them appear to be fake.

The following, however, are all real: cougars (and their cubs) have Urbancougar, CougarLife, Date A Cougar, Cougarfling, and Toyboy; while the more traditional variety of age-incongruent relationship— sugar babies and sugar daddies—can be sought out on Seeking Arrangement, where sugar babies, who list compensation demands ("open— negotiable," "$3,000 to $5,000 per month"), emphasize that they are "easy" and "drama-free." The CEO of SeekingArrangement, Brandon Wade, also owns What'sYourPrice, where rich men bid on dates with beautiful women; and MissTravel, which pairs "generous travelers who hate to travel alone with attractive travelers who would love the opportunity to travel the world for free." Wade, a Chinese American with two degrees from MIT, says his sites are not about prostitution but are simply being "honest" and more efficient, by treating the dating game as it really is—an exchange of female beauty for male resources.

Honesty, particularly when it comes to expectations about lifestyle, is crucial to the success of any relationship. For the marijuana enthusiast in search of a mate who won't see red flags in his bloodshot eyes, there's LonelyStoner. Those obsessed with their iPhones, but who also want to find love, can scroll for mates at Cupidtino ("find other Machearts around

---

* FindYourFaceMate: A dating site for the "facially compatible." (See, e.g., a study of this phenomenon, by Liliana Alvarez and Klaus Jaffe, published in 2004 in Volume Two of *Evolutionary Psychology*, and titled, "Narcissism guides mate selection: Humans mate assortatively, as revealed by facial resemblance, following an algorithm of 'self seeking like.'")

† TrekPassions: "Feel like you are always wearing a red shirt in your relationships? In Pon Farr?"

‡ CowboyCowgirl, SinglesCorral, HorseandCountryLovers, FarmersOnly. One FarmersOnly member testifies: "The city folks that dominated these online dating sites couldn't relate to my lifestyle. They wanted to meet at 9:00 p.m. for a cup of coffee when I would typically be preparing for the next day, which started at 5:00 a.m. Caffeine at that hour was the last thing I needed!"

§ SeaCaptainDate. "In the unforgiving ocean of love, let us be your lighthouse."

¶ FitnessSingles: "Where relationships workout!"

you"). Lest one overlook the bonding power of shared virginity, abstinence, too, is a niche. Those choosing to retain their V-card until marriage have We Waited: "Before you ever get into any relationship at all, you need to be right with God." In the niche dating world there are all kinds of ways to be right with God. Liberal Christian swingers have libchrist: "Hell fire and save the matches, fuck a duck and see what hatches." Beautiful people date through BeautifulPeople, which expels users who transgress into ugliness, becoming, say, too fat after the holidays. Not even those with sexually transmitted diseases need remain lonely with niche dating, what with PositiveSingles, STDFriends, and Herpes Online, to name but a few of the sites that have, as one dating executive put it to me, "niched out everything from crabs to cottage-cheese discharge, a veritable Sunday buffet." Speaking of eccentric tastes, vampire enthusiasts can sink their teeth into dating profiles at Vampire Passions where, in addition to selecting among blood types, the garlic-averse daters must choose between "sanguine vampirism" and "psychic vampirism." If your thing is minimalism, Diapermates ("No scat videos please!") boasts of more than eleven thousand diaper-loving members, among them, WetBabyGirl, a twenty-nine-year-old who poses with a pink pacifier, a bib, and, of course, a diaper, and in her profile explains that she's looking for "a strong daddy" to take her to the movies. World Singles specializes in nationality niches, with sites like ArabLounge, IranianPersonals, RomaniaKiss, and VietVibe. A white-label dating company called Dating Factory has over three hundred sites for people with disabilities. Toy collectors once dated through PlasticSouls, but it folded for lack of subscribers—too niche-y.

Again, some of these sites are spoofs, but many niche sites are very real; and even if a niche site doesn't have a sufficiently large community, the member can always be fed into a larger database, such as Ross Williams's Singles365 or Markus Frind's Plenty of Fish, and introduced to people whose behavior indicates they're a good match.

The suburb of Windsor lies twenty miles west of London, south of the Thames River. Home to Windsor Castle, a royal residence, along with some of the most expensive real estate in the United Kingdom, Windsor doesn't seem like a hotbed of mate seekers. But just off Windsor's cute cobblestone strip, Global Personals, one of the largest online-dating companies in the world, does business from a comparatively bland office building.

Inside, an open-desk plan is divided among departments with names like Global Development, Business Intelligence, User Experience, Retention, and Fraud Moderation. Nearly one hundred employees chug coffee and fluorescent-colored energy drinks as they shift between an in-house deli, a miniature golf course, and a pool table. When they need a break, they relax in beanbag chairs and play video games. A sign by the door says: YOUR BRAND. YOUR SITE. OUR PLATFORM.

"Ultimately online dating is about understanding yourself," says Ross Williams. He's seated in a zebra-striped beanbag chair between the pool table and the flat-screen TV. "What online dating does, in my opinion, is allow me to experience more encounters and relationships. You can condense what would be years or decades of learning into months."

Going small and local, Williams effectively went large. In 2011, White Label Dating had more than six thousand affiliate sites across seven countries, from England to New Zealand, and was making $70 million a year in revenue. Some in the industry call Williams the Ray Kroc of dating, after the founder of McDonald's. There's also a more modern analogy. By creating a platform on top of which others build their own sites, Williams did for online dating what Mark Zuckerberg is attempting to do for the entire Internet by opening his Facebook platform to outside developers to build their own applications within the site. The affiliates of White Label Dating, some of whom make tens of thousands of dollars per month in revenue, operate niche sites such as the infamous Ugly Bug Ball ("If you are one of the millions of people that don't always like what they see in the mirror, then this is the place for you!"), and GILF Dating, a site that features thousands of British grandmothers in various states of froufrou and frippery.

"We've got a platform for people to create whatever they want," says Williams. "Life's too short. They should enjoy themselves."

Williams racks the balls for a game of pool. He's tall and lumbering, with a ready smile and jolly red cheeks devoid of judgment. Shortly after Williams started the main site, Singles365, he met a woman through it, fell hard for her, and proceeded to block messages from other guys until he'd solidified the bond. They dated for four years, then broke up. But he says that's just life, nothing to do with the site. (Williams's business partner, Steve Pammenter, met his wife through Singles365.) At the moment Williams is in a long-distance relationship with a woman from Arizona, whom he met offline. "I'm not totally sure about it," he says, cracking the balls apart. "I'm a homebody and she loves to go out all the time." A month from this interview she'll move to England to be with him, the relationship will fall apart immediately, and she'll return to the States.

"You don't learn much in life when things go perfectly right," says Williams, pragmatism unifying his sensitive side with the renegade businessman. "You need to experience some bad things. Hopefully we'll see a reduction in divorces, because people will be making smarter choices. Online dating is fantastic for building the confidence you need to date the person you want, and also for realizing that we're all in the same boat. We're all a bit nervous. We're all a bit shy. Some are better actors than others."

Many White Label sites seem very much on the fringe. But in a way, niche dating, whether it be GILF or LonelyStoner, is no different than general dating sites. Just as your Google searches become increasingly tailored to your interests and opinions, and your Pandora account tries to predict your music taste, relationship search engines also put you in a box. Niche dating simply markets, individually, the thousands of options out there. As the Internet grows vaster, technology is allowing us, and in some cases forcing us, to be more specific. This means John Dater can find people who are like him, and quite easily. It also means that, out of necessity, he will exclude those with qualities he may not realize he needs or enjoys. Opposites like Kelly and Tom are more likely to run into each other on Match, perhaps, than on CollarMe or Date My Pet. On the other hand, Atheist Passions or SingleParentMeet might have been good options for Carrie and AteoBoriqua.

But niche dating will likely have the largest impact on the lives of people who, for reasons beyond their control, lack choice. "If your dating pool is limited," says Trish McDermott, "online dating in its 'miniform' has been amazing in reducing some of that limitation."

Growing up gay in a suburb of New York City during the 1990s, Joel Simkhai faced a limitation. At the dawn of the Internet he would meet other gay teenagers through Compuserve's gay channel, an early version of a niche chat room, striking up long-distance relationships with people in places like Minnesota, Boston, and Washington, D.C. It was thrilling to make these connections, but also impractical. Simkhai's father would yell at him about the long-distance phone bills. There had to be a better way.

Not only does the gay community amount to a small fraction of the heterosexual community, but it can be hard to tell who's what. "I walk into a place, I don't necessarily know who's gay," says Frank Mastronuzzi, the former Match business developer. "This is why gays have always been on the cutting edge of technology. It's so much harder for them to connect. If their family casts them out, then it's also crucially important for them to connect."

Simkhai thought he had a pretty good "gaydar" until he realized, in his midtwenties, that both of his brothers were also gay. "With problems," he says, "come solutions."

He wanted to make it very easy to meet the gay people right around him, to see if there's chemistry, and move on if there's not. In 2009, Simkhai released a smartphone application through Apple's new app store. He gave his app a bold name: Grindr. On their smartphones, Grindr members are shown the profiles of other members within several hundred feet. Grindr has a reputation for facilitating sex on the fly, but Simkhai rejects the notion. "Here's the deal: The name 'Grindr' was chosen because it embodied the idea of 'grinding' people together in the same way that a coffee grinder grinds coffee beans," Simkhai explains at conferences and on the Grindr Web site. "The name is also a combination of the words 'Guy' and 'Finder.'"

Whatever the original intent, the app took off, and Simkhai became something of a rock star in the gay community. By 2012, Grindr had more than 3.5 million users in 192 countries, including in many with cultures that are intolerant of gays, such as Sri Lanka, Djibouti, Haiti, Iraq, and Iran. The UK is Grindr's biggest market, with 1 in every 60 male Londoners using the app. Assuming a 10 percent rate of homosexuality, that's 1 in 6 gay men. At the 2012 summer games, when the first Olympians arrived in London, Grindr melted down from overuse.

After her recovery from cancer, Laura Brashier spent the better part of a decade inside her head, wondering what she was meant to do with this hand she'd been dealt. She told no one of her condition, instead throwing her energy into her garden in Orange County, where she would relax in the evenings with food and wine. One day, in her late forties, Brashier was at a restaurant when a friend asked her why she wasn't dating. For the first time she told someone: "I can't have sex."

"When I finally heard myself say it out loud," she recalls, "I could imagine others in similar situations." She researched the reasons why intercourse might not be possible: diabetes, high blood pressure, cancer, the list went on. "It turns out that there are all kinds of reasons why people either don't want to have sex or can't have sex, yet still seek intimacy," she says. "I suspected that the group of people out there, if I could find them, was large enough to warrant a dating site."

In 2011, Brashier introduced 2Date4Love, "a dating site that enables people who cannot engage in sexual intercourse to meet and experience love, companionship and intimacy at its deepest level." Members began signing up, slowly at first, then faster.

"We all want to portray that we're perfect," Brashier says. "With clothes and makeup we can hide a lot. But when you have to admit this, you have to admit you're not perfect anymore. My goal is to make this a subject that people no longer have to hide from."

Thank-you letters rolled in from people whom the site had coaxed out of isolation. "I am smart, fun and very social," wrote Renee, an ovarian cancer survivor whose treatments hindered sexual functioning. "However, until now, I've shied away from dating. When men approached me, I would immediately act uninterested even if I was. I anticipated rejection and found it easier to dismiss them. I also got defensive when topics related to sexuality and relationships arose, which made me feel like I was in my own little bubble, separate from the rest of the world."

"Unlike a traditional dating site, I'm focused on what I call 'digital lipstick,'" says Noel Biderman. "I realized early on that my role in this was twofold—create the connection, and help you not get caught. That's what the perfect affair is."

A law school graduate who became a sports agent, Biderman used to work out of Chicago and Italy, helping move basketball players around to keep their careers alive. "My fantasy was to be Jerry McGuire," he recalls, referring to the sports agent played by Tom Cruise in the eponymously named 1996 movie. "Instead I became the Jerry McGuire of Lebanon."

In 2001, after leaving sports agenting to join some friends in a real estate concern, Biderman (pronounced BEE-der-man) began thinking about online businesses. The first Internet bubble had just burst, meaning it might be a good time to invest. A Toronto native, Biderman recalls reading an article by a female journalist in Canada. The piece, he remembers, was about how, even though the bubble had burst, the Internet had made an irreversible impact on our lives. Napster changed how we thought about music. Online pornography meant no longer wearing disguises out to the video store. Online dating was changing the way we meet people. Anecdotally, the writer estimated that a third of the men on dating sites were married.

"I was in an entrepreneurial mind-set at the time," Biderman recalls. "That statistic jumped off the page. I looked at dating sites. They were all subscription businesses that promised better relationships. I thought, 'Hmm, who's more motivated than a married man to put down a credit card to get what he's missing in his marriage?' These people should have their own site." Biderman ran the idea by his friends. The response from men was the same—laughter, either nervous or excited. The response from women was more interesting. They were silent at first. "There would be this moment," he remembers, "when they sort of peered into my soul, as if maybe I was testing them, as if I'd found them out. I always suspected that a lot of guys cheated. But I would've never guessed that half my female friends had had affairs."

If you're on a niche dating site, you may lie about your height, weight, and income, but at least you're not lying about the one attribute that makes you eligible for the niche. If you post a profile on DateGinger, you're either a redhead or you want to date one. If you go on Grindr, you're gay. If you're on SalaamLove, you're presumably Muslim. What happens when the relevant qualification is relationship status itself?

In 2003, Biderman started Ashley Madison, naming the company after the two most popular names for baby girls. Ten years later, the site claims thirteen million members in seventeen countries. With slogans like "Monogamy is Monotony" and "Life is Short. Have an Affair," Biderman's advertising is often turned down, particularly for primetime television slots like the Super Bowl. So he compensates by going on TV talk shows, where he's often booed.

On these shows Biderman has become skilled at defending the societal contribution of his business: Affairs will happen with or without online dating to facilitate them, he argues. Would divorce cease if divorce attorneys couldn't advertise? Do limits on alcohol stop drinking? Workplace affairs, he says, jeopardize jobs and livelihoods. By creating a space for discreet affairs, you limit fallout and keep families together. The children—Ashley and Madison—are the ultimate beneficiaries.

After talk-show appearances, the traffic on Ashley Madison spikes.

Biderman sees himself as a crusader on behalf of the online-dating industry's taboo-busting efforts. "I'm happy to be a one-man wrecking crew making the industry better for everyone else," he says. But he's also careful to distinguish Ashley Madison from traditional dating sites. "eHarmony has a terrific trick up their sleeve. If you're patient enough to fill out hundreds of questions, then you might get along with someone who's also patient enough to do that. These sites want you to think that dating is about getting married. Yet a small percentage of people out there are seeking only permanence. Most of the rest of society is willing to date for lots of reasons besides dating-into-relationships-into-permanence."

Ashley Madison's success spawned copycats in North America and abroad. Gleeden, founded by two French brothers, got its start by serving a culture of infidelity in France. A Scandinavian cheating site called Victoria Milan prompted a record number of complaints to Sweden's advertising authorities after introducing a billboard campaign that read: "Are you married? Liven up your life—have an affair."

Since the mainstream advertising world treats Biderman's cheating empire as toxic, he does what a lot of online-dating businesses do. He puts out reports showing how popular Ashley Madison is. So while Match and eHarmony distribute studies showing that more marriages are originating from online dating, and that online-dating sites result in better marriages, Ashley Madison sends out press releases claiming, for instance, that Hispanics are "the fastest growing community when it comes to infidelity," and that, according to its own data, "Hispanic members have affairs at the youngest age: Average age of 27 for women and 34 for men (compared to 33 for women and 40 for men in the general U.S. population)." Another press release, quickly parroted by the media, announced that Washington, D.C., was Ashley Madison's biggest market. "Powerful men and women, particularly those in politics, tend to take multiple 'risks' on their way to the top," explained Biderman. "Taking a risk within their personal life, since they feel they are made of Teflon, is a natural extension. Simply put, the more successful you are, the more prone to cheating you are."

People scoff at Biderman for promoting a pastime still generally regarded as immoral by most of the population. But his efforts don't seem as outlandish when you think of the ways our views on relationships—from premarital sex, to divorce, to gay marriage—have progressed over the years. "As an entrepreneur, part of my responsibility to society is to help it evolve, the way an artist does," Biderman says.

This theme—helping society evolve past old traditions, whether marital fidelity (Biderman) or privacy (Zuckerberg)—runs through the world of social media. The message is: Conventions should be revised to conform with the behavior enabled by technology, which has been tooled to accommodate all possible behavior.

For at least a century, America has been "preparing to meet the challenges of a more permissive society" trumpeting some new "emerging culture of chaotic indulgence," celebrating and ruing another "conquering of taboo." Declaiming a sexual revolution is practically a generational rite of passage: From the perverse poetics of Catullus (80 B.C.) to the sixteenth-century Rabelaisians to the seventeenth-century libertines, the men and women of every generation have thought they reinvented fornication. For all we know, granny fantasies and diaper fetishes date to Catullus's *polymetra*, or at least to the invention of diapers.

And still, today *is* different. Even if there is nothing new under the covers, the mode of *finding* it has been revolutionized by the Internet, by the radical connection that is unique to *this* era. Perhaps a diaper fetishist is a diaper fetishist is a . . . and so on, all the way back, and what has been will be again. But a diaper fetishist living in a world with immediate access to similarly pampered people is a new baby. The player still suits up one leg at a time, but the game has changed.

It doesn't matter who you are or what you do. You can be a closet swinger, an out-of-closet deviant, or a U.S. congressman. You can be them all. Between Twitter and Facebook and Phantasy Tour, as well as the thousands of sites and smartphone applications designed explicitly for dating, there is bound to be someone in the cloud of faces who's interested in whatever it is that you've got. These portals not only present the whole human grid of desire and stimulation but make that grid real and attainable, nonvirtual, bounded by only the limitations of curiosity and imagination.

Although Biderman catches a lot of flak for branding infidelity, he is not alone among online-dating execs in his belief that monogamous marriage is at odds with the reality afforded by technology. With a courtside seat to the behavior of enormous mating populations, those who run dating sites see infidelity firsthand. "At the moment," says Dan Winchester, founder of Free Dating in the UK, "there's a glaring inconsistency between the old convention—in which people are still very much geared toward maintaining traditional relationships—and the way people are actually using the Web today to get together. Some of the most well-trafficked sites are those for affairs, swinging, or so-called deviant behavior of one kind or another. These are not tiny ecosystems, mind you. Sooner or later we reach a point where people say: 'What is actually wrong with this behavior? Why are we not openly engaging in it?' This is the real story of our industry."

When *The New Yorker*'s Adam Gopnik reviewed a bunch of books about life online in 2011, he argued that the Internet's first two decades sparked "a revolution less in morals, which have remained mostly static, than in means: you could already say 'fuck' on HBO back in the eighties; the change has been our ability to tweet or IM or text it." The Internet is certainly a revolution in means, but those new means are not properly identified as IM or text, which are merely updates of the letter and the telephone. What's revolutionary about the Internet is the way it combines communication with ever-enhanced search-and-discovery capability.

On HBO in the eighties you could hear people say "fuck," and you could see people have sex. What you could not do then, which you most definitely can do now, is crawl through the screen, meet anyone, go anywhere, even abroad, and forge relationships on whatever grounds the free market permits. The kind of online connecting that leads to offline relationships is an Internet breed apart. The measure of power that it abdicates to the user is unprecedented, far from theoretical, and it's changing the way people approach their relationship lives, giving rise to a new normal.

CHAPTER SEVEN

Like Everyone, I'm Looking for My True Love

MARRIAGE AND MIRAGE IN THE INTERNATIONAL DATE-O-SPHERE

I like women from countries that have sustained political turmoil. Western culture seems to forge women that are valueless and inane. OK. Not only women!

—OkCupid profile of WikiLeaks founder Julian Assange

The online-dating honchos in Europe and America are trying to free the date-o-sphere from its stigmatized roots. They want to expose the old encased world of online dating to the great wide open of social discovery, lose the pink hearts on the homepage, skirt the taboo, and make their product universal by conditioning the world that meeting new people online is amazing.

Neal Bryant, a British dating exec based in Moscow, is waging a branding battle that is similar and different. The site he represents, AnastasiaDate, claims that it connects Western men with women in Russia, Ukraine, China, Africa, Latin America, and beyond.

The stigma here is mighty, well, stigmatizing. Always has been. Even in the Old West of nineteenth-century America, when pioneers would strike out for the Territories, and then, once settled, advertise for wives in newspapers back east, it was assumed that the mail-order bride industry relegated prostitutes, old maids, and hopeless spinsters to the nation's grubby backcountry. As an Anastasia rep, it's Bryant's job to make over the mail-order bride industry, to convince the buying public that there's nothing weird about this, nothing untoward. It's just another way of meeting people.

It's early fall in Russia, 2011. This afternoon Bryant spoke at iDate Moscow, an international online-dating conference organized by the same people who handle Miami. The conference was sponsored in part by Mamba.ru, a dating site for Russians seeking Russians. "Mamba," states the corporate poster, "creates happy couples and families, makes people feel better, feel needed and important. Mamba is not just a business but, in a way, it's a business that helps children to be born." This local online-dating market is not substantially different from what goes on back home. I've come to Moscow, rather, to investigate this cross-border format in which the Russians specialize, to see whether it could really one day go mainstream, assuming it hasn't already.

The business is certainly cash-positive. In 2012, *The Daily*, an iPad publication owned by Rupert Murdoch, reported that the international marriage brokering business had reached $2 billion, making it equal in size to the entire online-dating industry in the United States. Although numbers are hard to substantiate, Anastasia appears to be grossing something on the order of $1 million per day, perhaps substantially more. As we'll see, it's also difficult to tell how much of Anastasia's revenue comes from scamming its clients. Its main competitor, A Foreign Affair, is owned by Americans and based in Arizona. Both companies are doing everything they can to get the word out. Times have changed, they say: You can find love at your local church, at work, in a pub, and now you can find it in the foreign country of your choice. This is the way of the world now.

"We don't say mail-order brides!" Bryant told his audience of online-dating colleagues. "People say Anastasia is about mail-order brides, but you can't order a bride by mail or the Internet. If you could, Amazon would be doing it!" The joke played well. He continued: "Many people ask what our clients see in Russian girls. From our research and understanding, we think the art of attracting a male is more developed in Eastern European culture. In Russia, it's frowned upon for ladies not to look after themselves. They walk more, eat less junk food. There's no gender-role confusion."

In the evening, the conference-goers—comprised of online-dating execs from the United States and Europe—convene at a cavernous underground restaurant across town, where they dine on vodka, beef, boiled potatoes, and smoked fish. Bryant sits down at my table with a bottle of Russian Standard. "Drinking," he says, "this is a serious problem here in Russia. Escaping the fate of an abusive, alcoholic husband is one good reason the Russian and Ukrainian women have for shopping their wares overseas."

Bryant's ironic smirk hardly bears the courage of conviction: He pours a shot of vodka, then another. A female dating exec from London joins us. "If you don't call it mail-order brides," she asks Bryant, "what do you call it?"

"We call it 'premium international online dating,'" he says.

But the question, coming from a Western woman, seems to rattle Bryant, almost shame him in some way. "Oh my God," he says, leaning hard on the Russian Standard. "I can't believe what I do for a living."

Following the 1991 collapse of the Soviet Union, the market for mail-order brides began to heat up. Many bridal agencies in the United States that had dealt mostly with women from the Philippines switched their focus to Russia and Eastern Europe. The business was mediated almost entirely by catalogs. New York–based Scanna International, a pioneer in the Russian mail-order-bride industry, set up an office in Vladivostok as early as 1989. Scanna published a five-dollar catalog every two weeks, with profiles of two hundred new women. The catalogs, which often featured poorly printed photos, didn't put much of a gloss on the industry, or help convince would-be customers that the women were real. Media reports about mail-order brides helped spread the word, but without a more efficient way to connect the market would remain limited. Throughout the nineties, and even into the early 2000s, the Internet didn't figure much in Russian life. Even in 2007, when Ericka Johnson wrote *Dreaming of a Mail-Order Husband*, only one of the hopeful mail-order brides she interviewed in Moscow had ever "surfed the Net."

Still, women found a way to connect. In 2003, when Anastasia started its Web site, many Russian women flocked to their local "bridal agencies" to have their photos taken and uploaded into profiles to be seen on the other side of the world. These local agencies, which are now said to exist in most Russian and Ukrainian cities, are essentially Anastasia's subcontractors, or white-label partners, feeding women into the main database. This model would prove handy as the mail-order-bride business spread across Eastern Europe, Asia, and Latin America, from 2003 to the present. Anastasia now partners with over one thousand bridal agencies around the globe.

In 2011, *Bloomberg Businessweek* reported that "venturing abroad for love has taken on a more acceptable mien," as international matchmakers comprise "a growing segment of the U.S. online dating industry." It's the poor economy in the United States—rather than the desperation of disadvantaged women abroad—that's responsible for the flourishing growth in recent years of premium international online dating, the magazine said: Struggling financially and losing out in the gender wars, American men were doing the rational thing by looking abroad for a low-maintenance alternative to that entitled and difficult American woman to whom he no longer measured up. Those who run Anastasia and A Foreign Affair don't disagree with this view. But they chalk up their success to a rising awareness among men that, yes, you can meet young, beautiful, *real* women from foreign places and actually pursue a relationship with them.

At the restaurant, Bryant and the female dating executive are joined by a fortyish man from Los Angeles named Tai Lopez. Like Brandon Wade, Lopez operates dating sites that target the sugar-daddy/sugar-baby niche. Bryant and Lopez don't see themselves as being in the same business. Yet they both match older men with younger woman, based either explicitly (Lopez) or implicitly (Bryant) on a financial imbalance. In the States, this is stigmatized as sugar daddies and sugar babies. When the connection is cross-border, it's mail-order brides, or premium international online dating.

"I was going to bring my Ferrari to Moscow," Lopez says. "After racing it across the States."

"Why would you do that?" Bryant asks.

"The women here are such gold diggers," Lopez says. "It's not like Sweden. If you go to Sweden, the women don't care what you have, because everyone in Sweden has the same amount."

Vodka is drunk. Lopez then asks Bryant: "Are the girls on your site real? Aren't you just selling them to a bunch of weirdos?"

This is the perception. Some high-profile murders of women who came to the United States via so-called international marriage brokers prompted President Bush to sign the International Marriage Broker Regulation Act of 2005, or IMBRA, which mandates background checks for men. Before flying abroad to meet a woman through one of Anastasia's Web sites, the client is required to fill out a form answering questions about restraining orders, domestic violence, arrests for prostitution, rape, kidnapping, stalking, and incest, as well as marital status, past marriages, and biological and adopted children. Clients must list all the states they've resided in, so the appropriate sex-offender registries can be checked. According to Bryant, Anastasia's staff in Moscow spends the majority of its time satisfying IMBRA regulations. Those in the United States who advocate on behalf of trafficked women say it's not enough.

"We're going to let the journalist decide," Bryant says. He and I had previously discussed the possibility of my tagging along on an Anastasia romance tour. "We've got a tour running down to Colombia in November. We'll send him along."

Like normal online dating, the international date-o-sphere is another venue for matching people who are looking for the same thing, optimizing market efficiency just as eBay does with goods bought and sold. But unlike local online dating—Match in the United States or Mamba in Russia—the technology in its cross-border format is as much about expanding one's options as it is about exploiting a gap in options. This gap is often financial, but not always. When Western men use the Internet to meet women in China, for example, the Chinese women who sign up for the service often come from well-off families. These women don't want to meet an American for his money, necessarily. Rather, they're looking abroad because they *can*. Female infanticide, part and parcel of China's one-child policy, resulted in a gender imbalance that left women in a competitively favorable position. Of course, this won't be the situation in Colombia, one of South America's poorest countries.

Welcome to Medellin, City of Eternal Spring. Seventeen of Anastasia's male clients have descended on Colombia's second-largest city for a weeklong romance tour. In the cultural primer provided by the company, the romance tourists have been warned not to be offended if they're called "gringo."

For the past several months, if not several years, these men have been members of Amo Latina (Find Your Princess), the Latin sister site of Anastasia, where they pay to correspond with women in Brazil, Colombia, Costa Rica, Panama, Peru, and Uruguay. Amo Latina is one of three Web sites owned by Anastasia. The other two are Asian Beauties, which markets relationships with women from Chongqing, China, as well as from select outposts around Southeast Asia; and Africa Beauties, the company's newest site. There are no monthly membership fees on these sites. Instead, male clients buy credits, which they dissipate in the sending and receiving of e-mail messages and instant chats. Bulk purchases bring the cost down: one thousand credits cost $399 ($.40 each), while twenty credits cost $15.99 ($.80 each).

The service is "premium" in part because all communication requires a human translator. One e-mail or chat correspondence—a message sent, a message returned—can cost the client between one and two dollars. Anastasia claims to exchange 2.5 million letters per day through all of its sites combined. The sites offer male clients other methods of mobile courting too, such as the delivery of flowers and chocolates. "When a lady you've corresponded with has a birthday upcoming," the Amo Latina Web site promises, "you will receive a birthday notification to remind you about the significant date."

As for the romance tours, they're billed as a very special experience for clients who see the value proposition: $1,595 gets you one week at the Dann Carlton Hotel, located in El Poblado ("the Beverly Hills of Medellin"); two "socials," at which women outnumber men 20 to 1; access to a support staff of Russian ladies, who function as dating concierges, suggesting restaurants and arranging in-country transportation should a client wish to swing through, say, Bogotá, to meet more women on his way home; and a crew of able translators for hire. For fifteen dollars an hour, a translator can accompany the client on dates. If he has a phone number written in the little black book that is provided for the purpose, the translator can even make the date. While the translator's presence jacks up the dinner tab, she becomes an indispensable third wheel, not only translating languages but arbitrating emotions, a kind of relationship mediator brought to the table to help hammer out terms.*

Poolside at the Dann Carlton, the gringos eat a buffet breakfast while discussing their motivations for turning to premium international online dating.

"American women took me to the cleaners," says Andy, a fifty-two-year-old window-installer from Florida. "They'll basically say, 'I'm going to fuck you up the ass and take 150 percent of everything you ever dreamed about.'"

In his Amo Latina profile, Andy calls himself a "Texas-raised gentleman" looking for his "Latin Princess." He enjoys dinner on his boat under the stars and bubble baths by candlelight. He warns all those seeking "rich sugar daddies" to stay away. Andy came to Colombia to find love, to be appreciated for who he is, not for what he can provide. He feels that his first two marriages were brought down by gold digging, not by his alcoholism; Andy says he's stopped drinking. His third marriage, which ended recently, was to a young Brazilian he met in a Miami bar. She offered him ten thousand dollars in exchange for a sham marriage and a green card. He turned down the money, said he'd marry her only for love, and two years after the wedding she disappeared.

"American women won't say, 'I want a relationship,'" agrees Bart, a fifty-four-year-old air-conditioner salesman from Alabama. "They'll say,

---

* The romance tours to Russia and Ukraine typically cover two cities and three socials. They cost twice as much as the Latin America tours.

'Fuck you, I want to see how much money you got first'—at least to a certain extent."

Bart is also coming off a difficult divorce. Despite giving his wife of thirty years "horses in the barn, vacation cruises, and cars," she became addicted to crack and left him for her dealer. But Bart is eager to accept responsibility for the failed marriage. Through a regimen of competitive ballroom dancing, hunting trips, and attendance at relationship seminars, such as those run by guru David Deida, author of *The Way of the Superior Man*, Bart's been striving to improve himself for the next woman. "You must be passionate enough to understand we have a very short window to make a connection," says Bart's Amo Latina profile, "and do whatever you must to make that connection unbreakable."

The opacity of Bart's actual intentions speaks to a basic divide among the group. While decorum requires all of the men to express hope of a relationship, only about half of the seventeen romance tourists (sixteen Americans, one Canadian) are in Medellin to find a wife, I am told by Charles, a former bodybuilder who became an Anastasia rep after going on a romance tour. The rest, he says, are here for "a week of fun."

A third romance tourist, a fifty-six-year-old doctor from California named Richard, says, "Women in the States are confused. They don't know if they want to be the man or the woman. I sure as hell don't want to be the woman."

"Burn the bra and everything else," Bart says. "Gloria Steinem started all that stuff."

"It'd be nice to find a girl who thinks gym clothes are for the gym," Richard says. "That's why I'm down here."

Bart, Andy, Richard, and several other men on the trip say they came to Amo Latina after failing to find happiness on mainstream dating sites like Match and eHarmony. They came on the romance tour because it's easier and more efficient than planning a trip on your own.

After breakfast, the gringos convene in a hotel conference room for the introductory session. "These tours serve as huge public relations tools," they are told. "We don't really make any money on the tour. It brings you here to meet women, but also to understand that these women are for real, so that you can return home and hopefully spread a good word about us, dispel any naysayers who think the women on our site are just pictures. Remember: If you can think of it, if you can imagine it happening, we can help you make it happen."

Historically, the media has written off the mail-order bride industry as a business that services the West's most undesirable men— ignoramuses, racists, misogynists, repeat offenders. In press accounts, the red-faced lecher with a walrus mustache is a standard of the genre. A few of Amo Latina's clients fit that bill. But what's unique about the foreign niche's stigma is the perception that only older men use it. If the stereotype was ever true, it's no longer. According to sources who work for the local bridal agencies in Medellin, the women in foreign countries who sign up for these sites are getting younger and younger, and so are the men. On this trip there is Derrick, a soft-spoken twenty-seven-year-old Hispanic American from Houston. Derrick came on the trip because his job at a petroleum company keeps him long at the office and he wants to settle down with a Latin woman. Eddie, a thirty-two-year-old Hispanic American chef from Brooklyn, also speaks Spanish, also works long hours, and is determined to marry a Latin woman. Eddie worked two jobs to support his ex-fiancée in New York, until she cheated on him with his best friend. The group contains three additional members under thirty-five. Almost half the group is under forty.*

The men, showered and dressed, gather in the lobby of the Dann Carlton. Brody, a thirty-year-old nurse from Michigan, wears jeans and an untucked black button-down. A tour veteran, this is Brody's third trip to Medellin. "It's a little overwhelming at first," he explains, referring to the unusual ratio at the socials. "But then you get used to it, and all the

---

* This comes as a shock to Norma Ramos, the executive director of the New York–based Coalition Against Trafficking in Women. The paradigm of the older troglodytic male preying on the underprivileged foreigner makes a more compelling argument in favor of her agency's work against trafficking and exploitation. When told that male clients are getting younger, Ramos said it "just demonstrates the increasing commodification of women, based on intense poverty and dramatic inequality."

attention makes you cocky. You go back to the States and not even the girl behind the McDonald's counter smiles at you."

Almost goofy with optimism, Brody is not a particularly good-looking guy, though he's not unattractive. His last American girlfriend, whom he met on eHarmony and planned to propose to, was unfaithful. Now, according to his Amo Latina profile, he's looking for a woman who is "worth the white dress," one who knows that "matrimony is not a game but a glorified dimension if we obey our heavenly father." His colleagues at work rib him about these trips, suggesting that he comes to Colombia to sleep with prostitutes. Like Bart, Brody's mission is a matter of some urgency: His previous tours have earned him a reputation as a player among Medellin's bridal agencies.

"I can't find a woman at home," he says. "Yet thanks to the Internet I can develop a reputation as a player in a foreign city where I don't speak the language."

A trim man with a perma-smile slaps Brody on the back and says, "Ready to go, buddy?" This is Tony, a poster child for Amo Latina. "I'm already with a girl down here," he explains. "But I'll be doing the same thing as you tonight, walking around and talking to them."

Tony is a forty-nine-year-old emergency-room doctor from Oregon. Last week he proposed to a thirty-seven-year-old woman he met on an earlier Amo Latina tour. They're commencing paperwork for a K-1 visa, known as a fiancée visa, which allows a woman to live in the United States for ninety days. (During that time she must either marry an American or leave the country.) Once married, she can apply for a green card. Whenever the paperwork for the fiancée visa gets processed, she can return to the States with Tony. In the meantime he rents a condo in Medellin and flies back and forth. "I'm addicted to these tours, man," he says. "You'll see tonight at the social. You can't put it in words. You go in there, and it's like you're punch drunk. You feel like a rock star. See, I don't work for the company, but I help promote the company. And for these girls to come back to the Amo Latina socials, they've got to be able to say, 'Hey, I came here and I met some guys, and it was okay.'"

Tony will repeat these lines many times over the next few days. Billing himself as a perennial promoter seems to help Tony maintain a risky illusion—that he can send his fiancée shopping, or tell her to wait at home and study English, while, in the name of keeping Amo Latina in business, he trawls for women at the socials.

The gringos are now in a tour bus heading to their first social of the week, at a nightclub called Mango's, where, according to the *Lonely Planet* travel guide, Medellin's "rich and beautiful come to show off."

"This city has a history, sometimes a rough history," the gringos were told during the introductory session. Medellin was home to the late drug kingpin Pablo Escobar. Much of the city doesn't feel safe. Vendors return change in counterfeit bills. Taxis stray from course. Nicer areas are guarded with guns. "You have a safe in your room—use it. Only take as much cash as you need. Don't flash your cash, don't bring your bling, don't go anywhere without a buddy. It's more fun to double-date or even triple. It's also a courtesy to the ladies, because many don't speak English, so they'll feel more comfortable with another girl at the table."

Bart, the air-conditioner salesman from Alabama, is giving a counterhistory of the Confederate War. "Redneck," he says, "is as insulting to whites as nigger is to niggers. I tell you, there should be no quotas or affirmative action, because on the sports field the most powerful wins, the best wins. Why should it be turned around in life? It's like they want to eradicate any form of a moral code."

Andy, the window guy from Florida, is more focused. Though divorced three times, Andy's spent most of his adult life as a married person. The prospect of mingling with dozens of women makes him more nervous than excited. He carries a digital pocket translator. Compounding Andy's angst is an experience he had a couple days before the rest of the crew showed up. He came down to Medellin early to meet a woman he'd been communicating with through the Amo Latina Web site.

"The only downfall was that she's twenty," he explains. "But man, did we click. I tried to shoot her down right away when she invited me to chat online. 'What are your parents going to think? What are your friends going to think?' I tried to give her something to really think about. I even said, 'If we're together in the States we wouldn't have a lot of friends, because they wouldn't agree with our arrangement.' A thirty-two-year age gap. People look down on that shit. I even mentioned that she's seven years younger than my youngest daughter. But she said, 'I don't want to talk about age.' Then she started talking about things she liked. She liked everything I like: swimming, the beach. And man, she don't look twenty. And she conducts herself like a lady, not like a kid. When we went out, she had a sore throat. I said she should go home and sleep. But she said, 'No. I want to spend time with you.' So we went to dinner and to the mall to shop. She wanted pictures of everything. A picture of the translator. A picture of her and the translator. A picture of me in front of the fountain. Of me in front of the Christmas tree. She wanted all these pictures for memories. So I thought, 'Man, that's pretty good.'" With the pocket translator, Andy told her she should call him when she got done with work the next night. But she never called. He sent her a letter through the site. He knows she opened it yesterday. "Maybe with being sick she couldn't respond," he speculates. "But it went so good. I don't know what happened."

Dave, an Amo Latina client liaison, asks Andy what the company can do to help.

"Maybe you can get me her phone number," Andy says, "so I can text her, and if she doesn't text back, then at least I can move on."

"Okay," Dave says, "we'll take care of you, buddy." Dave is a former Amo Latina client who met his girlfriend on an earlier tour. Now he owns a vacation house on the beach in Cartagena. Dave says he made it "to the top of the tree" in the nightclub business back in London, where he "banged pretty much everything." Dave's girlfriend runs one of the local bridal agencies. She's responsible for the rumor going around that Brody is a player.

Tony intervenes. "Trust me," he tells Andy. "After tonight you won't even remember her."

Andy's misfire with the twenty-year-old is a reminder that, just like other online-dating portals, the reality of international online dating is complicated: For every Western man looking not for a wife but for quick sex abroad, there is a woman looking not for a relationship but for a free night out in her hometown, shopping for shoes at the mall, and eating at restaurants that she and her family could never afford. As for explicit scamming, it's well-known among Web site users that the staffs of local bridal agencies will often pose as the women in the profiles, responding to incoming messages in order to keep the rubles rolling in. Shortly after the original publication of this book, Anastasia confessed to *Fortune* magazine that some women also get kickbacks for participating. Nearly every man on the tour has a story of chatting up a beautiful woman on-line and then offering to fly down, only to be told, suddenly, that she'll be out of town or busy working during those dates. Two of the romance tourists on this trip came specifically because they'd been corresponding with women they wanted to meet. In both cases, the men explained, with more pride than disappointment, the women were away doing a modeling tour and couldn't meet up.

According to Neal Bryant, about 80 percent of male clients are so-called keyboard Romeos, lonely guys looking to make pen pals and nothing more. Therefore, much of the scamming goes undetected by Anastasia's users—no harm, no foul.

But Arturo, a Mexican American truck driver from Fresno, has found the Amo Latina Web site frustrating for this reason. That's why he came on tour. "I no want no woman with kids," he says. "In States, the young girls with no kids—they think I'm too old. But if I date older, then she already have kids. That mean father come to my house to get kids on Saturday. I don't like that." For tonight's social, he's dressed in white polyester pants, a bolo tie, a beige leather jacket with brown leather shoulders, and a cowboy hat. Arturo records every minute of the trip on his Tablet's video function and then replays clips over breakfast.

As the tour bus pulls into the dirt parking lot of Mango's, Dave cries out in his cheerio English, "Alllllrrrrrrighty gents! Pace yourself. This is about endurance. Don't let conversations go too deep too soon," he says, as if such were possible between people who don't speak the same language. "Move, flow. They'll all have the same names. You'll meet ten Luisas and twenty Cristinas. So get phone numbers and e-mails and Web site IDs, if possible. And remember, when you're walking away from a table after getting contact info, rip the sheets out of your little book so the next girl doesn't know she's actually twenty-third on your list!" Bart—who has chosen black dancing shoes, gray slacks, and a white tuxedo shirt open at the chest—is incredulous, his mouth open in giddy disbelief like a twelve-year-old being told about porn for the first time. "Good luck hunting, guys! We wish you all the best!"

The inside of Mango's looks like a Western-themed bar. It's as if a Hard Rock Café merged with Hooters, Johnny Rockets, and a rodeo. Clint Eastwood posters adorn the wall. Red-and-white-striped mannequin legs hang from the ceiling. Urinals are shaped like Rolling Stones lips. In the entrance, by the registration table, stands a three-foot midget. The registration table ensures that the women who enter the social are authenticated Amo Latina users, not simply passersby looking for a night of free food and drink.

The women trickle in, wearing jeans or minidresses, blouses, and high heels. Colombia's females are staggeringly beautiful, the product of a transnational genetic slosh that includes mestizo, Spanish, Italian, Portuguese, German, and African heritage. Even the least attractive girls are curvy. Botero didn't lie. Much of the beauty is natural. Some of it is engineered. In addition to romance tourism, Colombia specializes in vanity tourism, attracting American and European travelers in search of cut-rate deals on liposuction, rhinoplasty, wrinkle removal, and breast and buttocks augmentation.

Steve, a skeletally svelte accountant from Sacramento, stands by the bar holding his umbrella like a beat stick. He's becoming visibly upset over a scheduling glitch. "Look," Steve says, glaring at the door. "Look at this. It's going to take at least an hour for them to get all the girls in. So you lose an hour right there." Steve is drinking a six-dollar can of Red Bull, a noncomplimentary item. He's been on Amo Latina tours several times before, and has a few tips. "Listen, if you sit down at a table with a group of girls, and you wind up liking one of them, you can't just ask for her phone number and not ask the friends. So what you do is you leave and then send over one of the translators to ask the one you like to come to a table with just you. But don't be too obvious about it, because that's just wrong."

At the translator table, ten college-aged women, most of them more conservatively dressed than the other women in the room, chat with each other, drink soda, and wait to be deployed.

"People ask a lot of standard questions," says Valentina, a twenty-year-old translator majoring in international business at the local university. "They both want to know if the other has been married and if the other has kids. That's the first thing. Then they want to know about the person's expectations for the future. The guy wants to know why she's interested in an American man, and she wants to know why he's interested in a Colombian woman."

"It's weird," adds Juanita, a brainy twenty-one-year-old who's majoring in physics and fashion and has a cat named Aristotle. "As translators we have to, like, channel the emotions back and forth. It's not just words. If you're doing it well, it's also expressions and gestures. Like we flirt for them. But if the conversation doesn't go well, it's hard for you to go well. This is like an internal joke we have between the translators."

Mango's is now full, with well over one hundred Colombianas present for perusal by seventeen gringos. To get things started, two Colombian Chippendales—shirtless, oiled-up beefcakes—do some choreographed bumping up on stage. The midget from reception, who is now dressed like a construction worker, dances inside a cage, swinging stiff-limbed from the top bars. Tony, the ER doc, joins two bikini-clad dancing girls on a high railing.

Dave says that most of the clients who come on tour are surprised by the possibilities for age gaps: twenty years is nothing; thirty years is not unusual. But these tour clients seem to be plenty aware. In their profiles, Andy, fifty-two, says he's looking for women twenty to thirty-five; while Arturo, fifty, wants to find a woman between eighteen and twenty-eight. Rod, a fifty-six-year-old Japanese Canadian architect from Vancouver, says that no matter how old he gets he still goes for the twenty-three-year-olds. "Where I live," he says, "that's just not possible anymore. The girls up there, they have certain what they call mores."

This is the real selling point of premium international online dating. Like fine leather bucket seats or truffles on pasta, you'll pay a little extra, go a little farther, for the tonics of youth and beauty. Anastasia emphasizes the health benefits that accrue to men who marry younger women. They cite a 2009 study by Germany's Max Planck Institute, which found that a man's chances of dying early are reduced by 20 percent if his bride is between fifteen and seventeen years younger. The study found that men who marry older women are more likely to die early.*

That marriage, as an institution, is on the rocks back home is not in doubt: In America, the average marriage age is rising while the marriage rate plummets. But in places like Moscow and Medellin, where tradition reigns, it's still frowned upon for a woman to be single past her midtwenties.

On the tour the men talk of fleeing gold diggers up North, a legal system whose alimony rules unfairly favor women, and/or a misguided culture of feminism. But the gold-digger rationale falls apart under the lightest scrutiny. The men are in Colombia to meet women who are interested in them for no other reason than what they can provide. And yet, for most of the romance tourists, squaring this incongruity requires little effort. He is here to meet women who both value the controlling, masculine gender role that he enacts and embrace the servile, "family-oriented" femininity without which his own role would not make sense to him. His desire to be captain of his own ship finds validation in an image that is necessarily vague: the beautiful but unstable Colombiana who deserves better than her circumstances provide. It's not that she's so poor, nor her options so limited, that she's willing to sell her youth to a man more than twice her age. A parity of power must be assumed. This is why the neat geopolitical overlay—i.e., the obvious fact that the power hierarchy between these two gender roles happens to conform with the hierarchy that binds developing nations to the industrialized world, so long as they agree to adopt their benefactors' ideas about democracy, or capitalism, or family—proves not to be a popular subject of conversation for the romance tourists, when brought up. The view among the Amo Latina reps, a view that filters down to its clients, is that it's all about enjoying oneself,

---

* Women don't experience the same benefits, reports the Max Planck Institute. Women with husbands older *or* younger by between seven and nine years *increase* their chances of dying early by 20 percent.

seeing what happens. You're the man. Be assertive. Take control. But don't stress.

"You won't find a more open-hearted place," Dave says. "All these Colombian girls want to do is have a good time. Medellin is called the City of Eternal Spring for a reason. Men come here and have years added to their lives. That's not bullshit."*

Late that night, back in the lobby of the Dann Carlton, Bart and Andy are new men. "To pull off something like that!" Bart says. "To have a bar where they supplied *all* the booze and *all* the food and *all* the girls. Boy, it was like . . . you can't do that at home! The possibility of romance was in the air for all those women. You could see it in their eyes."

For Andy's part, he's no longer carping over the twenty-year-old who blew him off. His mind is fixed on Paola, a twenty-four-year-old he met at Mango's and spent all evening speaking to via interpreter. "I tell you, we just clicked," Andy says. "I asked her at the very beginning: 'I'm fifty-two, do you have a problem with that?' You see, I was trying to shoot her down. But she didn't see the problem. She asked if I could cook, 'cause she doesn't. I said I make a really good spaghetti, a couple Mexican dishes, and a champagne brunch."

"You think she was running a game on you?" Bart asks. "You never know in these third world countries, when you're out at these places meeting girls."

"Nope," says Andy. "I don't think so. I said to the translator, 'This girl seems very special,' and I asked the translator for her feedback, and she said, 'You know, I think you've found the one. She's very simple, very affectionate, and very caring.' And then I said to the translator that I would consider selling everything I have and moving down here, instead of taking her up to Florida and turning her into a fucking gold digger."

----

* Medellin is called the City of Eternal Spring because its moderate mountain climate and proximity to the equator mean the temperature hovers around 77 degrees Fahrenheit all year round.

In the eighteenth century, Bogotá—Colombia's capital—was the cultural and political center of the Spanish empire, a territory that comprised what today are Colombia, Panama, Ecuador, and Venezuela. Three centuries later, Colombia has South America's second-most unequal distribution of wealth after Paraguay. Structurally it has one of the most stratified social systems in the world. It is split into six "stratos." Strato one is the poorest, six the richest. Only people from stratos four, five, and six pay taxes. Most of the women who register with bridal agencies are from either strato two or three. As with the women of Eastern Europe and the men of the West, the women of Colombia who turn to bridal agencies have a standard narrative too: A third world economy combined with Colombia's machismo culture, its drug wars, and *la violencia* have depleted the supply of eligible males.

So when Amo Latina tour clients praise "the beautiful simplicity of these women," they are speaking really of grinding poverty, of the narrow aims and provincial ambitions imposed by a life that has never known anything beyond Medellin. After all, there's no gene for "traditional family values," or "femininity." Rather, they are norms and expectations engendered by culture and circumstance, including class structure, race, ethnicity, nationality, and other aspects of identity that determine who people are and what they want. Through this lens, one understands better how the eyes of a Colombiana could go bright at the sight of, say, Nick, a thirty-four-year-old machinist from small-town Indiana who says almost nothing, except when he's high on painkillers, and then he says things like, "My brother's married to a Jew, so he thinks he's got to get everything half price and then sell it back to the family at three times what he paid for it."

Norma Ramos, the executive director of the Coalition Against Trafficking in Women, suspects that many Colombianas do not understand the degree to which they'll be dependent on their husbands for support and social integration. "What about their precarious legal status in the States?" she says. "Or the possibility of violence and exploitation?"

To what extent does our very modern ideal of marriage as a nonfinancial arrangement account for the natural revulsion we feel when we think of American men descending on the world's final frontiers of development to search for that perfectly young and beautiful and submissive wife, the one who will never ask for more than she gets, who will never doubt his command, will never leave him when he's old and sick, and will certainly never drag him over the coals and take all his money like that evil ex-wife? When we turn our noses up, what are we feeling? Do we mock what we don't understand? Or do we mock what we understand all too well: lonely/desperate/horny people trying to be less lonely/desperate/horny?

Anastasia and A Foreign Affair have been successful companies, and are becoming more so, because they meet a demand that they help create. How different is their stigma from the one that once attached to Gary Kremen's Match.com? Given the social iniquities and power dynamics on display in Colombia, one could argue that the two stigmas are sufficiently different. So a big question is whether increased access and availability, along with more widespread use among younger people, will, over time, be enough to change how these cross-border relationships are perceived.

Premium international online dating? Mail-order brides? Sex tourism? Human trafficking? "There is nothing that indicates they are mutually exclusive explanations," writes Ericka Johnson in *Dreaming of a Mail-Order Husband*, "and I think it is quite possible that the industry is made up of consenting adults who know what they are doing at the same time as the international framework of inequitably distributed wealth and migration regulations are influencing the options available to these 'consenting' adults."

The potential influence that Steve or Nathan or Bart or Andy could have on these women's lives might, to the women, seem trivial compared with the dismalness of what awaits at home. But when this view is presented to Norma Ramos, she insists that trading one vulnerability for another makes premium international online dating no different from any other form of human trafficking: "It's about those with power and choices shopping around for those without power and choices."

The second social takes the form of a beauty pageant. In order to document the event, and drum up publicity, Amo Latina has invited journalists and film crews to Museo El Castillo, a renovated castle on a hill in the center of Medellin. Pageant contestants have been invited from all over Colombia, though how closely tied to Amo Latina they are is in question: According to several sources, the best-looking ladies are professional models who've been paid by Amo Latina to participate in the pageant. This is standard operating procedure. In the States, Anastasia pays Dasha Astafieva, *Playboy* magazine's fifty-fifth anniversary playmate, to tout the company in interviews and photo shoots.

Tonight's judging panel is comprised of four Amo Latina tour clients and a local television celebrity named Patrizia, whose body has been biomechanically engineered to distract the male eye. The freckled blonde to my left touches my arm. Such is my state of mind after a few days of romance touring that I simply assume she wants me, or wants something from me. "*Qué lástima*," she says, shaking her head. *What a shame.* I see her Telemundo press credential. She, like me, is here to cover the event.

The contestants first traipse around in dresses and then in swimwear. Andrea is studying economics. Karina hopes to become a veterinarian. The men's faces melt into smiles.*

The pageant's winner is a nineteen-year-old model from Bogotá. The Telemundo reporter rushes onstage with her film crew. "You have many more choices now," the reporter tells the winner in Spanish. "What are you looking for? What do you want?"

"*Como todo el mundo*," the winner responds, "*yo estoy buscando el amor de mi vida*." ("Like everyone, I'm looking for my true love.")

Love can emerge anywhere. Anastasia says 20 percent of its tour clients find a long-term relationship—about half of those are marriages; the other half are nonmarried relationships lasting over four years. But the situations in Medellin share themes of disillusion and hopelessness.

---

* Colombia prizes the beauty of its women. In addition to the Miss Independence pageant and the Miss Colombia pageant, juries award many lesser titles: Miss Plantain; Miss Coal. Cellblocks in a Bogotá women's prison have their own pageants. One town in northern Colombia puts makeup and wigs on its donkeys and parades them for the annual Miss Burro celebration.

Take fifty-three-year-old Marc Bovet, another Amo Latina poster boy, whose forthcoming marriage to a Colombiana is being used as a promotional tool for the company, plastered across billboards and television. Bovet, who says he was a former mercenary in the Middle East, came to Colombia because he had to declare bankruptcy in the United States after his properties were foreclosed on. He says he owes his ex-wife a million dollars he doesn't have. He says one of his cousins invented Velcro and that another cousin is a well-known Wall Street mogul, but that no one in his family will help him financially. He says that having his face on the Amo Latina ads has made him a kidnapping target in Colombia. He regrets leaving his gun collection in Oregon. An alcoholic with a seething, hostile energy, Bovet comes across as a psychopath even to the tour's more fringe figures. And yet Bovet's marriage to a woman who cannot understand a word he says is Amo Latina's biggest success story.

An American video crew is now interviewing the Telemundo reporter. "What makes the women sign up?" she's asked.

"*Mucho dinero*," she says, rubbing her fingers together in the universal sign for money. "I think eighty percent of girls want travel, money, clothes. Not love."

Andy is falling in love with Paola. She's from strato two and has diabetes, he's discovered. "But she seems like she would be the type of girl, when she falls in love, that will be there at my bed in the nursing home when I die, and not just take my money and run off with another guy," he speculates. "And you know, that's an issue I have." On the back of Andy's white denim button-down, with the sleeves torn off, an American eagle wrapped in stars and stripes flies above the words RIGHTEOUS RULER.

Nearby, Juanita the translator has been facilitating a conversation between Bart and a Colombiana, which she describes as strange: "He said that for every child she has, he would give her one plastic surgery," Juanita reports. "I don't know if he was making a joke. I've never heard that one before. I just told her he said she was very pretty."

Tony, the ER doc, bought his fiancée new shoes and a dress for the social. But he ignores her and flirts with other women. One wonders whether Tony intends, at the subconscious level, to see how poorly he can treat his fiancée, and for how long, until she leaves him, an outcome that would confirm his view of himself as a no-good shmuck. He is telling a group of people about his new Corvette when his fiancée walks by. "Tony," she whines, "I no enjoy alone. I no enjoy alone."

Over cocktails, Marc Bovet and his fiancée are meeting with a real estate agent about buying a condo in Cartagena, the beachside town where, in a few months, several of President Obama's Secret Service agents will clash with Colombia's legalized prostitution industry.

A Colombian camera crew has been told I'm a journalist. The producer asks me to do an interview with Patrizia, the television personality with the mechanically enhanced figure. Since neither her English nor my Spanish are good enough for the camera, we agree that she will speak in Spanish and I will reply in English, having been told beforehand what the questions will be. The camera rolls. Patrizia reels off something in Spanish that I know means, "Why did the American men come to Medellin? And what have they found here?"

I could say I've been sent to Medellin as a corporate shill, to report on what will likely become known as the love junket. I can say it's good or I can say it's bad. I can say whatever. ("We expect that whatever you write will fall somewhere between neutral and positive," I was told by an Anastasia rep during the journalistic negotiation that preceded the trip.) It's not that they don't care what I say. Rather, it's that they care more that I say *something*. The point is not: This is good or this is bad. The point is: *This is happening.* Whatever Anastasia actually believes about the relationships it facilitates, the company believes strongly, and based on the numbers, justifiably, in the allure of its product to overcome a little societal disapproval.

I could say that, for the time being, this particular technology seems to be satisfying the needs of tough cases, but that for all I know, in five or fifteen years there could be tours of Ivy League graduates coming here to date the daughters of strato six families. As for Western women, well, they don't use international online-dating sites yet. But they can be seen paying for sex and companionship in the Caribbean. As the financial status of Western women continues to improve in a local relationship market that resembles, increasingly, the competitively favorable situations of successful African American men and in-demand Chinese women, who's to say they won't be shipping back commitment-minded husbands from somewhere like Tibet, a historically polyandrous country* whose males are said to be found attractive by Western women.

I could mention that Anastasia and its ilk are merely brands in an undifferentiated communications industry, and that in the course of research I met several middle-aged Western men who, by simply changing the zip code on their searches, use traditional online-dating sites to date women in other countries. On one such Match-facilitated journey from London to Manila, George, a forty-three-year-old architect, was stood up, so he salvaged the trip with a couple days of scuba diving in Boracay. I could say it's no big deal. That, as shocking as it all seems, the rise of international online dating is just another slide toward the end of a long-vanishing moral arc in the West, where the rule of sexual conduct by authority has been dissolving for one hundred years. If history is any lesson, a new set of guiding conventions will come along soon, just in time to be overthrown once again, antiquated before they can ossify. All that is holy is profaned. All that is solid melts into air.

The shift is happening now. Neither Anastasia nor its main competitor, the Arizona-based A Foreign Affair, will divulge its profits or registration numbers. However, in the six years between 2005 and 2011, Anastasia says the number of Russian and Ukrainian women joining its site has tripled, while the number of Western men signing up has more than quadrupled. A Foreign Affair says its business has grown by an average of 25 percent a year over the last decade. Both companies say male clients are skewing younger.

In places where international online dating operates, it's powerful enough to recruit high-quality talent on the ground to run the agencies, maintain the Web sites, and host the tours—even in a place like Ukraine, where the local stigma that attaches to the business is so strong that staff members are embarrassed to tell their friends and family they work in

---

* Women have two or more male partners.

the bridal industry; if pushed, they're likely to explain that the hopeless women they broker abroad are from a different Ukraine. Natalia Pankova, a Ukrainian woman who works for a Kiev-based bridal agency named Charming Brides, never admits where she works. "They have a very negative view that we are selling girls to rich foreign men," she says. "But there is no buying or selling. And it is not mail-order brides. You can't pack a girl and send her. It's just another way of meeting people."

ALEXIS, PART VI

↓

A Searing Chronicle

WHEN A PTER ASKS ALEXIS WHETHER SHE'S WORRIED THAT BEN might find out about his role in her second life and exact retribution, she writes: "Yes, but you guys would probably love me more for all the lulz if a random boy came to air dirty laundry/pics, and at least I would see his true colors."

In fact, he does know. Shortly after Ben met Alexis, a friend of his, who happened to check out Phantasy Tour from time to time, forwarded Ben the link to one of Alexis's threads about online dating, because he knew Ben was on Match. Even though PTers post under handles like Wonderbrah and McFly, it was clear to Ben, from the details provided, that he was dating the person who was leading these conversations. It struck him as a bizarre coincidence, until he thought about it. The Internet had expanded his social circle, but perhaps not as much as he imagined. The kinds of people he met online were similar in their tastes and background to the friends he had.

Ben was amused by Alexis's habit. Her sharing compulsion wasn't atypical. Every day he watched his friends on Facebook broadcast all kinds of information about their families, relationships, marriages, and children. But then Alexis's reports become increasingly revealing. "I am seeing him on Friday and Saturday," she writes on Phantasy Tour, "making for dates 4 . . . and 5!"

It's uncomfortable to see his private life broadcast like this, even if he is kept anonymous. Alexis, he feels, is crossing some boundary of loyalty or trust. This goes beyond Facebook-style sharing. What bothers him is that she seems to be prioritizing this public persona over their actual relationship. It also bothers him that her reports stray from the facts. They already slept together, on the third date. Why not tell it like it happens? Then again, he wasn't being entirely honest when he told Alexis that he'd been on Match for one only month prior to meeting her. In fact, he'd been on Match before, and also had an account on OkCupid.

Casually, Ben mentions to her that one of his friends follows chat room discussions on a site called Phantasy Tour, and that the friend recently sent him a thread discussing online dating. "Do you ever read that site?"

Alexis blushes, says yes, she loves Phantasy Tour, and may have even participated in some of those threads about online dating.

The next day she relates this coincidence on Phantasy Tour. "He does not have a handle," she writes, "but his friend sends him funny threads occasionally. Including, he told me, a thread entitled 'Match .com.' That. Is. Crazy."

"Epic!" writes a PTer, in a comment typical of many others expressing giddy dismay.

"And a bit embarrassing," Alexis writes. "Not to mention that he could very well be reading this, which is scary."

When Ben sees this, it becomes impossible for him to take the relationship seriously. Who is he dating? The Alexis of an online-dating profile? The woman he's spent a few dates with? Or the Phantasy Tour persona? Is there a difference? He cancels the fifth date and never calls back to reschedule.

Alexis is distressed, but briefly. A week later she's back on Phantasy Tour, posting enthusiastically about another potential boyfriend from Match. "I had a really fun first date last weekend," she writes. "Delicious dinner/drinks, fun conversation, ordered 3 desserts . . . quite tipsy by the end. He called my bluff about singing, so we went around the corner to a karaoke bar, got more drinks, raged it. Super fun. He asked for another date yesterday."

"This isn't the one who originally inspired these threads, is it?"

"No, a freshie."

"What happened to the first guy?"

"I just got a case of the meh. I think he did too, or he sensed it, because we both stopped making the effort."

"Poundtown?"

"I slept with him," she writes. "It was a lackluster experience though. Felt totally disconnected."

Alexis's opinion of online dating soon cools, when the second guy from Match stands her up. "When I texted to confirm," she writes on PT, "he cancelled, said he was sick. Then no call back. Very perplexing. But I've been flirting with my date for tomorrow and he's a stud." After a first-date hookup, that guy disappears as well.

On PT Alexis announces she's quitting Match.

"What happened?" asks a PTer. "Didn't like what you were finding?"

"It was an entertaining venture," she explains, "but it always seemed forced. Mostly it was an experiment and a way to get me out of the house during winter. I also needed the confidence boost. But I'm feeling better now. The weather is getting nicer and it will be easier to meet people out and about. Sundresses get me farther than Internet profiles." She continues: "I've decided to stop trying in the life partner department. If it happens, it happens. But focusing on it too much is draining and that energy should be put toward my career right now."

"Someone should make a weekly Internet dating thread so we can all continue to discuss/share experiences," writes a PTer. "I used a lot of helpful tips in here."

For Alexis, too, the sharing compulsion remains strong. "I'm considering starting an anonymous personal blog," she writes, "a searing chronicle of my dating life. I just started writing the first entry."

CHAPTER EIGHT

Knowledge Is Sour

HOW TOO MUCH INFORMATION
TURNS US INTO *THAT KIND* OF GIRLFRIEND

Online relationships are vulnerable to a "boom and bust" phenomenon.... Relationships can get quite intense quite quickly.

> —"Romance in Cyberspace:
> Understanding Online Attraction"

There is an optimal pace at which intimacy develops, and too great a change might have the effect of undermining the relationship.

> —"A Second Chance to Make a First Impression: Factors
> Affecting the Longevity of Online Dating Relationships"

When Trish McDermott was hired to market the first iteration of Match, she wrote an advice column called Tell It To Trish. One female online dater wrote to Trish with a problem. The woman had always operated on a "five-date rule"—no sex till date number five. She found it took the pressure off getting to know the other person, and also helped build some anticipation if things were going well. On the first date with someone she met through Match, she told him about her five-date rule.

Okay, he told her, the rule's been satisfied.

Huh?

Well, he explained, they'd exchanged two e-mails apiece on the site and spoken on the phone twice. Since those conversations had been at least as revealing as face-to-face dates would've been, their first date was, in theory, their fifth date, and therefore they should sleep together.

"Even as rudimentary as the service was back then," McDermott recalls, "it felt like we were living in a Wild West of technology. No one knew what the rules were."

This new way of meeting someone surely meant new behavior online. But should it also alter the way you conducted yourself offline? What was a woman to do? "So many people had this problem," says McDermott. "It was hard to know what to say, except to remind them that behind the technology they were dealing with real people."

For centuries, relationship-advice givers have debated how much "togetherness" is the right amount. In a twelfth-century advice manual, *Treatise on Love and its Remedies*, Andreas Capellanus warned that too many opportunities to see or chat with the beloved diminishes love, another way of saying absence makes the heart grow fonder. Today's technology means more communication. But online dating adds a new wrinkle: What *is* togetherness? Do e-mail and text messages count? How about interaction on social networks? What happens when the opportunities to see or chat with the beloved are commitment-free, nonexclusive opportunities to see or chat not with the beloved per se, but with the beloved's self-extension, or simply to watch the beloved chat with the self-extension of some other person?

Internet-mediated relationships aren't just about pheromones giving way to CMC, or competing algorithms, or the splintering of PXRs into SEOs and PMXs. It's also about an entirely new set of rules and signaling in a digital world that enables not only more communication but also a new broadcasting capability, which can be disastrous for things like intimacy and trust.

Fifteen years after online dating first subjected the five-date rule to scrutiny, the spread of dating sites and social media have accelerated connection and sharing. Today's togetherness is often instantaneous, and then constant. You begin dating someone you met online, or off, and in a matter of days you are Facebook friends who also follow each other's Twitter feed and show up on each other's Tumblr dash and chat throughout the day via IM and text. By midday you've opened ten tabs on your browser, and on five of them the avatar of your paramour is blinking and winking and typing and poking and accepting and liking and smiling and frowning and inviting.

In the first months of Facebook, the site established a new system of signals for students at Harvard. "Now," wrote David Kirkpatrick in *The Facebook Effect*, "if a girl met a guy at a frat party, an elaborate set of electronic rituals was set in motion. They took on even more significance if you had already hooked up. The first key question was whether the guy immediately friended you. . . . If he didn't, that was a disastrous sign."

Similar rituals occur with online dating. "The first thing you do when you meet someone online," explains Dara, a twenty-eight-year-old documentary filmmaker in San Francisco, "is exchange a couple messages through the dating site. Then you send texts and e-mails to coordinate the first date. Then, after the first date, if things go well, there's the question of who's going to add who first on Facebook. Then you look at each other's pictures and all their stuff. You Google them, read their résumé, maybe an essay written ten years ago. It feels intimate, but also really distant. You have a ton of information, but you've only met them once. Maybe just thirty minutes for coffee. So there's a huge disconnect between what you think you know about each other and what you've actually established in real life."

San Francisco's proximity to Silicon Valley has resulted in a particularly gadget-crazed, heavily connected culture that seems to dovetail perfectly with online dating. It's always been one of OkCupid's best markets. "There are more techies, more early adopters than anywhere else," says Sam Yagan.

A self-described tomboy with a chilled-out California vibe, Dara sticks to a simple philosophy of life: Don't blame people for being the way they are; but if they're really stupid, then go ahead and blame them. She moved to the Bay Area from San Diego. "I'd just been through that one devastating breakup that everyone goes through. I had this big plan for my life, and then the bottom dropped out."

In San Francisco, Dara found a group of friends, but no one she was interested in romantically. So she had a choice: remain single or go on-line. "Everyone in San Francisco is too busy to date. But everyone owns an iPhone. So dating becomes one more thing you access through an app. I have one app to get my music, another to suggest movies, another for news, another to keep up with friends, one to show me where a good bar is, and another app to help me find a date to go to that bar with. I used to think of dating as this special thing. Now it's mixed in with all these other things. In a way, dating is easier. It's definitely more efficient. But it's also really confusing."

Through Match, Dara went on a few lackluster dates, and then she met someone she liked. She thought, "Well, he's still on Match. So I guess we're not exclusive?" They dated for a couple of months before hitting what Dara calls "the Great American Drop-Off." They would hang out from time to time, with long gaps in between.

But then the relationship picked up again. She looked on Match and saw that his profile had been taken down. So she quit Match too. She figured they were an item, even though no one had said anything. "It was based on what I guess you might call appearances."

Over the holidays, while Dara was visiting her parents, she noticed he'd popped up on Match again. That's when she found herself monitoring him on Facebook, puzzling over the identity of new female "adds," and trying to deduce the nature of the relationships he had with the Facebook friends who posted on his wall. Why hadn't she met these people or heard about them before? Were they other women from Match, or just friends? Was he trying to make her jealous? Did she need to do the same?

Dara thought she was alone in her confusion until one night when, after several glasses of wine, she and her girlfriends began discussing Facebook stalking. They noticed a cycle to San Francisco's dating scene:

meet online; go on a few dates; then try to decide whether a relationship exists by checking back at the dating site and monitoring Facebook behavior. Less than ideal, but there it was.

The ladies' wine-fueled chat was itself a mating tradition. "To guard against deception, women spend hours discussing with their friends the details of interactions they have had with their mates or with potential mates," writes David Buss in *The Evolution of Desire*.* In the past, the girlfriend consultants might've had some previous knowledge of the guy whose intentions were being scrutinized. The special modern problem faced by Dara and her friends, all of whom used online dating, was that they often had no idea of the guy being discussed. Thanks to technology, their social circle lacked coherence. Often guys were referred to by their professions, or just by their online-dating screen names. Everyone was meeting everyone, it seemed, and yet no one knew anyone. They discussed every man in San Francisco, it seemed, and no one at all.

The solution, they decided, was to cultivate a Facebook presence of what they called hot-and-wanted. This entailed posting pictures of yourself doing fun things, featuring flirtatious comments on your wall from guys, and generally exuding the image of a fantastic life. Hot-and-wanted: This was their hypothesis. A little immature, they all agreed. But desperate times called for desperate measures.

"Humans," says Gian Gonzaga, the director of eHarmony's relationship lab, "evolved in tightly interwoven groups, where everyone knew each other's business. So you could argue that today's hyperconnectedness is actually a lot more natural than what we've gone through over the last hundred years, with the geographic dispersal and breakup of families. On the other hand, there is something quite different about the social interweaving of today. We have so many more people in our social network, and our brains aren't all that big."

The next day, before Dara could implement the hot-and-wanted strategy, her paramour texted her a picture of himself standing on a golf

---

* "Men," writes Buss, "are significantly less inclined to devote effort to this problem of assessment."

course, wearing a pair of silly plaid pants that she'd encouraged him to buy. She felt the special bond of an inside joke. When Dara logged onto Facebook she saw that he'd posted the same picture. She watched while other women plastered his Facebook wall with flirtatious comments about how great he looked in the silly plaid pants.

"But I'm the one who told him to wear those pants!" Dara fumed.

Her girlfriends told her she had a right to feel hurt. Her male friends said he probably hadn't even considered it. He was trying to seem hot and wanted too.

If a third of American singles are meeting through Web sites that are explicitly for dating, how does the rest of one's online presence complement or complicate relationships? In the past, certain things were only shared with your lover, while some details of your relationship may have been shared with a few friends. But now it's natural to broadcast every encounter to a group of strangers.

Technology, writes Sherry Turkle in *Alone Together: Why We Expect More from Technology and Less from Each Other*, "supports an emotional style in which feelings are not fully experienced until they are communicated. . . . [T]here is every opportunity to form a thought by sending out for comments." Turkle finds teenagers who send text messages to friends all day and wait, with palpable anxiety, for a response to validate the feeling. "We are stimulated by connectivity itself," she writes. "We learn to require it, even as it depletes us."

Each person's social network—whether Dara's Facebook or Alexis's Phantasy Tour—becomes a kind of Greek chorus sounding off on the dramatic action of her life. When word escaped on Facebook that Jennifer, a twenty-seven-year-old fashion designer, had left a physically abusive relationship, her ex's Facebook friends booed him down publicly after he posted about the breakup on his wall. On 4chan.org, the message board called /b/ is where young hackers come to collude, trade n00dz (porn), and discuss how to prank pedos (pedophiles). In her 2012 book, *We Are Anonymous*, about a famous hacking organization, Parmy Olson observed that even while constant insults between posters on /b/

create a "throbbing mass of negativity," beneath it all there is a supportive side. In so-called bawww threads, hackers appeal to the sympathetic side of 4chan with titles such as "gf just dumped me, bawww thread please?" This is the rare instance when users offer sincere advice, comfort, or funny pictures to cheer each other up, converting the social network into a self-help network.

Perhaps Phantasy Tour members suffer from no classifiable disease or pathology. They're not overcoming any psychic trauma, like Mothers Against Drunk Driving. Nor are they committing to a course of improvement, like Jenny Craig or Weight Watchers. But they are coming of age in a world where relationships are discovered, initiated, and maintained in ways that are starkly different not only from their parents' era, but from all of human history.

"We're not married and we're not having kids," Dara says. "But we're still trying to make the same kinds of connections our parents made when they were our age and perhaps had already had us."

Dara went back to monitoring her paramour's online behavior, as if more Facebook stalking was the answer to incomplete information on Facebook. A couple of days later he deleted the silly pants picture with the flirtatious comments beneath it. This made her happy. But then she got to thinking: "Did he delete the picture as a gesture of care toward me? Or was he trying to hide something?" Was his profile meant to speak to Dara, individually, or to his five-hundred-plus Facebook friends?

Second-order information, writes communications professor Ilana Gershon, is the meaning of a message beyond its explicit terms, "the information that can guide you into understanding how particular words and statements should be interpreted." Linguistic anthropologists refer to this as metapragmatics. In *The Breakup 2.0*, Gershon's 2011 book about how things like Facebook and text messaging complicate relationships, she gives the following examples of second-order information. A woman refuses to e-mail her ex-husband's personal e-mail account, sending all correspondence to his work e-mail instead. Translation: *I mean to emphasize my wish that the relationship remain over.* In another case, a twenty-one-year-old doesn't know if her boyfriend is serious when he breaks up with her, because he did it via text message. During the relationship they'd used texting only to send jokes. The exact same message, sent via e-mail, would've been clearer. The second-order information conveyed by the medium—this is a text, therefore this is a joke—was at odds with the message. Texting, Gershon's female interviewees say, is a medium men use, because it's so low stakes.

Facebook is a rabbit hole of second-order information. Take Dara's paramour's willingness to flirt with other women on his wall. Did that communicate second-order information that he was interested in them? Uninterested in her? Unwilling to commit? Very likely, but who knows. She wouldn't have been wrong to take it that way. Public signals, writes David Buss, are one of the foremost indications of a man's intent to commit.

The Facebook effect ripples across cultures. In *Tales from Facebook*, digital anthropologist Daniel Miller's study of Facebook's impact in Trinidad, we learn that Facebook is called *Fasbook*. The name is less a variation on pronunciation than meaning: In Trinidad, to be *fas* is to try to get to know someone too quickly. *Fas* is likely derived from *facile*, which means shallow, simplistic, superficial. And yet Trinidadians believe that the truth of another person is more readily discerned on *Fasbook* than in real life. The shield of the screen means people talk more openly and reveal unintended truths. Trinidadians believe in "truth by construction": The labor a person puts into crafting her *Fasbook* profile is more suggestive of her truth than concrete facts could ever convey.

Research indicates that when it comes to building trust and nurturing romantic relationships, Facebook, along with other social portals that link lovers in a nonprivate forum, often play a negative role, particularly for those who try to balance risk and commitment in their relationships by evaluating Facebook profiles for signs of infidelity. The problem with Facebook-as-relationship-facilitator is that it simultaneously offers *too much* information and *not enough*. Facebook, writes Gershon, promotes a "contextless promiscuity." In *The Breakup 2.0*, one of Gershon's male interviewees says his girlfriend gets upset when his

Facebook friends post pictures of him with other women. He tries to appease her by "untagging" (deleting) his name from the picture. But it does no good. She can still see the picture on Facebook, and see that he's untagged himself. Then that looks even worse.

Young women tell Gershon that the ease of monitoring their boyfriends on Facebook changed them, "made them into *that kind of girlfriend*, the one who is ever suspicious and constantly asking her boyfriend to prove he only thinks of her."

A journal paper published in *CyberPsychology & Behavior*, entitled "More Information Than You Ever Wanted: Does Facebook Bring Out the Green-Eyed Monster of Jealousy," explains the vicious cycle that is Facebook-stalking:

> With the vast majority of our sample reporting that their partners have unknown individuals and past romantic and sexual partners as friends on Facebook, the potential for jealousy in this environment is evident. The qualitative data we collected indicates that participants recognize that increased exposure to information on Facebook without proper context can increase their experience of jealousy. What is perhaps more puzzling is that despite this knowledge, many of these same participants also engage in a high degree of personal disclosure on Facebook.

Total information versus total control: This has been the tension driving Facebook's business model, and the recipe for its seemingly limitless growth potential. "The problem Facebook is solving is this one paradox," a twenty-one-year-old Mark Zuckerberg told *The New Yorker* magazine. "People want access to all the information around them, but they also want complete control over their own information. Those two things are at odds with each other." In an article entitled "Saving Facebook," New York University law school professor James Grimmelmann phrased the paradox in terms of socializing: "There's a deep, probably irreconcilable tension between the desire for reliable control over one's information and the desire for unplanned social interaction."

As Zuckerberg made the previous comment, in 2006, he was planning a major change to the architecture of his site, one that would shift the user experience further toward total information exposure, endowing her with a kind of social omniscience that was as addicting as it was anxiety inducing. Facebook introduced a feature called "News Feeds." Upon logging into Facebook, the user would now see a cascade of his friends' latest entries—comments, photographs, news about new Facebook friendships, etc. Prior to News Feeds, Dara would've had to visit her paramour's Facebook page to see that he'd posted the plaid-pants photo. With News Feeds, the plaid-pants photo would be the first thing she'd see upon logging in. Facebook would inundate her with every move her lover made on Facebook, plus every move made by anyone else— whether she knew that person or not—that referred to him.

The problem with News Feeds, writes social-media anthropologist Danah Boyd, is that it collapses "disparate social contexts" into one. "How one behaves in a pub differs from how one behaves in a family park, even though both are ostensibly public," Boyd writes. "Social convergence requires people to handle disparate audiences simultaneously without a social script."

For Gershon's Facebook-addicted women, the only way out was to call it quits, delete their profiles, and walk away, but this was harder than it sounds. Humans have evolved to express proprietary attitudes toward their mates. Men have had more success using public markings. Women tend to rely more on vigilance, through which they detect signs of defection and send their mate the message that consequences await.

"You're left feeling a little shameful," says Dara. "You don't know how you're supposed to interpret these things. We can obviously choose to communicate better than we do. But there's no protocol. It's not like it's been written down in a Jane Austen novel."

A novel no, a blog yes. At How About We, bloggers Chiara Atik and Scott Alden have written extensively on how to prevent technology from capsizing a relationship. Atik provides the woman's perspective on subjects such as things you shouldn't do until you're exclusive (friend each other's friends on Facebook), the crazy things women do on Facebook ("They will continuously monitor your Facebook page. If another girl writes on a guy's wall that girl will also get stalked."), and how to properly manage a Facebook relationship so you don't annoy your friends (don't write personal messages on a public space; limit the amount of "together" photos and the number of partner-focused status updates). Alden proposes reasons why Facebook might be ruining your dating life (keeping you in touch with old flames; public flirting), when it's appropriate to become Facebook friends with someone you're casually dating ("Talking on the phone as opposed to texting is a step. Gchatting is a step. And Facebook *is* a step."), the crazy things guys do on Facebook (purposely pissing off the boyfriend that she's too good for by, say, "posting a clip from last night's Rachel Maddow on her wall, which you know will lead to like 14 comments back and forth between you and her, and a decision to get coffee soon to discuss it further, but nothing from the boyfriend, cause he's more a *Big Bang Theory* kind of guy, you know?"), and why Gmail's instant-messaging function, Gchat, is terrible for new relationships: "brb" is hardly the language of love.

In her 2006 book, *The Joy of Text*, Kristina Grish lays out the elements of digital style, urging her readers to think carefully about punctuation, grammar, spelling, and the signals they send. For example:

> **Exclamation points:** Assign yourself a quota of two exclamation points per message. . . . If six out of seven of your sentences end with this overzealous punctuation mark, most guys will assume they don't have the energy to keep up with your cheery attitude. NEVER (yes, I'm screaming) use more than one in a row unless you want the reader to think you're on some really good crack.

> I had such a great time last night. I've never seen the original King Kong, but I'm so glad you made me watch it. Next time, I'll call shotgun on movie rentals. It's only fair . . . Talk soon!

All this code seems downright explicit compared with some of the texting schemes reported in 2011 by the *Wall Street Journal*. Following fights with her husband, a wife sends him blank text messages to create an air of mystery and score a callback. Other power plays include replying, "who is this?" when you receive a text from someone you know, and having a friend text you repeatedly while on a date in order to paint a picture of popularity. A twenty-three-year-old woman writes texts to new boyfriends while pretending to be drunk. She writes something honest, such as "I really like hanging out with you," but spells words wrong and mentions her drunkenness. If the guy responds in a gentlemanly fashion ("I like you, too. Why don't we talk tomorrow?"), he's proved himself. If he writes something inappropriate, he's dead. The *Journal* coined such behavior bluffting.

To which a frustrated *WSJ* reader responded: "I don't know who thinks that they're going to start a successful relationship by trying to mess with someone's head."

But to live as a single adult in today's postrules world of techno-relating is to play a nonstop game of puzzle-and-parse. To derive meaning from an abstract web of ambiguous connections. To look for clues and relevance in effortless gestures, such as an offer of inclusion in one's social network. To interpret the meaning of a four-hour lag in e-mail response versus a one-day lag versus a one-week lag and so on. To read romantic intent into the late hour of a text message or flirtatiousness in an abbreviated salutation. To glean entire emotional states from messages hammered out in text-speak, punctuated with emoticons, all nuance rendered down to *me happy, me sad.*

Or ...

:O (me surprised), :S (me confused), >_< (me angry), =_= (me bored), -_- (me annoyed), -_-' (me nervous), ¬_¬ (me suspicious), O_O (me shocked), ._. (me intimidated), =^_^= (me blushing).

Yet all the Facebook stalking and bluffting in the world won't change the fact that while new relationships can be discovered online, trust and loyalty are established IRL, based not on how well or poorly someone manipulates text and images on a screen but on how he or she behaves offline.

Before leaving town for a work trip, Dara erased the lengthy paragraphs in her OkCupid profile and wrote simply: "I'm sick of online dating. Let's just meet in a Laundromat."

When she returned home she had a message from a guy named Chris. He was tall, blond, into rock climbing, and had photos of himself on camping trips. "Want to go for pizza at 7:30 on Wednesday?" he wrote. "If so, send me your phone number and I'll give you a call."

"He actually called!" Dara says. "No one had ever taken the reins like that."

It turned out they had several friends in common, but probably wouldn't have run into each other had it not been for online dating. Pizza lasted several hours, and then became dessert, then a drink, and then a weekend date that lasted all day.

She was never planning to put her relationship status on Facebook, but he asked her early on to be his girlfriend. No one had ever been so direct. Boundaries had never been set. But they had dated enough people online to know what they didn't want. He'd also had communication problems in past relationships, in part because online dating had been the catalyst. They both wanted to trust someone, establish a connection, and then say, "That's it, we're done looking."

By the time they moved onto Facebook, Dara couldn't have cared less what he did on Facebook.

ALEXIS, PART VII

↓

The Battle of Least Interested

ALEXIS OPENS UP A NEW ACCOUNT ON TUMBLR, THE BLOGGING site, and begins writing a searing chronicle of her dating life in New York City. The first entry details her relationship with the law student, their intimate moments, their fights and escapades, and what she learned about the dangers of dating a person for his money. She writes another entry about the forty-year-old, and then posts a link to the blog on Phantasy Tour, expecting it to give her fellow PTers lulz. Their responses surprise her.

"That story kind of makes you seem like a bitch," one writes.

"I'm no expert (that's a lie)," writes another, "but I think you should work on making yourself a more likable and reliable narrator. You sound like a total gold digger."

"I am sorry about your dad," writes another, "I really am," implying that Alexis's dating problems might be tied to unresolved issues with her father, the straight-edge tax attorney who seems to be a model for some of the men Alexis pursues.

These comments are hurtful. "Hmm???" she replies. "My dad's the man." She begins writing more, but then decides to delete the whole thing.

During the summer Alexis begins dating a guy she meets through a music industry connection. He introduces her to his friends and family. A few months into the relationship his birthday arrives. She makes him a mix of her favorite music and prepares dinner. When he shows up he says they shouldn't see each other anymore. He travels too much for work, he says, and he doesn't have time for a relationship right now. It sounds like he just doesn't like her enough to work through these obstacles.

"Happened literally minutes ago," she writes on Phantasy Tour— starting a new thread under the title "And I just got dumped"—"and I needed to tell someone, somewhere."

As the short ribs and gnocchi cool in the kitchen, she continues: "I feel just awful. I am sure he sniffed that I liked him more than he liked me, and that he'd rather just be alone than feel obliged. I wish I knew how to play hard to get. I blow off everyone I'm not into but if I want to tap it I tiger pounce with all my loving. Now I lost the battle of least interested and I'm paying for it." While Alexis posts about the breakup on PT, she watches online porn and gets drunk on the wine she bought for supper.

A week later she posts a new dating profile on OkCupid. "At least the Internet is always there for a confidence boost via messages, or some quick dates to get out of a slump in my single times," she thinks.

She's heard rumors that guys think it's weird when women message them first, that it makes the woman seem desperate or somehow less desirable, so she waits to be contacted. Several messages per day come in, some from kind-seeming suitors and some from repulsive slimeballs.

"Your general pretentiousness is quite irritating," writes one suitor on OkCupid, "but I think I'd enjoy pounding you senseless. Up for a drink? I'd even consider taking you somewhere exclusive."

"The idea of even having a conversation with you makes my skin crawl," Alexis responds. "Why don't you stick with Craigslist hookers and gold digger sluts. Maybe they'd be impressed by 'somewhere exclusive.' Fuck off and die you arrogant little prick."

Another message comes in from mw_01: "How are you? My wife and I saw your page and thought we'd say hi since you were really attractive. Hope that's not super weird. Sorry we don't have any pictures up—our friends don't know we are into other women—but we can send some. Anyway, how is your weekend going? Do anything fun for the holidays? Hope all is well!"

A PT colleague starts a new thread, "How to get laid online," and writes: "How does this shit work? The most I got was a couple dates from chicks who were lame or fat. The last chick I met left after 5 minutes, claiming she got a phone call and her friend was having her wisdom teeth removed so she had to go pick her up."

"That's 5 minutes longer than my date lasted last night," replies a female PTer. "Guy hits me up and we chat a bit, trade some pics. He asks me out. I go to meet the guy. He gets there and abruptly tells me he changed his mind on the drive over, but he came to meet me anyway because he didn't want to be a dick. Then he left. WTF?!?!"

"Post your pics," someone tells the original poster.

"Let's just say I've been told on several occasions that I look like Jake Gyllenhaal," the OP replies.

"If you looked like Jake Gyllenhaal you would not be resorting to online dating. Someone lied to you."

The OP posts his Plenty of Fish profile.

"You look like a fucking pedophile in your picture and your profile is boring as shit," someone advises.

"For God's sake shave that chode stash!"

"There is some really trite language on there," writes another. " 'I am always seeking the next level!!' What does that even mean?"

"I'm fucking crying over here."

"Switch to OkCupid. They have all these questions girls answer. You can specifically view questions about sex. It's easy to tell if you're going to have your dick sucked within an hour of meeting them."

"My wife and I split up back in September. She recently told me she joined OkCupid and went on a horrible date. I of course got jealous and joined. Who does it match me up with? HER!!! Like a 95% match or something. If this was a paid site I'd be demanding my money back. My female friends are saying it's a sign we are meant for each other and need to get back together . . . FUCK that."

Alexis contributes some suggestions for the OP: "Don't tell her she's cute. It's creepy. Also don't list your salary. It just makes you look like an asshole. Short, funny, and positive. Casual is the way to go. Don't plead your case or ask for a date right off the bat. I ignore almost all those messages. There needs to be a little banter and buildup before you ask someone out. Just point out a common interest and ask a follow-up question."

Over the next two months, Alexis goes on what she calls an Ok-Cupid bender. These dates seem strange after a while. Each time out feels like "a performance of herself," she says, acting out the qualities that she thinks the guys expect her to have based on her profile—bubbly, sarcastic, funny.

"I've gone out with like 10 dudes," she writes. "Nice guys. Lots of entertainment. I'd like to meet a guy who's into Phish, but I feel like a lot of guys keep that off their profiles."

One day, her most recent ex, who recently joined OkCupid, pops up on the site. Turns out they're a 90% match. It's painful for Alexis, but also reassuring. At least she knows the system works.

CHAPTER NINE

Let's Keep This Fucker Coming Back

WHEN A HAPPY CUSTOMER IS BAD FOR BUSINESS

If you succeed, you lose.

—Aaron Schildkrout, chief executive officer, How About We

Dating sites, like the behaviors and matches they facilitate, don't come out of nowhere. There is a geek behind the technology. That geek has a vision. That vision is shaped by his unique geek background.

Although Gary Kremen was born in the sixties and became one of the Web's earliest entrepreneurs, a tech pioneer in every sense, he came of age in the print era, during the eighties, when newspaper personals were enjoying a resurgence. Kremen's dating site, Match.com, reflected those classifieds: anonymous profiles with a checklist approach. The eHarmony of Dr. Neil Clark Warren adapted the paternalistic, hands-on approach of the midcentury marriage-guidance movement that produced Warren. The White Label Dating of Ross Williams grew out of his belief in the efficiency gains of targeting niche networks. With Plenty of Fish, Markus Frind stood on simplicity: Make it easy; make it free. Plenty of Fish became the Costco of the date-o-sphere, the place where other name-brand sites advertise to the masses. Before OkCupid, Chris Coyne and Sam Yagan made their name by putting information on the Web, in the form of study guides. They came to online dating with a particular geek sensibility—that data was king.

Despite their differences, these innovators have been successful for the same fundamental reason: They made profitable businesses out of the search for love and companionship.

The rise of online dating as the dominant way to meet people means that many of the economic principles we've long applied to dating, in a theoretical way, are now *actually* applicable. It used to be that by living in a certain place and moving in a certain crowd we participated in "a relationship market" that operated on scarcity and demand. Now that market is owned and managed by people with a profit motive, people whose interests might diverge from ours. To varying degrees, they want satisfied daters. But they also spend their days focused on maximizing nonromantic metrics, such as "customer acquisition," "conversion rates," and "lifetime value."

Is a conflict of interest inevitable?

Explaining the mentality of a typical dating executive, Justin Parfitt, a British dating entrepreneur, puts the matter bluntly: "They're thinking, 'Let's keep this fucker coming back to the site as often as we can, and let's not worry about whether he's successful.' There's this massive tension between what would actually work for you, the user, and what works for us, the shareholders. It's amazing, when you think about it. In what other industry is a happy customer bad for business?"*

Indeed, getting daters to come back to the site is a point of pride at Match. Virtually every Match CEO, including former CEO Greg Blatt and current CEO Mandy Ginsberg, have on multiple occasions boasted to the media that most of their users are return customers. It's a PR talking point meant to suggest customer satisfaction, sort of like tracking the number of hamburgers sold nationwide. Even back in 2003, then-CEO Tim Sullivan told the *New York Times* that although his subscribers tended to leave Match after about five months—having either found a

---

* Psychiatry? The weapons trade? Plastic surgery? Pharmaceuticals?

mate or had no luck—many of them come back to the site. Sullivan, who now heads the genealogy juggernaut Ancestry.com, said 40 percent of Match subscribers are returnees. "Match.com," observed the *Times*, "does not necessarily benefit if its users pair off for good."

As the first mass-market site, Match established the industry's business-model prototype. It's a bizarre, inherently conflicted system of incentives that's been more or less replicated by every pay-based site to succeed Match in the last fifteen years. Outwardly, the industry sells a promise of customer satisfaction. Inwardly, it understands that profits can be inversely proportional to that satisfaction guarantee. The faster the user makes the site work for him, the faster he finds a mate, the faster he deletes his profile, ends his subscription, and walks away.

"We can sum up the paid dating industry pretty easily," wrote Markus Frind on his blog. "Screw your customers . . . and extract as much money as you can."

The success of free dating sites between 2005 and 2010 sparked a new debate in the industry. When daters are not being charged, when sites get paid by advertisers instead of users, are the interests of the daters and the business more closely aligned? Did the free business model therefore mean a more effective site for users?

To understand what the debate over free versus paid means for dating, it's necessary to know a little about the business itself. Most paid sites let people post a profile and search the site for free. These people are called "free users," or simply "registrations." The business of running a paid dating site therefore depends entirely on what the industry calls "conversions": convert the free user into a paying subscriber, and then maximize his "lifetime value" by getting him to come back to the site as often as possible.

Conversion rates for most paid sites dwell in the low single digits. A paid site will spend perhaps $120 in advertising to acquire one paying subscriber. That subscriber then pays the site anywhere from $20 to $60 per month. The site must keep him on long enough to recoup the original $120 investment required to get him—two to seven months, on average. Every subscription month beyond that is profit. It's a cycle: The site needs to get the original investment back as fast as possible so that the money can be funneled back into advertising to get more subscribers.

So the question becomes: What's fair in love and business? What tactics should a paid dating site use to convert its free users?

Until 2001, Match took a generous approach with its free users: If the free user received a message from a paying subscriber, he could open the message and respond to it without subscribing himself. He didn't have to put down a credit card until he wanted to initiate contact with someone. If he had a good experience messaging with a subscriber, then he might be convinced that the site worked, that there were good people on it, and it was worth subscribing himself. This business model, called "pay-to-initiate," removed a barrier to meeting for all of Match's users— paying and free—but it did so at the expense of the bottom line.

So Match instituted a new model called "pay-to-respond." Now when the free user received a message from a paying subscriber, he would get an e-mail alerting him that he had a message in his Match in-box from a wonderful woman who was eager to meet him. To read the message, and respond to it, he'd need to pay up.

The pay-to-respond model can create headaches for Match's paying customers. If they send a message to the profile of a free user, there's a slim chance they'll get a response. Yet it's often difficult to tell who's paid and who isn't. According to several former Match employees, the majority of "new profiles" seen by users in their search results belong to people who haven't paid and therefore cannot respond.

But when asked about the typical balance between free and paid users in the search results, Match's current head of product, Sharmistha Dubey, says she doesn't know. "It's not something we measure or keep track of," she says. Although she adds that "close to 80 percent" of messages exchanged on Match are sent to subscribers, and that "the bulk" of Match's users are not looking at inactive profiles.

"In our experimentation around conversion rates," Dubey explains, "we've found that it doesn't pay very well to manipulate subscription status. Instead, we've found it's more beneficial to play with factors like relevance, recency, and freshness." Dubey defines "relevance" as how well a profile fits with the searcher's stated criteria and browsing habits, "recency" as how active a profile is on the site, and "freshness" as how new a profile is, and/or when it was last updated. "We've found that emphasizing these factors [in determining search results] increases message initiation and response rates," she says. "Fortunately for us, we've found these factors to be good for monetization, too. If it hadn't worked out that way, then, well, it would've been a much more contentious thing of balancing monetization with user success."

However the economics work out, online dating is a give-and-take: In order to access a big network of potential mates, the user helps the company build an ever larger network of potential mates.

It's difficult to know exactly how any online-dating company drives conversion rates and manages the tricky balance between the success of its business and the success of its users. But it's clearly an issue. A 2011 industry report, published by *Subscription Site Insider*, found that nearly 90 percent of U.S. dating executives polled were "highly concerned" about unethical practices: "Dating sites rely heavily on personalized e-mails—supposedly triggered by individual profile activity—to convert free registered users into paying members," the report explains. "We say 'supposedly' because many in the industry suspect that some sites send non-genuine e-mails. For example, a new registered user may receive several e-mails from the site indicating women are interested in his profile, when no women actually have responded to the profile yet."

Match's former head of marketing, Trish McDermott, says that while Match's business model may be skewed in favor of Match, and against its users, there's nothing wrong with that. "I don't think there's anything illegal or unethical about pay-to-respond," says McDermott. "It just makes the barrier to connecting a lot higher. It becomes much more common to not get responses to your messages."

McDermott says Match's database is padded with the profiles of people who are no longer active on the site. In industry-speak, these profiles are called "date bait." Match makes it difficult to delete profiles, she says, because the more profiles left on the site, the more messages get sent. The more messages get sent, the longer you remain on the site. Mc-

Dermott says Match never posted fake profiles when she was there. "The sense that Match is loaded with fake profiles"—profiles representing nonexistent people—"grows out of the experience many users have of sending lots of messages and not getting replies."

But Match's CEO differs. "The truth," says Mandy Ginsburg, "is that a lot of the people who don't respond to your messages *are* paid users. They got your message. They didn't respond because they're not interested in you. Unfortunately, we can't come out and say that."

The online dating business can run afoul of its users in other ways. In the Brooklyn offices of How About We, CEO Aaron Schildkrout combs his site for scammers, people who post fake profiles in order to con real daters out of money in romance scams. Some clues? They often come in through a Google search, have registered under a Yahoo or Hotmail e-mail account (never Gmail), and use particular words and phrases that most genuine daters would find peculiar in an introductory message: blessing; companion; wife; sincere; open-minded; I am; you look gorgeous; God; children; caring; love.

Schildkrout stops at the profile of a man claiming to be from Brooklyn. He posted what appears to be a stock photo of a golfer in midswing. He calls himself a Christian conservative and writes form messages along the following lines: "Hello: I am looking for someone who I can love and will love me back, someone to support me in all my endeavors and dreams. I am a caring man with a college degree who is looking for a wife and children. I abstain from smoking and drinking."

Another likely scammer has posted a picture of a busty and seductive Latin woman. The scammer has written fifteen form messages that say: "Hi, I am Shantel. Single and ready to mingle. I want you to know that you look gorgeous. If you want a real relationship and are serious about meeting, holla!"

"Every time I throw a scammer off the site I lose money," says Schildkrout. "Not only do I lose the scammer's subscription, but I lose the subscriptions of the free users the scammer would've duped into converting."

In theory, scammers could be helpful to a dating site, by luring in real users and getting them to convert to subscribers. In 2012, Ross Williams's niche-dating empire, Global Personals, was called out for scamming. Two whistle-blowers said they'd been part of a thirty-strong team of "pseudos"—industry lingo for a dedicated staff that uses stolen photos and information from social-networking sites to set up and run fake dating profiles. "You'd take Helga from Iceland and make her into Helen from Manchester and write a profile," said one whistle-blower. "You'd use her features and invent a whole new person." Each pseudo would run as many as fifteen different fake personalities. On the other hand, many of the execs I met were obsessed with ridding their sites of scammers. "A clean site, with no scammers, is always a better long-term business proposition," says Schildkrout. Match says it spends millions on antifraud efforts.

Still, romance scams are rampant. Dotti Gale is a Chicago-based woman who helps operate sites such as Scamwarners.com and 419eater .com, where victims of romance scams come to commiserate with each other and seek support. Gale says that a single scamming outfit in Nigeria might operate up to fifty thousand dollars worth of online-dating memberships at one time. Scammers harvest information from online forums, chat rooms, dating sites, and social-networking sites. They use software designed to spot keywords that betray vulnerability ("lonely"), wealth (the name of an expensive car), depression, and old age.

In the typical West African scam, the scammer poses as a charming, affectionate, but down on his luck lover. There's also Vlads, short for Vladimir, the scamming world's nickname for scammers who target men looking for Russian brides. The newest is the Soldier at War scam, wherein the scammer poses as a U.S. soldier in need of a laptop, a plane ticket, or money for an operation the military won't pay for.

Here's how the standard scam works: The scammer strikes up a steamy online relationship, pulling the victim close and gaining his or her trust. Men are lured with sex, women with love. If the scammer is good, Gale says, he'll put in some extra time to "whiplash" his victim, alternating between hot and cold. The scammer might use a stolen credit card to send flowers, as if to say he can't possibly be a scammer, because he's spending money. Meanwhile, he's now confirmed the victim's mailing address, through which he can find out more information, plus get a fairly accurate sense of his victim's net worth.*

Once a victim has been lured in, he or she is often passed up a chain of seniority within the scamming organization, sort of like buying a car. Over the course of a fraudulent online relationship, the scammer's writing often magically improves. In the typical case, the scammer broaches the money issue by asking for a large sum to finance a fictive life-or-death medical operation for his son or mother, or to complete a crucial business deal that will allow the two of them to finally be together. He might direct the victim to a bank account, alleging that he's owed money and simply needs a temporary loan.

In 2009, a fifty-eight-year-old man in Britain threw himself under a train after losing nearly one hundred thousand euros to a Nigerian woman. In 2010, a fifty-two-year-old woman in rural England was scammed out of three hundred thousand euros by a prolific Ghanian romance fraudster named Maurice Asola Fadola, who posed as a strapping sergeant serving in Iraq. When Britain's Serious Organised Crime Agency, working with local Ghanian authorities, caught up with the thirty-one-year-old Fadola, he was living in a gold-plated, marble villa on the outskirts of Accra, complete with a gym, a pool, and Rottweilers as guard dogs. In 2012, a Nigerian man and an Argentine woman were nabbed for separating fifteen Americans from more than five hundred thousand dollars in romance scams. Several victims, including a sixty-nine-year-old woman in Minnesota, were taken on Match. Jim Arlt, an agent with the Minnesota Department of Public Safety, said, "We all have a need to have somebody in our life, and these suspects prey upon that."

Like an aspiring politician, any innovator seeking to disrupt an industry must choose an injustice sufficient to hang his ambitions on. For Sam Yagan and his OkCupid team, it was paid dating.

Free sites, led by Plenty of Fish and OkCupid, began eating up mar-

---

* If you own property, put your address into Google to see how much a stranger could learn about you.

ket share in 2007, eventually coming to own about a third of the U.S. online-dating market. In 2008, Match offered $175 million for Plenty of Fish, but Frind turned it down. At iDate 2009, Frind won the Darth Vader Award, suggesting his site was the Dark Star crippling paid sites like Match and eHarmony. Still, paid sites insisted on their superiority, defaulting to the female-friendly argument that willingness to purchase access to a dating database is a proxy for commitment. Men who pay are more likely to stay.

"Paid sites signal fundamental seriousness and mate value," says Jim Talbott, a Match strategist. "I don't know how you replicate that on a free site."

It's the velvet rope theory, and proponents of free call its logic absurd. A dater's intent, say the Frinds and Yagans, can be measured only from within the relationship. If willingness to buy access to a dating pool signals anything, it signals naiveté and/or desperation.

"Match does a fundamentally bad job of matching people up," said Yagan at iDate 2011. "They just show you every person you want to see, based entirely on looks, even if that person doesn't want to see you. All they care about is that their paid users send lots of messages to free users so that the free user signs up. Most of the people they show you aren't even active on the site anymore. They waste everyone's time."

In 2010, OkCupid's blog published a well-read article, written by Christian Rudder, entitled "Why You Should Never Pay for Online Dating." It made an argument that Coyne, Rudder, and Yagan had been refining for years: Paid dating sites—Match and eHarmony being the best examples—misrepresent the size of their memberships, bamboozle their subscribers, and have "a unique incentive to profit from their customers' disappointment." Using public information about eHarmony and Match, Rudder concluded: 1) 96 percent of eHarmony's twenty million profiles are "dead"; 2) 6 percent of eHarmony's users get married; 3) the odds that a Match profile is active are 7 percent; and 4) Match collects $137,000 in user fees for each marriage it produces.

The hatchet job hit a vein of populist outrage in the online-dating user community. A couple of weeks before iDate 2011, Match was sued in its home state of Texas by people claiming the site uses deceptive practices to separate online daters from their money. The plaintiffs claimed that Match "takes virtually no action to remove" inactive profiles and that, "with regard to the thousands of fake or fraudulent profiles, Match likewise makes little to no effort to vet, police, or remove these profiles and thereby permits, condones, and acquiesces in their posting." After iDate, another deceptive trade practices suit was filed against Match in California, alleging similar improprieties.

The cases, which were consolidated, were thrown out by a Dallas federal court in 2012. The language in Match's user agreement, wrote U.S. district judge Sam Lindsay, "in no way requires Match.com to police, vet, update the Web site content, verify the accuracy of all profiles submitted and contained on the Web site, or to undertake any of the actions that Plaintiffs allege Match.com failed to do. . . . There is nothing in the Agreement that obligates Match.com to conduct its services using only current or 'active' profiles."

In other words, it's a jungle out there. Buyer beware.

The theory of free dating goes like this: Since free sites make a vastly smaller marginal profit off each user, they can't afford the massive marketing initiatives of sites like Match and eHarmony. Therefore, free sites rely on word-of-mouth advertising, which incentivizes them to focus entirely on user satisfaction rather than conversion rates and date baiting. On a free site the user pays with his time and information, which the site then catalogs, analyzes, and sells to marketers that, theoretically, will pay a premium for targeted marketing opportunities.

Online dating should be an advertiser's dream. Sexual orientation, religion, politics, food and drink preferences, travel habits, pop culture and media consumption—it's all there. Yet despite OkCupid's success at iDate, Yagan found the advertising market a tough nut to crack. "Yes," he says, "we know whether you smoke and how many hours a week you play video games. We know everything. But when it comes to businesses like ours, businesses that have historically carried a stigma, advertisers are risk averse. Their opinions lag behind the population at large. The chief marketing officer of Coke is probably fifty. He doesn't get it. And if you're the ad agency, then your job is to get approval from the CMO. So you've got to be even more risk-averse than he is."*

At present, the Cokes and Nikes of the world have no interest in associating their brands with a Web site that queries its users on everything from their preferences regarding oral sex to their thoughts about threesomes, strap-ons, masturbation, pornography, and how they'd feel if asked to play out someone else's rape fantasy. What gained OkCupid a loyal following and made it one of the industry's most admired sites also capped its upside. As a result, the biggest advertisers in the online-dating industry are not Coke or Nike, but rather *other online-dating companies.*

Two weeks after iDate 2011, OkCupid announced it was selling itself to Match for $90 million, an astounding figure for an advertising-based business that had good but not great traffic and brought in little more than $4 million per year in revenue. "We know that many people who start out on advertising-based sites ultimately develop an appetite for the broader feature set and more committed community" of subscription sites, explained Greg Blatt, CEO of Match parent IAC.

During the deal negotiations at OkCupid's Manhattan headquarters, Yagan brought up the infamous article, "Why You Should Never Pay for Online Dating," that gave fuel to the lawsuits against Match. Blatt, the man Yagan was trying to convince to pull out his checkbook, unloaded with a stream of sentiment that you wouldn't exactly call collegial. Outside the conference room, OkCupid's employees suddenly took a great interest in their keyboards. Who was this person keelhauling their fearless leader? It was their new boss, Barry Diller's right-hand man, and it was just business, nothing personal.

---

* Any dating-site partner—whether advertiser or investor—must also be more risk-averse than the credit-card companies, which label all dating sites as "adult services." For paid sites, this means that in "charge-back" situations—when a consumer contests a billing, arguing, for instance, that he thought he had canceled his subscription—the dating site is given no leverage, no credit, in the dispute. Charge backs are the bane of the dating business. Pretty much any charge can be disputed successfully by a customer.

On the day the deal was announced, Yagan removed the piece from OkCupid's site. When asked about the capitulation, he back treaded. "I chose to take that down," he said. "Match didn't ask." The article's claims—that Match profits by duping its customers—were pieced together from public information, he said. Some of the assumptions made, he'd since learned, were untrue. "It's a common sense thing to do," Yagan added. "We're joining a bunch of new colleagues; there's no need to have that post." Why ruffle more feathers? In due time Blatt will appoint Yagan, now thirty-five, head of Match Inc., where he'll oversee IAC's entire online-dating operation, paid and free—nearly $500 million of business, a quarter of the North American market. In 2013, *Time* will name Yagan to its annual list of the 100 most influential people in the world.

So maybe free versus paid wasn't such an important distinction after all. Don't free sites want you coming back as often as possible too? Isn't "socializing" the product being sold and guaranteed by all social-media portals, regardless of their profit model? The message is always: *Come back! Hang out! Find someone new!*

In 2011, as dating sites came under pressure from the government to improve security, a high-profile rape allegation turned the issue into national news. A fifty-three-year-old woman in Los Angeles alleged that she'd been raped by a man she met on Match who turned out to be a convicted sex offender. Days after she filed a lawsuit against Match, demanding that it screen its database for sex offenders, Match announced that it would be checking all members against the national sex offender register. Match hoped the announcement would mollify politicians and stave off legislation; the added expense of statewide regulations, it worried, would gouge profits. A few months later, California's attorney general issued "a joint statement of business principles" that was signed by Match, eHarmony, and Spark Networks, which operates Jdate. The companies promised "to help protect members from identity theft, financial scams and sexual predators" and "to proactively educate members about safe online dating practices."

"The whole thing was pathetic," recalls Brian Bowman. "All these sites had to do was bring in the social graph"—the rest of one's online identity. "But that'd mean the end of anonymity in online dating, which would mean risking hundreds of millions of dollars for a business model change that's probably inevitable anyway."

Bowman is a particularly well-pedigreed geek. He majored in math and art at Purdue University. In the early nineties, he started his career in the world of computer-generated visual effects. He handled Internet products at the Cartoon Network, the Disney Channel, and ABC. After his stint as head of product strategy at Match, in the early 2000s, he worked for Yahoo! and a search engine called InfoSpace, where he tried to improve online search results by blending everyone's results together. In 2012, Bowman returned to the dating industry with a new idea that caught the attention of many.

For Bowman, the next phase of online dating is not about free versus paid but about open versus anonymous. Based on Bowman's experience at Match, he claims that "about 97% of the profiles" on Match belong either to free users—people who've posted a profile, are searching the site, but haven't paid yet and therefore can't send messages or respond to messages—or to former users, people who never removed their profile when they discontinued membership. According to Bowman, Match never goes out of its way to signal to users which 3 percent of profiles belong to paying subscribers. In fact, he says, Match doesn't go out of its way to authenticate much of anything about its users, and for a good reason: While user success thrives on efficiency, business success requires some inefficiency.

In the early years, he explains, promising anonymity was crucial for dating sites. It was not until later that the industry realized how important anonymity was to a paid business model that relies on message volume: keeping profiles anonymous meant a lower response-rate to messages sent. A lower response-rate to messages sent meant . . . *more messages sent.* Meanwhile, for the user, anonymity works to her detriment. While anonymity assures privacy (your boss will never find out you date online, unless he too is on the site and sees your picture), it also theoretically *diminishes* security and efficiency by withholding what Bowman calls "badges of authenticity." *Are you really not a criminal? Are you really not married?* By failing to distinguish between free users and subscribers, sites can also represent much larger membership numbers. A site that claims a membership of ten million might actually have only three hundred thousand active subscribers.

For a 2012 segment about the online-dating industry, CNBC's Amy Robach interviewed eHarmony's Dr. Gian Gonzaga. "Just how big is eHarmony's haystack?" Robach asks in a voiceover. "The company told us forty million—until we got specific." The interview continues with Robach asking Gonzaga how many daters are currently using the site.

"I'm not quite sure how to answer that question," Gonzaga replies after an awkward pause.

Later, when Robach asks if it's possible that eHarmony matches paying subscribers with non-paying subscribers, Gonzaga says, "It is possible they're not a subscriber and would have to subscribe in order to communicate with you."

In all cases, says Bowman, the concealment of your true identity becomes the site's main asset. Bowman would eventually marry. Ten years later, his Match profile was still on the site. Those who looked at it could discern only that he hadn't been active on Match in the past three weeks.

In the early days of Match, social media was not yet big. Privacy on the Web was taken much more seriously than it is now. Then Facebook came along. On Facebook, the presumption is that you go by your real name, and even provide an e-mail address and phone number. This is the opposite of most dating sites, where a few photos accompany generic, heavily edited, anonymous profiles. Bowman argued for "lifting the veil": dating sites would be more authentic, and therefore more effective, if they became more social by, for instance, encouraging users to post more pictures and information, and even perhaps linking their dating profile to the rest of their online identity. What would it take to move users in this direction?

As Facebook and other social-networks pushed society past its privacy concerns, some dating entrepreneurs wondered how they could leverage more of a user's online identity to make dating more like meeting in the real world, and move away from the old model of a private transaction between anonymous avatars. While the online-dating stigma still existed, online dating seemed neither novel nor extreme to a generation raised online, nurturing networks and watching each other's lives play out in a cascade of Facebook status updates. Privacy was something old people fussed over. *Who cares if your boss finds out?*

To the extent that Facebook is used for dating, it's the biggest dating site in the world. Dating-minded Facebookers will browse through the friends of their Facebook friends, letting interesting profiles lead to others. This way of dating was the main draw of Friendster, a Facebook predecessor. In 2003, after Friendster amassed 1.5 million members in just three months, the *New York Times* described it like this: "users sign up and post a picture and a list of interests. They also provide e-mail addresses of friends, who are invited to join. Users can search the service for their friends, then contact their friends' friends for dating or simply socializing." This "is more reflective of reality," said Friendster founder Jonathan Abrams, who also claimed to be chasing Match's market share: A friend of a friend felt less anonymous, more safe; the implication was that he or she had been vetted by someone you knew. This is precisely the argument that Bowman makes today. Though his timing may be more auspicious.

Friendster would fumble the ball, getting overtaken by MySpace, which in turn gave way to Facebook. These social-networking sites stole a significant chunk of online dating's market. Between 1998 and 2005, the online-dating industry grew at an average rate of 9 percent a year by revenue. Over the following six years, from 2006 to 2011, year-on-year growth slowed to less than 3 percent. At the same time, however, social-networking sites helped online dating by chipping away at privacy concerns.

Bowman hoped to leverage some of that behavioral evolution for dating when he started theComplete.me in 2012. On theComplete.me, the user clicks a button and his information gets sent over from Facebook. (If your relationship status on Facebook is "married," then you're not allowed on the site.) The user begins anonymously, in his "second skin." Then he can pull back that second skin as much as he wants. This might mean minor additions to his identity, such as posting more pictures. Or it might mean major reveals, such as linking to his LinkedIn page. As on Facebook, users control who sees what. Maybe every dater who is one degree removed from him on Facebook is permitted to see his complete online identity.

Rather than a static profile, theComplete.me hopes to "tap into the sites that consumers use every day"—such as Netflix and Amazon—to create "a more dynamic interest graph." In Bowman's unique geek vision, as Internet use rises, and people define themselves increasingly by where they go, who they talk to, and what they post and buy—*online*— their dating profile will evolve with them.

"The first version of the Internet," he says, "was based around 'It'—an index of linked Web sites, like Yahoo directories. Web 2.0 was based around 'We'—me and my human relationships, my social graph. Facebook won that round. The next iteration will be about 'Me'—who I am, my interests at this time, based not on what I say but on what I do. Mate selection will no longer be driven by looks. The average-looking person could become a great person, because you see the complete package."

There's a paid element to theComplete.me, making it a "freemium" site. Like Google, users can pay small amounts for premium placement in search results. Otherwise, the site is free, sort of: You pay with your privacy. Through a reward system—referred to as "gamification"— Bowman induces his free users to do what he wants them to do by giving them the tools to do what they want to do. For instance, a new user may be allowed five free messages after he transfers his profile from Facebook and fills out some basic information. If he proves himself to be a quality user—by, say, not sending overtly sexual messages—Bowman might offer him another ten free messages, but only if he posts two more photos or sends invitations to ten Facebook friends. Bowman compares it to frequent flyer miles.

Bowman's innovations caught the industry's attention, in part because many sense that, given the friction created by anonymity, something has to give. His early investors included Plenty of Fish's Markus Frind and Intel Capital, the investment arm of the semiconductor maker.

Mark Brooks, the dating industry consultant, is helping Bowman get the word out. "There are a lot of social norms that need busting," says Brooks, who moonlights as an "antiprivacy advocate." "Look at me, I've got nothing in the way of secrets. It's a nice, stress-free way to live." Leading by example, Brooks posts his credit-card transactions to a Web site called Blippy. When the *Times* ran a front-page story about Blippy in 2010, Brooks was featured in the lead: "Mark Brooks wants the whole Web to know that he spent $41 on an iPad case at an Apple store, $24 eating at an Applebee's, and $6,450 at a Florida plastic surgery clinic for nose work."

Like Badoo—whose stated goal is simply to maximize real-world interactions, whether for dating or some other purpose—Bowman and Brooks, among many others in the business, also believe online dating will get consumed by a broader world of social discovery. By taking the pink hearts off the homepage and rebranding the industry, dating execs expect to have an easier time reeling in not only Madison Avenue and investors, but users as well.

"There's still so much more social data that could be included in these algorithms to make them smarter," says Amarnath Thombre, Match's algorithm geek. "I'm sure the world will be more open in a few years from now."

By encouraging transparency—"mutually assured disclosure"—the innovators in online dating are blazing a path toward ever greater accuracy and choice. These innovators are not so much refining some science of compatibility as they are optimizing the Internet's supreme asset: search and discovery. Which is to say, the ability to combine several kinds of technology into one, the same virtue that captivated Barry Diller when he stood on the selling floor of his home-shopping network twenty years ago.

"What's cool about the social Web is that, unlike old dating sites, you're not trying to be a generically perfect person," says Bowman. "You're just living your life, in a fairly transparent manner, while looking for someone who is looking for someone like you. The goal, of course, remains the same: finding great first dates as efficiently as possible."

It's unrealistic, however, to believe that the openness of the social Web will cure all online-dating ills, particularly the problems of fraud and deception.

The need to connect deeply with others is a "fundamental human motivation." Whether subscription- or advertising-based, anonymous or authenticated, online dating or social discovery, any technology claiming to offer an antidote to solitude will always present opportunities for misdealing.

On Facebook, Rose, a multilingual artist in Switzerland, was contacted by a profile that appeared to belong to an olive-skinned forty-four-year-old Hispanic man living in New York.

"Hello," he wrote, "you look gorgeous. There is a saying that a picture is worth a thousand words, but when I saw yours I was speechless. Well my name is Dean Morris. I will be glad to communicate with you. Maybe we can chat."

Rose heard a voice counseling prudence. At fifty-two, she'd never been married and had attracted a string of guys who'd been interested only in "superficial relationships, bed stories."

Rose recalls: "The message was weird. But I thought it was interesting and fun to be in touch with someone from abroad. It felt like an escape from my life at home, which hadn't been going too well."

She sent a tepid response. Dean Morris said he was married for fourteen years, then widowed; and had an eleven-year-old son, a fact that appeared to be corroborated by his profile photos.

"You must be a fake," she wrote. "You can't be real."

But within a week, Rose and Dean Morris were calling each other "dear" and wishing one another sweet dreams. He expressed interest in Rose's artwork. No one had ever done that. Her weight never came up. He would ask: "Did you sleep well?" "How was your day?" "Take care," he would sign off at night, "and God bless your heart."

After two months, Dean Morris sent Rose a bank-account number. He asked her to log into the account so she could see that the bank owed him money. In the meantime, he needed a temporary loan to complete a crucial business deal in Africa. The money he would make on the deal would allow him to come see her in Switzerland. She should wire the loan via Western Union, or MoneyGram, her choice.

In the end, Rose gave Dean Morris—an identity concocted by an organized-crime organization in Nigeria—a total of eight thousand dollars. After she wired the money to the account in Africa, Dean Morris said his son needed a kidney transplant in Hungary. That's when she said enough. He got angry. Her last word to him was: "Fake."

It's tempting to shake one's head at Rose's fiasco. What was she *thinking*? But this isn't about education or IQ. It's about the power of loneliness, and the unthinkable ways we'll delude ourselves when offered even the thinnest hope of beating it.

In 2012, Ralph Gagliardi, a state policeman in Colorado who heads the identity fraud unit, led a bust of two American women, a mother-daughter team, who helped a Nigerian organized-crime organization run romance scams around the world. Through dating and social networking sites, the defendants helped defraud 374 people, mostly women, out of $1.4 million. That money, accumulated in one year, went to a single scamming "cell" in Nigeria. Gagliardi estimates that one scamming enterprise, comprised of dozens of cells, could bring in $50 million a year through romance scams.

"No one has any idea how much money flows out of the country every year in these scams," Gagliardi says. "It's massive, and there's not a lot dating sites can do about it. The Internet is so vast. When people go looking for love and companionship online, it almost seems like some disappointment is the price to be paid for opening you up to so much, and much of it great. There's always going to be something that cancels something else out."

ALEXIS, PART VIII

↓

In Terms of Sheer Numbers

IT'S MIDSUMMER 2012, AND MONTHS HAVE PASSED SINCE ALEXIS last posted on Phantasy Tour.

In the previous year she's worked as a set and costume designer on several films and advertisements, and is ascending in the business. Her twenty-sixth birthday is a month away, and she's in her longest relationship ever: For six months she's been seeing a thirty-year-old comedy writer who works at the production company where she works. They flirted for a long time at the office, while she scoured every post on his Facebook wall to figure out which women he'd slept with. Finally he gave her his cell number and casually suggested that she send him a text sometime.

"WHEN ARE WE HANGING OUT?" she texted immediately.

Now, over a glass of sangria, Alexis reflects on her first years in the city. "My past relationships had this one-foot-in-one-foot-out kind of thing," she says. "I never set any boundaries. I'd sit in my apartment clutching my cell phone and waiting for whoever the guy was to call or text. We'd sleep together, hang out, and it would never progress." She continues: "This relationship"—with the comedy writer—"developed more organically. I never had to set boundaries with him because nothing was rushed. He came right out and said, 'I really like you.' And I was like, 'Oh yeah. This is how it's supposed to be. I'm not supposed to have to chase you down and wonder if you're going to call.'"

Alexis realized that music isn't as important as she thought. "I don't even spend much time listening to music," she says. Her boyfriend has been sober seven years, so Alexis doesn't take him to concerts because the temptation is too much. "When it comes to guys, I think temperament is more important." She likes that he's a creative type, like herself, and works hard at what he does. "I don't know why I didn't realize until now that this is the kind of person I should be with."

Alexis recently moved to Brooklyn, where he lives. She hopes their respective living situations—they both share apartments with multiple roommates—will be incentive for them to get a place of their own. "I think we could be engaged within a year," she says, "if we can get our shit together."

The sticking point seems to be Alexis's past. He's concerned that she's been with too many guys in too many quick relationships.

"Our sexual histories, in terms of sheer numbers, are comparable," she explains, frustrated. "But when we get in arguments, or he's angry, he'll often lash out and say something like, 'Well I'm just another one of your boyfriends, and pretty soon you'll move on anyway.' I know I'm supposed to soothe his worries, but I get defensive. I mean, it worries *me* that he's had two long-term relationships, lived with one of them, and had butt sex with another, and *we* haven't reached that level of intimacy yet. The fact is, there's no such thing as perfect compatibility, and there is no perfect person for you, whom when your powers combine will make a totally effort-free relationship. If you've got a good thing going, with love and respect, where you treat each other well, you stay and make it work."

Alexis thinks there's more good than bad. Still, it's hard to discuss the problems without uncertainty creeping in. "I want someone stable and he needs someone who understands his demons," she says. "And what do I find myself doing sometimes? Itching to get back on OkC, to see who's there this time around. Of course it's good to know that if it falls apart it's not like it's the end of my whole romantic existence. The thought/fear/curiosity of someone better around the corner is always there, Internet or not, especially when you live in a big city. But I try not to let these thoughts bother me."

Dating Starts Here

n the heyday of Operation Match, Jeff Tarr appeared on a CBS game show called *To Tell the Truth*, where he and two other young men—all claiming to be Jeff Tarr, for purposes of the show—faced a table of judges. The judges asked questions, then guessed which one was the real Jeff Tarr.

"I guess number two," said the female judge. "Because he looks like the kind of boy that would want to take all the romance and the mystery and the uncertainty out of dating!"

Whether Tarr looked like that kind of boy was up for debate. But she guessed correctly.

Tarr had big plans for Operation Match. He opened offices across the country and hired more staff. Colleges looking to match freshmen roommates, he predicted, as well as businesses looking to optimize hiring would provide the next markets for Tarr's matching service. His competitor, David Dewan, had similar ambitions for Contact. In the end, both men would make their fortunes elsewhere. Shortly after Tarr and Dewan left Harvard in the midsixties, as the sexual revolution was gaining steam, they abandoned their companies. "It was easier when we had a captive audience, people at single-sex colleges with time on their hands and high hormone levels," an Operation Match employee recalled. "We all felt it was time to go find real careers."

Tarr and his partners set up an office in New York, but struggled. Tarr sold Operation Match to a student marketing company, then headed for Wall Street, where he pioneered the use of computers in stock arbitrage. Optimistic as Dewan was about the future of computers, he folded Contact, cut up his credit cards, and embarked on a two-and-a-half-year journey around the world, eventually returning home to a very lucrative career as a software entrepreneur, selling two companies in deals worth over a billion dollars combined.

Two of Tarr's Operation Match partners found success in the law. Returning to Texas, David Crump became a law professor, politician, poet, novelist, and online-dating success story. A few years ago he met his wife, a German, on Match. He was in Houston. She was in Hamburg. Douglas Ginsburg became a federal judge. In 1987, Ronald Reagan nominated him to the Supreme Court, but Ginsburg withdrew the nomination from consideration after admitting to smoking pot.

There was a third fellow, however, who couldn't leave the dating business behind.

In the sixties, a Yale student named Chris Walker helped Tarr advertise Operation Match around the country. Among Walker's PR gambits: He convinced a nineteen-year-old model named Shelley Hack to pose as an Operation Match user in photos taken for Gene Shalit's *Look* article. Hack later became the face of Revlon and appeared in the TV show *Charlie's Angels* and in the Woody Allen film *Annie Hall*.

Walker's interests in matchmaking extended to the laboratory as well. In his senior year, Walker wrote a psychology thesis entitled "An Experimental Investigation of Heterosexual First-Impressions." Walker's paper, a study of attraction, drew a conclusion that would inform the rest of his life: "Each person approaches others from an essentially exploitive angle," he wrote, "and judges others according to an inflexible self-centered set of standards."

After Yale, Walker picked up law and business degrees from Harvard, then became a real estate mogul in the D.C. area. He also tinkered on the side, inventing EXSYS, a hydraulic fitness machine. Politically,

Walker became a prominent libertarian who championed environmental causes. As for relationships, he kept the lab going, entering into an open marriage with the same woman for forty years.

It is late October 2010, when Walker arrives in the restaurant of the Tribeca Grand Hotel. He wears a blue suit, an iPhone around his neck, and is dragging a suitcase behind him. He settles into the leather banquette, splaying his arms and legs like a fighter down on the ropes. He has a leading chin, a small underbite, huge ears, and the sort of tumescent lips that don't always notice when specks of food stick to them. A broad forehead and high cheekbones carve out of Walker's face a look of permanent bemusement. The deep-set ocular structure makes it seem as though his eyes are always searching. When a scantily clad cocktail waitress walks by, he cracks a crooked smile, and says: "Cappuccino."

"I believe in the European tradition," Walker explains. "There's marriage, and then relationships on the side. Here, in the States, most women, if they get wind that you're even laying eyes on a third person, they go ballistic. My wife and I decided a long time ago that there are certain things not worth fighting about. She doesn't say, 'Who have you slept with recently?' And I don't say, 'Where did you spend that last bit of money I gave you?' Most people fight over sex and money. If you can get those two things out of the way, there's nothing left to fight about. You save so much time."

Walker often travels abroad alone, using newspaper personals and online-dating sites, including Craigslist, to meet women near and far, including Rio de Janeiro and Tokyo. "I've recently had a string of successes with Japanese women," he says. "I love the Japanese culture. They're the most uninhibited about sex, and they have the most sex. Japan pioneered the love hotel."

At sixty-six, Walker is stooped, yet moves with the cricked wiriness of a man who carries on vigorous exercise without regard to stasis. In fact, he's very sick: Walker was diagnosed with leukemia and told he had five years to live. That was six years ago. It was after diagnosis that Walker decided his last business venture would entail a return to what he calls the "digitally intermediated introductions business." He hired consultant Mark Brooks to help him execute his idea for a site called Dating Starts Here.

This is why Walker is in New York. He's meeting with one of Brooks's consultants, Eric Resnik, to discuss the site launch. Resnik is a thirty-three-year-old red-haired man who used to handle public relations for the tomato industry, once worked for Match and eHarmony, and now runs a service that helps online daters polish their profiles.

On an iPad, Resnik shows Walker the test version of Dating Starts Here. Walker wants Dating Starts Here to be an aggregator of dating sites. In the same way that Kayak.com makes it possible to search airfares from the Web sites of several different airlines, Dating Starts Here (slogan: "We Cover the Field") aims to be the umbrella site of dating sites, offering users the ability to search scores of sites at once before deciding which one to join. The red-and-white homepage looks pretty much like any other dating site, with a picture of a couple laughing and having a good time, but Walker likes what he sees.

"It'll be like a dating choose-your-own-adventure!" he says, and then asks Resnik: "Did you add the feature we discussed?"

"Nope," Resnik responds, a little annoyed, "didn't add that one. Come on, Chris. We agreed we weren't going to discuss this anymore."

For weeks, Brooks and Resnik have been trying to dissuade Walker from his idea that Dating Starts Here should ask female users to measure their clitoris, in order to improve matching. "I just read," says Resnik, eager to change topics, "that Japan is so worried about the low birth rate that they're doing a government-sponsored matching service."

"We've got to talk to those guys!"

As with some other dating entrepreneurs, it is difficult to tell where Walker's sexual prerogatives end and his business interests begin. Well versed in the literature of evolutionary biology, he believes humans are closer to bonobos—a famously nonmonogamous species—than they are to gorillas and orangutans. He peppers his language with phrases like "mixed reproductive strategy," "diversification," and "mating in peer populations."

"Ornithologists used to think birds were monogamous," Walker says. "But then they started doing DNA studies on bird eggs, and they found that these supposedly monogamous female birds had mated in peer populations. You spread your risks. What if the guy turns out to have a genetic defect or gets killed? Most of the animal world works like that: You have a main squeeze, but it turns out that, medically, from an evolutionary point of view, it's more stable to mate around."

Much of the human world finds Walker's views distasteful, or at least impractical—including, it seems, the waitress, who overhears Walker's monologue and votes with her feet.

Whatever one thinks about the lifestyle Chris Walker promotes, some version of his libertarian sexual morality is gaining ground in America. The change happens so quickly that official declarations of right and wrong fade shortly after they're enshrined. In 1986, when considering whether the Constitution protected sodomy, the Supreme Court laughed off the notion, concluding that a right to engage in such conduct was "facetious." To hold otherwise, sneered Chief Justice Warren Burger in his concurring opinion, "would be to cast aside a millennia of moral teaching." Just seventeen years later, in 2003, the Court pulled an about-face in *Lawrence v. Texas*. Now the Constitution did protect sodomy.

In *Lawrence*, the Court's scrappiest member threw a fit over the ruling. If, fumed Justice Antonin Scalia in dissent, promoting Texas's "majoritarian sexual morality is not even a *legitimate* state interest," then criminal laws against bigamy, incest, and bestiality could also fail constitutional challenge. Justice Scalia exaggerated in order to make his point, that the Court was killing off all possibility for "laws based on moral choices."

But the Court's opinion in *Lawrence* contained a subtler message: Sexual norms evolve. It makes no sense to speak of some collective American mating tradition, because there is none. Modern conceptions of sexuality are far removed from the categories through which earlier generations made sense of their urges and behavior. The concept of the homosexual as a distinct category of person, the majority in *Lawrence* pointed out, did not even emerge until the nineteenth century.

The evolution of computer dating, and then online dating, coincided with a period of great change in American mating norms. The trends are disparate, of course: There was no more a link between Jeff Tarr's Operation Match and Supreme Court decisions that constitutionalized contraception than there was a link between Chris Walker's lifestyle and the cheating site Ashley Madison. But we do know that the technology developed in unison with, and abetted some of, this rapidly changing value system.

Gay marriage has recently been constitutionalized. What will the next legal battle be over? Does it matter?

Surely legal recognition of lifestyles—of moral choices—matters to the interest groups backing them. But the idea that judges or politicians control who has sex with whom, and how, is, in this connective age, as facetious as Justice Burger's millennia of moral teachings. To the extent moral legislation ever regulated sexual conduct, that regulatory torch is now passing, increasingly, to technology.

So, what are my feelings about it? I believe strongly in online dating. Any technology that helps people find companionship, helps them not be alone, *offline*, is something to be thankful for. But it's not all sunny days. Handing relationships over to technology and business has its downsides. Scamming, exploitation, and infidelity are the big ones. The more subtle drawbacks are paranoia and anxiety, which have surely always featured heavily in dating. Some people believe that online dating has heightened dishonesty, largely by making promiscuity an easy secret to hide. I agree. But I also believe that re-lationship technology reveals our true intentions as often as it hides them: what we choose to highlight about ourselves on Facebook; whether we send someone a text or pick up the phone; how long into a relationship we wait before deleting that dating profile—all these decisions surrounding how to use technology send strong messages to the people in your life.

It's hard to be more specific. Online dating is so ubiquitous, and is being used in so many ways, that to talk about any one iteration as good or bad would be like talking about "sex" or "marriage" as good or bad. It works great for some people, less well for others. My goal, instead, has been to chronicle how, in a time when technology seems to define social norms, our conceptions of meeting, mating, and love are adapting to the new choice and control provided by these revolutionary means.

And since I've been looking at relationships through the lens of how online dating changes them, I've also tried to avoid passing judgment on all the many behaviors, new and old, facilitated by the date-o-sphere.

Again, this is not because I don't have feelings about infidelity, commitment, monogamous marriage, or diaper fetishes. But rather because the technology is neutral, largely undifferentiated, and therefore it's only how people use it that matters.

I wouldn't use Tai Lopez's or Brandon Wade's sugar-daddy/sugarbaby Web sites, and I don't agree with Wade's view that all relationships are exchanges of beauty for money. But it doesn't really matter what I think, nor even what Justice Scalia thinks. All that matters is that Wade is offering a channel and people are connecting through it.

"I'd like to think of myself," says Wade, "as a telecommunications service provider more than enabling a specific lifestyle." It's a false distinction. He's doing both. But point taken. I abhor infidelity and exploitative relationships, but I also know that Wade does little more than slap a brand on a universal communications network.

Universality, and the advancement of a common good, were two of the Internet's founding principles. In 1980, a physicist named Tim Berners-Lee, working in a cabin near the French-Swiss border, wrote a computer program for organizing information. Entitled ENQUIRE—short for "Enquire Within Upon Everything"—Berners-Lee's project would, ten years later, become the World Wide Web, the most popular application for the Internet.

In *The Master Switch*, Tim Wu explains the genesis of WWW:

> Accessed through a browser, the Web was originally just an agreement to store information in a common format (HTML), coupled with a means of connecting pieces of information by so-called hyperlinks. The supreme value of the Web was, and is, its *universality*. The idea, as Tim Berners-Lee told me, was that "the Web has to work on everything: any hardware, any software, every language, all kinds of different media, any quality level of data, be accessible to people with disabilities, and work with any culture. Not just different languages, but different cultures."

In Berners-Lee's utopic vision, the Web would be a place where personal identity could flourish, unconstrained by monopolists or regulators but directed by "a firm sense of some common good." Wikipedia, YouTube, Facebook: All were founded on some collaborative endeavor, whether it be connection, knowledge, or entertainment. "Even Google," writes Wu, "can be understood, particularly in its inception, as a consequence of the Web's natural evolution, a faster way of getting around when the terrain became too vast to be navigated by human faculties alone."

Among these tech giants, Facebook is perhaps closest to the Internet's original vision. During its rise to prominence, Mark Zuckerberg shunned buyout offers from many media conglomerates because he intuited a difference between those "media" companies and Facebook, which he thought of as simply a "technology" company. The difference was one of control. Facebook didn't produce content or make assumptions about what people ought to be interested in. It didn't offer to get you married or arrange a fling. It was nothing more than the collective actions of its users. It was agnostic, like a public utility, but even more so. Tearing down anonymity on the Web by encouraging as much openness and sharing as possible—this was the mission.

Brian Bowman's idea for theComplete.me, in which users sign up through Facebook and their dating profile encompasses part or all of their online identity, was not a success. The site shut down shortly after the original publication of this book because it couldn't get enough users. But he was on to something. Many new sites, such as Three Degrees, are following his lead. Judging from recent history, transparency in the "social graph" appears to be the final destination for online dating, or social discovery. Tinder, the new Match-financed dating app that allows you to swipe through potential dates at hyper-speed, has been successful partly because users must log in through Facebook, the gold standard of authentication. But whatever label we use to describe the process of meeting new people online, introducing more openness will be at least as important as the switch to mobile. Taking the long view, anything that inhibits efficiency is likely to lose out.

In the summer of 2011, as Dating Starts Here is preparing to go live, Chris Walker receives an invitation to the Harvard Club in New York.

Jeff Tarr and his wife are throwing a dinner party. There's no special occasion, other than that Tarr has recently reconnected with a couple of his old Operation Match partners, Professor David Crump and Judge Douglas Ginsburg; and also that the Tarrs' daughter, Jennie (Harvard '99), is eight months pregnant with her second child. In a twist, Jennie married Harvard classmate and OkCupid cofounder Chris Coyne, whose interest in the dating business predated his relationship with Jennie. His father-in-law stays out of operations.

The old guard sits at one table, the new at another. Jennie Tarr and Chris Coyne sit with Coyne's business partners, including OkTrends blogger Christian Rudder. Also present is the journalist Nick Paumgarten, who last week published a story about online dating in *The New Yorker*.

Walker, severely stooped now and walking with a cane, hobbles over to Coyne in the middle of dinner. Coyne stands; his father-in-law introduces them. Walker denounces OkCupid and the rest of the industry, insisting that there's no algorithm or "black box" that can forecast compatibility. The best a dating site can do, he says, is provide its users with as many choices as possible.

"I'm going to shake things up with my new site," Walker promises, and Coyne nods respectfully.

Walker's philosophy of matching is not entirely out of sync with industry thinking. Still, no one quite understands how Walker's site can be successful. Even if Dating Starts Here "scrapes" the profiles of hundreds or thousands of dating sites, there would be no "reciprocal indication" of the user's matches: The searcher might be able to see everyone on fifty dating sites who lives within twenty-five miles and fits his criteria, but he'd have no idea whether those people wanted to see him. Even Walker's own consultants are doubtful that a dating-site aggregator will work. The sites that are aggregated would need to agree to be included. Only a couple have expressed interest.

After dinner, Tarr, Crump, and Walker, along with a few other dinner guests, head to the Harvard Club's bar for beers and coffees. It's the first time the three of them have been together since their undergraduate days, over four decades ago. The gathering feels like a warm but awkward date between men who once shared very memorable experiences.

Tarr peels off. Crump and his wife hail a cab. Walker stays to discuss a book called *Sex at Dawn: The Prehistoric Origins of Modern Sexuality*. One of many recently published books that attacks monogamy, *Sex at Dawn* argues its case via evolutionary biology. "In the West," Walker says, paraphrasing the book, "we inflate the value of sex by restricting supply. The illusion of scarcity is what makes us so possessive and jealous. We're not naturally that way." *Sex at Dawn* suggests that, given the relaxation of social codes—from hook-up culture to sexting to recognition of legal rights for gay couples—the arc of history seems "to be flowing back toward a hunter-gatherer casualness," assuming, of course, that hunter-gatherers were casual in their approach to mating, which is a matter of scientific debate.

And yet for those who believe that technology might carry us away from the monogamous ideal, recall not the dawn of sex but the dawn of the information industry. Like religion, which aims to overcome human suffering through togetherness, a similar ennobling ethos accompanied the rise of broadcast technology: It was thought that social interconnectedness would free man "from his baser unmediated impulses," that connection itself would have some kind of civilizing effect.

Well, yes and no. As the world adjusts to the new reality that technology provides, many traditions and taboos surrounding meeting and mating are on their way out, and more will likely fall, replaced by whichever new theories of relationship happiness win out in a marketplace of possibilities that never in history has been so vast. Monogamy is not going away, and neither is infidelity. Rather, it is the way we make sense of these behaviors, the values and labels and portent we place on them, that will evolve.

"The way I work my marriage," Walker explains, "is that my wife always gets first shot at everything. You want to attend a political convention? You want to go around the world? And if she doesn't, then I either go by myself or I take someone else. But you've got to have your priorities straight when you're in a marriage."

The lifestyle that Chris Walker pursued was extreme, or ahead of its time, or both. At the Harvard Club, Walker bids his audience good night. Clinging to a brass rail for assistance, he heads toward the elevator. In two months, Walker will succumb. Dating Starts Here will die with him.

ACKNOWLEGMENTS

My gratitude to Mickey Rapkin, formerly of *GQ*, for suggesting that a book be done, and to my friend and mentor Farley Chase, of the Chase Literary Agency, for making it happen.

At Current I thank Adrian Zackheim and Will Weisser for their sponsorship, as well as Julia Batavia, Jackie Burke, Tiffany Liao, Bria Sandford, and Margot Stamas for their faithful cheer and hard work on this book's behalf. Rachel Burd put a mean copyedit on the manuscript, and Joe Perez turned out a banging design. Deepest thanks to my peerless editor, Brooke Carey, for enriching this book with her prodigious talents and unswerving sensibilities; from start to finish Brooke's enthusiasm and insight nourished my own. Any flaws are the author's entirely.

The construction of *A Million First Dates* relied on cooperation from the men and women of the online-dating industry, as well as the daters who spoke so frankly about their personal lives. I am also indebted, in the most fundamental of ways, to Jeff Tarr and David Dewan, and to the examples of fortitude set by my parents—all people without whom this book would not exist.

Many thanks to the editors, journalists, lawyers, and other teachers around town who've made the world of writing a friendly place to toil: Jess Bravin, Jason Feifer, Jennifer Forsyth, Vanessa Grigoriadis, Jamie

Heller, Neil Janowitz, Ashby Jones, Yvette Kantrow, Nathan Koppel, Patty Larson, Peter Lattman, David Marcus, Bethany McLean, Joe Nocera, Katie Pollet, Laurie Sandell, Dawn Schneider, Summer Shirey, Andrew Simon, Andrew Ross Sorkin, Bob Teitelman, Binky Urban, William Wallace, Jesse Wegman, Lizzie Widdicombe, Dick Winfield, and Elizabeth Wurtzel.

I've found refuge in some wonderful places. I'm especially thankful for all my families, adopted and biological, past and present, in Minnesota, on both coasts, and abroad, including but not limited to the Afshars, Bakers, Heaneys, Hunters, Mellons, Ryders, Shelskys, Simmonses, and Speerts. To think I might've never been lost and found in a Canadian snowdrift, hunted for morels in Cannon Falls, cast for trout on the Deschutes, enjoyed mutton on a stick in Abruzzo, defaced a pig's head in Park Slope, or known that the best secondhand items in Connecticut are found at Furniture on Consignment, located in Westport, where you should always ask for Jim Klinko and he'll treat you right.

To the Herbert-Kostyra-Plimpton-Stewart clan for giving me the most important gift of all, my Sophie: thank you.

NOTES

Introduction: Liquidity in the Market

Page

vii **"The Internet did not develop":** Monica T. Whitty and Adrian N. Carr, *Cyberspace Romance: The Psychology of Online Relationships* (Basingstoke, UK; New York: Palgrave Macmillan, 2006).

1 **"needs about 3.8 dates":** Frind's 2009 appearance can be viewed here: http://www.youtube.com/watch?v=YjU4nE3K-To.

2 **His look:** Maryam Sanati, "The Vancouverite behind Plenty of Fish," *The Globe and Mail*, Aug. 25, 2011.

2 **reached $2 billion in North America:** Mark Brooks, "Online Dating in the U.S.," *IBISWorld* (Dec. 2011). Brooks, who tracks the industry for *Online Personals Watch*, confirms that U.S. revenues hover around $2 billion, with about another $2 billion being made abroad.

2 **service thirty million of America's ninety million single adults:** Ibid.

2 **the Facebook-led rise of social networks:** "Market Share of Monthly U.S. Visits Among All Sites," *Experian Hitwise* (November 2010).

2 **the science behind their algorithms is bunk:** Finkel, J., P. Eastwick, et al. "Online Dating: A Critical Analysis From the Perspective of Psychological Science." *Psychological Science in the Public Interest* XX (2012): 1–64.

3 **a graduate of Harvard and Stanford Business School:** Don Aucoin, "Digital Man: Eight years out of Harvard, Sam Yagan has helped build two online companies and he says he's not done yet," *Boston Globe*, Sept. 5, 2007.

3 **a Canadian who comes from German-farmer stock:** Max Chafkin, "And the Money Comes Rolling In," *Inc.*, Jan. 1, 2009.

3 **Frind owns 20 percent of the world's online-dating traffic:** May 2012 data on market-share by visits from *Experian Hitwise*, reported by Irena Brooks at the online-dating consultancy Courtland Brooks.

10 **With around 1.5 million paying subscribers:** Julia Boorstin, "The Big Business of Online-Dating," CNBC, Feb. 12, 2010.

10 **OkCupid makes less than $5 million:** "Inc. 5000," *Inc.*, Jan. 2011. Available online at: http://www.inc.com/inc5000/profile/okcupidcom.

11 **"We don't know anything about dating":** Aucoin, "Digital Man."

Chapter One: Your Pleasure Is Our Business

13 **"It is clearly the most unusual entry":** Philip Shenon, "Nominee Left College to be Matchmaker," *New York Times*, Oct. 30, 1987. A spokesman told the *Times* that Ginsburg was a twenty-year-old vice president of Operation Match, which once had offices in New York; Cambridge, MA; Chicago; and Los Angeles. The *Times* reported that Ginsburg was a founder, and his initial investment was about eight hundred dollars.

13 **Shalit, then twenty-nine years old, to investigate:** Some of what I know about the development of computer dating at Harvard comes from Gene Shalit's article for *Look*, "New Dating Craze Sweeps the Campus" (Feb. 1966). The rest comes from a series of interviews I did between 2010 and 2012 with Jeff Tarr, David Crump, Chris Walker, and David Dewan; as well as other media reports from the era, all cited below. To a limited extent, some of the material in Chapter 1 appeared previously in an article I wrote for *GQ*, "The Social Network: The Prequel" (Jan. 2011).

13–14 **In 1959, two Stanford engineering students:** C. Stewart Gillmore, "Computers in Love: Stanford and the First Trials of Computer Date Matching," 26, nos. 2–3, *Sandstone & Tile* (Summer/Fall 2002). Available online at http://www.mgb67.com/computersinlove.htm.

14 **In the early sixties, some colleges used computers to optimize:** Erin Rosacker, "Before Internet Dating . . . ," *Time*, Feb. 15, 2008. See also "216 Meets 14," *Time*, Oct. 25, 1963.

14 **Harvard had owned computers since 1944:** IBM's online archives, available at http://www-03.ibm.com/ibm/history/reference/faq_0000000011.html, describes the Automatic Sequence Controlled Calculator, known as the Harvard Mark I, "as the first operating machine that could execute long computations automatically . . . the industry's largest electromechanical calculator."

15 **In sixty-three, a Defense Department employee:** J. C. R. Licklider, "Memorandum for Members and Affiliates of the Intergalactic Computer Network." Apr. 23, 1963. Available at http://www.kurzweilai.net/memorandum-for-members-and-affiliates-of-the-intergalactic-computer-network.

15 **raised $1,250 in start-up capital:** Timothy Leland, "2 Harvard Men Replacing Cupid With Computer," *Boston Globe*, Mar. 14, 1965.

16 **In March, just weeks before the official launch:** The scene in Tarr's dorm room was re-created using both Leland's *Globe* article and Tarr's recollection of events.

17 **"A computer-dating service?" laughed Ginsburg:** Douglas Ginsburg, now a federal judge in Washington, D.C., declined my interview requests. The limited information about Judge Ginsburg that appears in Chapter 1, and later in the epilogue, was gleaned from public records as well as from interviews with Tarr and Chris Walker.

17–18 **"I approve of it as a way to meet people":** Shalit, "New Dating Craze Sweeps the Campus."

18 **"We're not trying to take the love out of love":** Ibid.

18 **from any given geographical area:** Interview with Jeff Tarr.

18 **Having followed the success of Operation:** Roger Doughty, "He Programs Futures of Young People," *Times-News* (Hendersonville, NC), Mar. 17, 1969.

18 **Over the summer he drafted his own dating questionnaire:** Interview with David Dewan.

18 **Dewan played the part:** "Young Man Rides Crest of Computerized Life," *Sarasota Journal*, Mar. 13, 1969.

19 **Operation Match's questionnaire was "less sophisticated":** "University Police Eject Man from Winthrop House," *Harvard Crimson*, Sept. 30, 1965.

20 **"If there's some chick I'm dying to go out with":** Shalit, "New Dating Craze Sweeps the Campus."

20 **"Funny," an Operation Match employee later recalled:** The employee was a Yale student, Chris Walker, whom I interviewed three times between 2010 and 2012. He remains nameless here because he doesn't reappear in the book until the epilogue.

20 **"The way I envision things":** *Sarasota Journal*, "Young Man Rides Crest of Computerized Life."

20 **Going back to the Newtonians:** Walter Lippmann, *A Preface to Morals* (Piscataway, NJ: Transaction, 1982), 241.

20 **"Back then I was going out with a girl from Wellesley":** Interview with Dewan.

20 **Meanwhile, on campus, a political science major named Gerry:** The correspondence between Nancy and Gerry was quoted directly from the author's trove of letters between them, which includes a copy of Gerry's completed Contact questionnaire and the Contact sheet he received with Nancy's name on it. All other information about the young lovers was gleaned from a lifetime of being their son.

23 **In urban areas across the country:** John D'Emilio and Estelle B. Friedman, *Intimate Matters: A History of Sexuality in America* (Chicago: University of Chicago Press, 1988), 304–5.

23 **one of the first bars that "respectable" single women could visit alone:** Nick Paumgarten, "Looking for Someone," *The New Yorker*, July 4, 2011.

24 **In some ways this world of urban nightlife:** My understanding of the sexual revolution of the 1920s, and how technology affected courtship then, came from many great books, including: Beth L. Bailey, *From Front Porch to Back Seat: Courtship in Twentieth Century America* (Baltimore: Johns Hopkins University Press, 1988); Paula S. Fass, *The Damned and the Beautiful: American Youth in the 1920s* (New York: Oxford University Press, 1977); Ellen K. Rothman, *Hands and Hearts: A History of Courtship in America* (Cambridge, MA: Harvard University Press, 1984); E. S. Turner, *A History of Courting* (New York: Ballantine, 1954); Frederick Lewis Allen, *Only Yesterday: An Informal History of the 1920s* (New York: Harper & Row, 1931); Ben B. Lindsey and Wainright Evans, *The Revolt of Modern Youth* (Garden City, NY: Doubleday, 1925); and Robert S. Lynd and Helen Merrell Lynd, *Middletown: A Study in Modern American Culture* (New York: Harcourt Brace Jovanovich, 1929).

24 **"had elicited pity, scorn or fear":** D'Emilio and Friedman, *Intimate Matters.*

24 **a "privileged, spotlighted, envied group":** Ibid.

25 **billed as "one of England's most reputable marriage counselors":** Eustace Chesser, *Love Without Fear: How to Achieve Sex Happiness in Marriage* (New York: Signet, 1962).

25 **a "right to privacy" could be divined:** The relevant text of Douglas's opinion in *Griswold:* "[S]pecific guarantees in the Bill of Rights have penumbras, formed by emanations from those guarantees that help give them life and substance. . . . Various guarantees create zones of privacy. The right of association contained in the penumbra of the First Amendment is one, as we have seen. The Third Amendment, in its prohibition against the quartering of soldiers 'in any house' in time of peace without the consent of the owner, is another facet of that privacy. The Fourth Amendment explicitly affirms the 'right of the people to be secure in their persons, houses, papers, and effects, against unreasonable searches and seizures.' The Fifth Amendment, in its Self-Incrimination Clause, enables the citizen to create a zone of privacy which government may not force him to surrender to his detriment."

26 **when men showed off their assets:** Bailey, *From Front Porch to Back Seat.*

26 **desire for security in an uncertain world:** Ibid.

26 **to act as if they were already married:** Ibid., p. 49.

26 **"was further breaking down":** Ibid., p. 52.

26 **"Through at least the first two-thirds of the twentieth century":** Ibid., p. 25.

27 **"great and mysterious motive force in human life":** *Roth v. U.S.*, 354 U.S. 476.

27 **Judge Lindsey held heart-to-heart meetings:** Turner, *A History of Courting*, pp. 184–85.

28 **The youth of past generations didn't have the same economic independence:** Lindsey and Wainright, *The Revolt of Modern Youth*, pp. 158–59.

28 **Before dating there had been "calling":** Bailey, *From Front Porch to Back Seat*, pp. 13–16.

29 **The idea was that women:** Rothman, *Hands and Hearts*, pp. 188–89.

29 **Henry Ford and his ilk believed:** Turner, 208-213. See also Lynd and Lynd, Middletown, *258*: "Here again the automobile appears to some as an 'enemy' of the home and society."

29 **In 1919 the country had seven million registered cars:** Allen, *Only Yesterday*, p. 6.

29 **which furnished girls with the school's rules:** Bailey, *From Front Porch to Back Seat*, p.19.

30 **The etiquette expert Emily Post wondered:** Emily Post, *Etiquette: In Society, In Business, In Politics and At Home* (Funk & Wagnalls Company: New York, 1922), p. 293.

30 **"With the old order of things":** Allen, *Only Yesterday*, p. 100.

30 **"the rule for young couples was conversation in pairs":** Duncan Aikman, "Amazons of Freedom," *Harper's* (June 1926).

30 **"A growing emphasis on personality":** Rothman, *Hands and Hearts*, p. 225.

30 **"were separated from their parents":** Ibid., p. 289.

30 **no amount of fast driving could outrun:** Allen, *Only Yesterday*, p. 97: "A time of revolution, however, is an uneasy time to live in. It is easier to tear down a code than to put up a new one in its place.... People who have been brought up to think that is sinful for women to smoke or drink, and scandalous for sex to be discussed across the luncheon table, and unthinkable for a young girl to countenance strictly dishonorable attentions from a man, cannot all at once forget the admonitions of her childhood."

31 **The trending divorce rate of today:** Ibid., p. 95. As the divorce rate continued increasing, wrote Allen in 1931, there "was a corresponding decline in the amount of disgrace accompanying divorce. In the urban communities men and women who had been divorced were not socially accepted without question; indeed there was often about the divorced person just enough of an air of unconventionality, just enough of a touch of scarlet, to be considered rather dashing and desirable." (See also Lynd and Lynd, Middletown, p. 121: From Muncie, Indiana, the Lynds reported a much higher divorce rate—in 1909, there were twenty-five divorces for each one hundred marriage licenses. That rate increased to forty-two in 1924.)

31 **That "they should distrust the new freedom":** Lippmann, *A Preface to Morals*, p. 17.

31 **"The inexperienced":** Ibid., p. 300.

Chapter 2: Delivering More Love than Jesus

35 **"We are the most important search engine on the Web":** Nick Paumgarten, "Looking for Someone," *The New Yorker*, July 4, 2011.

35 **As a youngster in Skokie, Illinois:** The facts of Match's history and Gary Kremen's background were taken from an interview I did with Kremen; a keynote address he gave at the 2012 iDate conference in Miami; a series of

interviews I did with his first publicist at Match, Trish McDermott; and the following articles, listed in order of their value to this book: Ron Jackson, "Be Careful What You Wish For: The Continuing Saga of Gary Kremen and Sex .com," *DN Journal*, Mar. 31, 2008; Todd Krieger, "Love and Money," *Wired* (Sept. 1995); Julia Angwin, "Love's Labor Lost: Online matchmaker still seeks love, money," *San Francisco Chronicle*, Feb. 12, 1998; David Gelles, "Inside Match.com," *Financial Times*, July 29, 2011; and Jeff Kauflin, "How Match .com's Founder Created the World's Biggest Dating Website—And Walked Away With Just $50,000," *Business Insider*, Dec. 16, 2011.

36 **Over in France:** I learned of the Minitel and early French dating chat rooms from an interview I did in Paris with the present CEO of Meetic, Marc Simoncini's successor, Philippe Chainieux.

37 **The BBS revolution began:** Peter Zelchenko, "Jack Rickard, editor of Boardwatch magazine, saw it coming," *Chicago Tribune*, Oct. 30, 1998.

37 **Early BBSs would be used by clubs and communities:** Dwight Silverman, "Once the forums of computer devotees, bulletin board systems are dwindling as the graphical, global appeal of the Net's World Wide Web lures away the faithful," *Houston Chronicle*, Sept. 29, 1996.

38 **"We had some awful press coverage":** Andrea Orr, *Meeting, Mating, and Cheating: Sex, Love, and the New World of Online Dating* (Upper Saddle River, NJ: Reuters Prentice Hall, 2004), p. 28.

38 **The Matchmaker network grew into a nationwide chain:** Jeff Corydon, "Computerized Singles Scene," *Tampa Bay Times*, July 20, 1992.

39 **In the early seventies, James Schur:** Jim Schur passed away in 2010. My knowledge of Phase II comes from an interview I did with his wife and business partner, Iris. Iris and Jim met in 1967 through a Boston-based computer dating service called Data Mate, while Jim was doing research for his own dating service.

39 **referenced computer dating in his debut novel:** Don DeLillo, *Americana* (New York: Houghton Mifflin Harcourt, 1971), p. 5.

39 **Dating services had a reputation for drawing losers:** Bruce McCabe, "Who's Dating By Computer?" *Boston Globe*, Jan. 18, 1970.

40 **compiled letters sent to computer-dating services:** Bill Adler, ed., *Dear Dating Computer* (New York: Signet, 1968).

40 **In 1976, Jeffrey Ullman, a handsome young techie:** My understanding of video dating comes from two interviews I did with Jeff Ullman and the following articles, listed in order of importance: Amy Wallace, "Love God from Hell: The Man Who Brought You Video Dating Hates to Date, Loves to Taunt and Has Himself Been Unlucky in Love. Would You Buy a Relationship from Jeffrey Ullman?," *Los Angeles Times*, Jan. 16, 1994; Washington Post Service, "'Great Expectations' Fulfilled by Videotape," *Tri City Herald*, April 30, 1976; Barry Siegel, "Videotape Takes Blind Out of Dating," *Milwaukee Sentinel*, Apr. 26, 1976; Associated Press, "Who You Callin' Zero?" *Times Daily*, Sept. 27,

1990; Dan Dorfman, "Love, Not Burgers, Is Latest Franchise Item," *Lakeland Ledger*, June 24, 1984.

41 **montage viewable:** Available at http://www.youtube.com/watch?v=0bom kgXeDkE.

41 **the sketch-comedy:** The clips can be seen at http://www.youtube.com/watch?v=FTBObmbe83A.

41 **He organized a demonstration:** Associated Press, "Who You Callin' Zero?"

41 **when TV talk-show host Montel Williams:** Wallace, "Love God from Hell."

42 **In 1690 in Britain:** H. G. Cocks, *Classified: The Secret History of the Personal Column* (New York: Random House, 2009).

43 **in Plato's ancient Greece:** Turner, *A History of Courting*, p. 16.

43 **The first known dating agency:** Cocks, *Classified*.

43 **It was not until the middle of the eighteenth century:** Aaron Ahuvia, Mara Adelman, and Elif Izberk-Bilgin, "Commercial Channels for Mate Seeking," *Encyclopedia of Human Relationships* (2009).

43 **"Everybody was letting it all hang out in other ways":** Patricia Morissroe, "Strictly Personals: Romance in the Want Ads," *New York Magazine*, Mar. 19, 1984.

44 **In 2011, *The New Yorker* observed:** Paumgarten, "Looking for Someone"; Marshall Sella, "iBone," *GQ*, (October 2011).

44 **Instead, we heat seek via search engine:** Eli Pariser, *The Filter Bubble: What the Internet Is Hiding from You* (New York: Penguin, 2011).

45 **he came to his first television interview:** Kauflin, "How Match.com's Founder Created the World's Biggest Dating Website."

46 **The Internet, writes communications historian:** Tim Wu, *The Master Switch: The Rise and Fall of Information Empires* (New York: Vintage, 2010), p. 266.

46 **Kremen's girlfriend met someone else:** Gelles, "Inside Match.com."

47 **remembers hearing about a couple who met online:** Lois Smith Brady, "The Vows at 20," *New York Times*, May 18, 2012.

47 **"It's really a bummer":** Angwin, "Love's Labor Lost."

48 **while standing on the selling floor of QVC:** Frank Rose, "Barry Diller Has No Vision for the Future of the Internet," *Wired* (November 2004).

48–49 **the young lawyer who:** Joy W. Wang, "Greg Blatt: A Perfect Match," *Columbia Law School Magazine*, (Winter 2010).

49 **average marriage age was twenty-three for men and twenty for women:** See "Median Age at First Marriage, 1890–2010." Available at: http://www.infoplease.com/ipa/A0005061.html.

49 **By 2011:** Anne Holland, "Dating & Matchmaking Site Benchmark Report" (Anne Holland: 2011), p. 15.

50 **attitudes toward online dating become more positive:** Doan, T. T. and S. A. Meyers. *Online dating: Determining the presence of a stigma.* Poster session presented at the meeting of Midwest Psychological Association, Chicago, IL.

Cited in Finkel, E. J. et al, "Online Dating: A Critical Analysis From the Perspective of Psychological Science," *Psychological Science in the Public Interest* (Feb. 2012).

50 **In 2010, nearly 33 percent of people between forty-six and sixty-four were divorced:** I-Fen Lin and Susan Brown, "Unmarried Boomers Confront Old Age: A National Portrait" 52(2), *The Gerontologist*, 1-13, Jan. 31, 2012. Available at http://www.documentcloud.org/documents/322105 -baby-boomers-confront-old-age.html. This study was cited in Rachel L. Swarns, "More Americans Rejecting Marriage in 50s and Beyond," *New York Times*, Mar. 1, 2012.

50 **accounting for 21 percent of the market:** "Dating & Matchmaking Site Benchmark Report," p. 15.

50 **The press release cited:** "IAC, Operator of Match.com and Other Popular Dating Sites, Unveils New Online Dating Site for Singles 50-Plus," *PR Newswire*, May 10, 2011.

50 **The top ten players:** Statistics for top visited dating sites comes from Irena Brooks at the online-dating consultancy Courtland Brooks, which aggregated data from *Experian Hitwise* for the month May 2012.

51 **one in five committed relationships originated online:** "Match.com and Chadwick Martin Bailey 2009—2010 Studies: Recent Trends: Online Dating Research Study." Available at http://cp.match.com/cppp/media/CMB_ Study.pdf

Chapter Three: The New Serendipity

59 **Back at Harvard, a math geek from Maine:** The foundation story of OkCupid was cobbled together from a series of conversations I had with Sam Yagan, Chris Coyne, and Christian Rudder, together and separately, between 2011 and 2012. The following news articles were also helpful: "A brief history of SparkNotes," available at http://www.sparknotes.com/about/ history; Catherine A. Zielinski, "15 Questions with Sam A. Yagan '99," *Harvard Crimson*, Feb. 11, 2009; Paumgarten, "Looking for Someone"; Aucoin, "Digital Man"; Lingbo Li, "Site Makes Matches with Math," *Harvard Crimson*, Jan. 31, 2008.

62 **OkCupid is premised on the idea:** See http://www.okcupid.com/help/ match-percentages for Coyne's overview of how the OkCupid algorithm works.

63 **researchers observed 109 "attraction tactics":** David M. Buss, *The Evolution of Desire: Strategies of Human Mating* (New York: Basic Books, 2003), pp. 103, 117.

64 **defines pheromones as:** Ibid, 244–48.

64 **scientists believed that because nonverbal cues:** Joseph B. Walther, "Computer-Mediated Communication: Impersonal, Interpersonal and Hyperpersonal Interaction" 23, no. 1, *Communication Research* (Feb. 1996).

65 **Potter's approach:** My interview with Potter was supplemented by Jordan Ellenberg, "The Netflix Challenge," *Wired* (March 2008).

68 **Dissonance, a popular concept in social psychology:** See Eastwick, P. W. and E. J. Finkel. "Sex Differences in Mate Preferences Revisited: Do People Know What They Initially Desire in a Romantic Partner?" 94, no. 2 *Journal of Personality and Social Psychology* (2008), pp. 245–64. Markus Frind, of Plenty of Fish, takes credit for introducing the concept of dissonance into online dating. In a rare 2007 appearance on the *Today* show, Frind said: "What people say they want and what they actually want are two completely different things. On my site, if someone is searching for clean-cut guys, but they really are messaging all the bad boys, I'll show them more bad boys than good guys." http://www.youtube.com/watch?v=3_eniyhXUZw.

68 **"If I had laid out criteria for what I was looking for":** Gelles, "Inside Match .com."

74 **"When I walk down the street":** Robert Andrews, "Google's Schmidt: Autonomous, Fast Search Is 'Our New Definition,'" *paidContent*, Sept. 7, 2010.

74 **Badoo was invented in 2006:** David Roman, "How Badoo Built a Billion-Pound Social Network," *Wired*, April 25, 2011.

74 **"It's no coincidence that Badoo was built in Spain":** Dan Slater, "How Badoo Bridges the Gap Between Online Dating Profiles and Real-Life Attraction," *Fast Company*, June 18, 2012.

75 *Bloomberg Businessweek* **called Tinder:** Summers, Nick, "Dating App Tinder Catches Fire," *Bloomberg Businessweek*, Sept. 5, 2013.

75 **"Any site that can be used for flirting will be":** Jenna Wortham, "New Apps Connect to Friends Nearby," *New York Times*, Mar. 8, 2012. Through a spokeswoman, Parker denied several requests to be interviewed for this book.

75 **which was bought by Facebook:** Stacey Higginbotham, "Facebook buys Glancee in another mobile play," *GigaOM*, May 4, 2012.

75 **"We are thinking more about ourselves as simply a dating site":** Meghan Walsh, "Dating Sites Aim for a Novel Idea: Actual Dates," *Bloomberg Businessweek*, July 27, 2012.

76 **Airtime, Parker told CNN:** YouTube video, "Sean Parker explains how 'Airtime' works," available at http://www.youtube.com/watch?v=LeVzvu1GB4U.

76 **The word "dating" appeared nowhere:** Jenna Wortham, "Airtime Adds to a Growing Choice of Video Chat Services," *New York Times*, June 6, 2012.

77 **found that the "natural equilibrium mechanism":** Hitsch G.. J., A. Hortacsu, and D. Ariely. "Matching and Sorting in Online Dating," *American Economic Review* (2010), p. 1,

Chapter Four: It Knows My Anal Preferences?

81 **"No one knows what chemistry is at work":** Reuters, "Erk! Eek! Bloop! He Loves You," *Washington Post*, Sept. 12, 1973.

81 **In an early scene:** Gary Shteyngart, *Super Sad True Love Story* (New York: Random House, 2011), p. 89.

82 **"People are going to have to have a device":** David Kirkpatrick, *The Facebook Effect* (New York: Simon & Schuster, 2010), p. 314.

83 **"There was a lot of randomness to it":** Interview with Dewan.

84 **Born in 1934, Warren was:** Warren's background and the foundation of eHarmony were gleaned from media reports, marketing materials, books, and radio interviews, many of which were cited in a 2006 unpublished dissertation by Stephanie Blake, entitled "A Virtual Love Triangle: Mainstream online dating sites, the companies that own them and women subscribers." The original source materials, in order of importance, are: Rebecca Traister, "My date with Mr. eHarmony," Salon.com, June 10, 2005; Neil Clark Warren, interview by Terry Gross, *Fresh Air*, National Public Radio: Aug. 17, 2005; Janet Kornblum, "eHarmony: Heart and Soul," *USA Today*, May 19, 2005; Valerie Reitman, "We Clicked," *Los Angeles Times*, Apr. 26, 2004.

86 **"We came to the conclusion":** Interview by Terry Gross.

88 **In 2012, a team of five psychology professors:** Finkel, "Online Dating: A Critical Analysis from the Perspective of Psychological Science," 2012. The Finkel paper, published halfway through the writing of this book, was instrumental in helping me synthesize the results of my own research into how online dating affects relationships. My summary of the paper, which distills the material on pages 38 to 44, captures the heart of the authors' argument.

89 **made famous in:** Malcom Gladwell, *Blink: The Power of Thinking Without Thinking* (New York: Back Bay Books, 2005), pp. 21–22.

91 **"A very anxious person":** "Is there a science to compatibility?" *Psychologies* (May 2012).

92 **Chemistry ran competing TV ads:** Paul Farhi, "They Met Online, but Definitely Didn't Click," *Washington Post*, May 13, 2007.

93 **Between 2007 and 2010, personality-profiling sites:** "Dating & Matchmaking Site Benchmark Report," p. 15.

93 **A 2013 study:** Cacioppo, J., S. Cacioppo, et al. "Marital Satisfaction and Breakups Differ Across Online and Offline Meeting Venues," *Proceedings of the National Academy of Sciences*, (2013).

94 **Cacioppo defended his potential conflict of interest:** Ingrid Wickelgren, "Meeting Your Spouse Online May Lead to a Better Marriage," *Scientific American*, June 3, 2013.

95 **two pioneering sex surveys:** D'Emilio and Friedman, *Intimate Matters*, pp. 55, 171. See also Christopher Turner, *Adventures in the Orgasmatron: How the Sexual Revolution Came to America* (New York: Farrar, Strauss and Giroux, 2012), pps. 215–17. Much of Davis's work was used for political ends. The information she gathered while running the Laboratory of Social Hygiene, an annex to a women's reformatory in Bedford Hills, New York, supported the eugenics campaign led by John D. Rockefeller Jr. Over

the next four decades, Rockefeller would direct nearly $6 million into sex research. Beneficiaries included the Planned Parenthood project of Margaret Sanger, who would become involved in the research that led to the development of the Pill.

95 **predicted that Kinsey's studies:** *Look*, Dec. 7, 1947, pp. 106–7, as cited in D'Emilio and Friedman, *Intimate Matters*, p. 286.

95 **their write-up of a ten-year study of sexual physiology:** Mary Roach, *Bonk: The Curious Coupling of Science and Sex* (New York: W. W. Norton & Co., 2008), pp. 42–43.

96 **He started writing a corporate blog called OkTrends:** I've cherry-picked findings from OkTrends posts that appeared between September 2009 and April 2011, all available at http://blog.okcupid.com. In chronological order: "Online Dating Advice: Optimum Message Length"; "Exactly What to Say in a First Message"; "How Races and Religions Match in Online Dating"; "How Your Race Affects the Messages You Get"; "Your Looks and Your Inbox"; "The 4 Big Myths of Profile Pictures"; "The Case for an Older Woman"; "What Is *Your* Best Profile Picture"; "The Big Lies People Tell in Online Dating"; "Don't Be Ugly by Accident!"; "The REAL 'Stuff White People Like'"; "Gay Sex vs. Straight Sex"; "The Mathematics of Beauty"; "The Best Questions for a First Date."

97 **Black women reply to messages at the greatest rate:** This appears to be a reflection of the offline reality that college-educated black women are twice as likely as their white counterparts to wind up alone. See Ralph Richard Banks, *Is Marriage for White People? Why the African American Marriage Decline Affects Everyone* (New York: Dutton, 2012). Banks, a black professor at Stanford Law School, argues that the decline in black marriages is due to a tangle of factors, including: 1) black women's outperformance of black men in high school and college; 2) high rates of incarceration among black men; and 3) the tendency of economically successful black men to forego commitment and maintain several concurrent relationships with black women and/or to marry outside the race, trading their professional status for the higher racial status of a white wife. Black women, Banks argues, should respond to the black marriage crisis by dating outside the race. But doesn't this conflict with Rudder's finding that black women are ignored by white men online? No, says Banks. But he explains that the truth about why black women are far less likely to date outside the race than black men is more complex than the OkCupid stat implies. For one thing, on OkCupid, Latino, Middle Eastern, Indian, and Native American men all responded to black women at rates substantially higher than did white men. Also, studies tend to understate black women's options because black women are a numerical minority—13 percent of the female population—while nonblack men account for roughly 87 percent of the male population. So even if two thirds of nonblack men refuse to date a black woman, there would still be at least two or three times as many nonblack men willing to date black women as there are black

women. Banks argues that the dating pools of black women are limited more by their own racial preferences than by those of nonblack men. Academic research suggests Banks is correct: A study of online mate selection showed that the same-race preferences of women are more pronounced than the same-race preferences of men.

99 **Online daters are, on average, two inches shorter:** In a separate study, social scientists found that the average deception for weight in online dating is 5.5 percent of actual weight. They also found the average deception for height to be 2 percent of actual height, and the average deception for age to be 1.4 percent of actual age. C. L. Toma, J. T. Hancock, and N. B. Ellison, "Separating Fact from Fiction: An Examination of Deceptive Self-Presentation in Online-Dating Profiles" 34 *Personality and Social Psychology Bulletin* (2008), p. 1032.

102 **"Vast digital trails of social interaction":** Jon Kleinberg, "What Can Huge Data Sets Teach Us About Society and Ourselves?" in Max Brockman, ed., *Future Science: Essays from the Cutting Edge,* (New York: Vintage, 2011), p. 80.

102 **Masters and Johnson relied on somewhat cruder instruments:** Roach, *Bonk,* p. 48.

102 **In 2010, the OkTrends blog served as fodder:** Scott James, "In the Calculations of Online Dating, Love Can Be Cruel," *New York Times,* Feb. 12, 2010; Jenna Wortham, "Looking for a Date? A Site Suggests You Check the Data," *New York Times,* Feb. 12, 2010; Jenna Wortham, "Three Steps to Demystifying Online Dating," *New York Times Bits blog,* Feb. 13. 2010; Catherine Rampell, "What We're Reading . . ." *New York Times Economix blog,* April 6, 2010; David Colman, "Me, Myself and iPhone," *New York Times,* June 30, 2010; Rob Walker, "Stats Appeal," *New York Times Magazine,* Nov. 5, 2010.

102 **the rights to Rudder's forthcoming book:** Rachel Deahl, "London Book Fair 2012: Crown Nabs Book by OkCupid Co-founder in Rumored 7 Fig Deal," *Publishers Weekly,* Apr.17, 2012.

Chapter Five: Better Relationships but More Divorce

108 **"If you were standing in front of a group of business school students":** E. B. Boyd, "Match.com Boss, Now Head of IAC: 'There's No Recession in Love,'" *Fast Company,* Dec. 20, 2010.

109 **To say that his roots are small-town:** The background of Markus Frind and the foundation of Plenty of Fish comes from two interviews I did with him in 2011 and 2012, his corporate blog, and the definitive magazine profile by Max Chafkin, "And the Money Comes Rolling In," *Inc.,* Jan. 1, 2009.

113 **that you have no control:** Barry Schwartz, *The Paradox of Choice: Why More is Less* (New York: Harper Perennial, 2004), p. 103. Schwartz cites M. E. P. Seligman, *Helplessness: On Depression, Development, and Death* (New York: W. H. Freeman, 1975); and C. Peterson, S. F. Maier, and M. E. P. Seligman, *Learned Helplessness: A Theory for the Age of Personal Control* (New York: Oxford University Press, 1993).

113 **It's thought that the "brain pain" of lost love:** Louann Brizendine, MD, *The Female Brain* (New York: Broadway Books, 2006), pp. 75–76, citing Eisenberger, N. I. and M. D. Lieberman. "Why rejection hurts: A common neural alarm system for physical and social pain," *Trends in Cognitive Science* 8 (7), 294–300. See also Eisenberger, N. I., "Why rejection hurts" in Max Brockman, ed., *Future Science: Essays From the Cutting Edge* (New York: Vintage, 2011). "Social connection," writes Eisenberger, "may have been so important for survival that the painful feelings associated with physical injury were co-opted to ensure that social separation was equally distressing—that individuals would be motivated by such feelings to avoid social disconnection and maintain closeness with others." Eisenberger argues that the dorsal portion of the anterior cingulate cortex, or ACC, registers the distressing aspect of physical (sensory) *and* social (distress) pain. Chronic pain patients who've undergone cingulatomies—the removal of the ACC—say they can still *feel* the pain, i.e., experience its felt aspect, but that it no longer bothers them, is no longer unpleasant. During episodes of rejection, heightened activity in the ACC correlated with self-reports of distress. In another study, Tylenol was found to reduce sensitivity to social rejection by reducing activity in the ACC. It's not yet been determined whether online dating's enhanced access to partners functions as natural Tylenol in the event of breakup.

115 **adopted by their peers in the face of "hook-up culture":** Kat Stoeffel, "Meet Your Gaggle: Crowd-sourced Love is Ready for Rom Com," *New York Observer*, May 31, 2011.

115 **each of whom fulfills a specific role:** Jessica Massa, *The Gaggle: How the Guys You Know Will Help You Find the Love You Want* (New York: Simon & Schuster, 2012).

117 **Abraham Maslow's Human Potential Movement:** Barbara Ehrenreich, *The Hearts of Men: American Dreams and the Flight from Commitment* (New York: Anchor Books, 1983).

118 **ten varieties of casual-but-emotional-sex:** Scott Alden, "The 10 Types of Non-Casual Sex," Aug. 12, 2011. Available at: http://www.howaboutwe.com/date-report/1633-the-10-types-of-non-casual-sex/#.

118 **any one of nine "pre-exclusive relationships":** Scott Alden, "The 9 Types of Pre-Exclusive Relationships," Dec. 29, 2011. Available at: http://www.howaboutwe.com/date-report/1402-the-9-types-of-pre-exclusive-relationships.

119 **elevates activity in brain regions associated:** Finkel et al., "Online Dating: A Critical Analysis from the Perspective of Psychological Science," p. 32.

119 **mate seekers are liable to become "cognitively overwhelmed":** Ibid., p. 33; see also Schwartz, *The Paradox of Choice*.

119 **three ingredients determine the strength of relationship commitment:** Le, B., and C. R. Agnew, "Commitment and its theorized determinants: A meta-analysis of the Investment Model," 10 *Personal Relationships* (2003), pp. 37–57.

126 **people will often overinvest:** Shin, J., and D. Ariely, "Keeping Doors Open: The Effect of Unavailability on Incentives to Keep Options Viable" 50 no. 5, *Management Science* (May 2004).

126 **have faced at least three constraints:** Buss, D. M., and D. P. Schmitt. "Sexual Strategies Theory: An Evolutionary Perspective on Human Mating" 100 no. 2, *Psychological Review* (1993), p. 207.

126 **change us by changing our perception of the world:** Marshall McLuhan, *Understanding Media: The Extensions of Man* (Berkeley, CA: Ginko Press, 2003).

Chapter Six: Diaper Daddies and Lonely Stoners

132 **founded in 1974 by John Broussard:** Lisa Belkin, "The Mail-Order Bride Business," *New York Times*, May 11, 1986. See also Melinda Henneberger, "Well, the Ukraine Girls Really Knock Them Out," *New York Times*, Nov. 15, 1992; and Christine S. Y. Chun, "The Mail-Order Bride Industry: The Perpetuation of Transnational Economic Inequalities and Stereotypes" 17 *University of Pennsylvania Journal of International Economic Law*, p. 4.

132 **his country had "become a real shopping market":** Kathleen Callo, "Philippine Mail Order Brides Are Booming Export," Reuters, Sept. 28, 1987.

133 **"There is a difference":** Wu, *The Master Switch*, p. 213.

138 **Wade, a Chinese American:** Marlow Stern, "Brandon Wade: The Man Behind 'Sugar Daddy' Web sites Miss Travel and Seeking Arrangement," *Daily Beast*, May 10, 2012.

142 **Simkhai released a smartphone application:** Background on Simkhai comes from my conversations with him, as well as Marshall Sella, "iBone," *GQ* (Oct. 2011); and Matt Kapp, "Grindr: Welcome to the World's Biggest, Scariest Gay Bar," *Vanity Fair* (May 2011).

143 **melted down:** Keir Mudie, "Gay app Grindr crashes as Olympic athletes arrive in London," *The People*, July 22, 2012.

144 **"Unlike a traditional dating site":** "Ashley Madison's Noel Biderman on the Profitability of Infidelity," *BlackBook*, Dec. 11, 2011. I interviewed Biderman in 2012. I was unable to unearth the article he refers to.

145 **particularly for primetime television slots like the Super Bowl:** Steve Mcclellan, "Fox Rejects AshleyMadison's Super Bowl Ad," *Adweek*, Jan. 20, 2011. The allegedly banned ad, which wound up running in Texas, depicts a beautiful woman celebrating her anniversary with her husband while he ignores her and ogles the waitress. The voice-over: "Have you ever been on a really bad blind date? Imagine that date lasting the rest of your life. Isn't it time for AshleyMadison.com?" And the tagline: "When divorce isn't an option."

146 **prompted a record number:** "Swedish 'Have an Affair' Ad Sets Complaint Record," *The Local*, Mar. 18, 2011.

146 **"the fastest growing community when it comes to infidelity":** "Ashley Madison.com Says Hispanics Are 'Fastest Growing Community When It Comes to Infidelity,'" *Huffington Post*, Nov. 11, 2011.

146 **Washington, D.C., was Ashley Madison's biggest market:** Brian Browde, "Washington, D.C. best city for cheating, online dating service finds," *New York Daily News*, Feb. 25, 2012.

148 **reviewed a bunch of books about life online:** Adam Gopnik, "The Information: How the Internet gets inside us," *The New Yorker*, Feb. 14, 2011.

Chapter Seven: Like Everyone, I'm Looking for My True Love

149 **"I like women from countries":** "Behold: Julian Assange's profile on Ok-Cupid," *Reddit*, posted Dec. 12, 2010. Available at http://www.reddit.com/r/politics/comments/ekgvz.

150 **had reached $2 billion:** Jessica Pilot and Julie Cohn, "Service With a Smile," *The Daily*, Apr. 23, 2012.

150 **perhaps substantially more:** Shortly after the hardcover publication of this book, AnastasiaDate told *Fortune* that it made $110 million in 2012 and predicted $140 million in 2013. Anne VanderMey, "The Mail-Order Bride Boom," *CNN Money*, April 9, 2013. Available at: http://tech.fortune.cnn.com/2013/04/09/the-mail-order-bride-boom.

151 **New York–based Scanna International:** Melinda Henneberger, "From Warm Letters to Cold Warring, Romance Fades," *New York Times*, Oct. 28, 1992.

151 **only one of the hopeful mail-order brides:** Ericka Johnson, *Dreaming of a Mail-Order Husband: Russian-American Internet Romance* (Durham, NC: Duke University Press, 2007).

152 **"venturing abroad for love":** "The Mail-Order Bride Trade Is Flourishing," *Bloomberg Businessweek*, Jan. 6, 2011.

153 **When Western men use the Internet to meet women in China:** My understanding of the Chinese mail-order bride market comes from interviews I did with various members of Anastasia's staff.

159 **Medellin's "rich and beautiful come to show off":** *Colombia* (London: Lonely Planet, 2009), p. 213.

161 **Some women also get kickbacks:** VanderMey, "The Mail-Order Bride Boom."

162 **Colombia specializes in vanity tourism:** Sergio de Leon, "Tourists Heading to Colombia for Plastic Surgery," *USA Today*, Mar. 14, 2006.

164 **which found that a man's chances of dying early:** Press Release, "Marriage and Life Expectancy," The Max Planck Institute, May 12, 2010.

166 **South America's second-most unequal distribution of wealth:** Simon Romero, "Dueling Beauty Pageants Put Income Gap on View," *New York Times*, Nov. 30, 2010, citing Center for Economic Development Studies in Bogotá.

167 **"There is nothing that indicates they are mutually exclusive explanations":** Johnson, *Dreaming of a Mail-Order Husband*, p. 154.

168 **to tout the company:** "AnastasiaDate Signs Playmate Dasha Astafieva as Spokeswoman," *Market Wire*, Oct. 7, 2011.

168 **juries award many lesser titles:** Romero, "Dueling Beauty Pageants Put Income Gap on View."

170 **will clash with Colombia's legalized prostitution:** Jackie Calmes and Matt Flegenheimer, "Secret Service Agents Accused of Misconduct," *New York Times*, Apr. 14, 2012.

171 **who's to say they won't be shipping back:** Mail-order grooms would not be unprecedented. In the mideightiess, Susie Carter, a woman who ran a day-care center in Anchorage, Alaska, noticed a surplus of single dads picking up their children. So Carter founded a catalog that became known as "Alaska Men USA." Several others followed, including "Bachelor Book." See Henne-berger, "Well, the Ukraine Girls Really Knock Them Out," *New York Times*. This market, however, was purely domestic, and it was still expected that the woman would be the one to move.

171 **the number of Russian and Ukrainian women joining its site has tripled:** Amanda Walker, "Western Men Look East For Internet Brides," *Sky News*, Sept. 20, 2011. Although Anastasia is not cited in Walker's article, I was told by the company that they provided her with those numbers.

Chapter Eight: Knowledge Is Sour

176 **"Online relationships are vulnerable":** Cooper, A. and L. Sportolari, "Ro-mance in cyberspace: Understanding online attraction," 22 no. 1 *Journal of Sex Education and Therapy* (1997).

176 **"There is an optimal pace at which intimacy develops":** Taylor, L. S., Fiore, A. T., Mendelsohn, G. A. and Cheshire, C. "A Second Chance to Make a First Impression: Factors Affecting the Longevity of Online Dating Relation-ships," Poster Paper. *Proceedings of the International Conference on Weblogs and Social Media*, 2010, p.4.

177 **In a twelfth-century advice manual:** Cited in Laura Kipnis, *Against Love: A Polemic* (New York: Pantheon, 2003), p. 60.

178 **the site established a new system of signals:** Kirkpatrick, *The Facebook Effect*, p. 91.

178 **"There are more techies":** David Weird, "SF Home to Next Generation of Online Dating Services, but Algorithm for Love Remains Elusive," *7x7SF*, Feb. 10, 2011.

180 **"To guard against deception":** Buss, *The Evolution of Desire*, p. 155.

181 **"supports an emotional style":** Sherry Turkle, *Alone Together: Why We Ex-pect More from Technology and Less from Each Other* (New York: Basic Books, 2011), p. 175.

181 **Turkle finds teenagers:** Ibid, p. 176.

181 **constant insults between posters on /b/:** Parmy Olson, *We Are Anonymous: Inside the Hacker World of LulzSec, Anonymous, and the Global Cyber Insurgency* (New York: Little, Brown and Company, 2012), p. 30. See also pp. 34, 35, and 38.

182 **Second-order information:** Ilana Gershon, *The Breakup 2.0: Disconnecting Over New Media* (Ithaca, NY: Cornell University Press, 2010), p. 18.

182 **A woman refuses to e-mail:** Ibid.

183 **doesn't know if her boyfriend is serious:** Ibid., p. 19.

183 **is a medium men use:** Ibid., p. 109.

183 **are one of the foremost indications of a man's intent:** Buss, *The Evolution of Desire*, p. 135.

183 **Trinidadians believe that the truth of another person:** Daniel Miller, *Tales From Facebook* (Cambridge, UK: Polity, 2012), p. 50.

183 **his girlfriend gets upset:** Gershon, *The Breakup 2.0*, p. 87.

184 **"made them into *that kind of girlfriend*":** Ibid., p. 83.

184 **explains the vicious cycle:** Muise A., E. Christofides, S. Desmarais. "More Information than You Ever Wanted: Does Facebook Bring Out the Green-Eyed Monster of Jealousy?" 12 no. 4 *CyberPsychology & Behavior* (2009).

184 **"The problem Facebook is solving":** John Cassidy, "Me Media: How hanging out on the Internet became big business," *The New Yorker*, May 15, 2006.

184 **"There's a deep, probably irreconcilable tension":** James Grimmelmann, "Saving Facebook," 94 *Iowa Law Review* (2009) p. 1137.

185 **"How one behaves in a pub":** Danah Boyd, "Facebook's Privacy Trainwreck: Exposure, Invasion, Social Convergence" 14 no. 1 *Convergence: The International Journal of Research into New Media Technologies* (2008), p. 18.

186 **things you shouldn't do:** Available at http://www.howaboutwe.com/date-report/1543-10-things-you-shouldn-t-do-until-you-re-exclusive.

186 **the crazy things women do:** Available at http://www.howaboutwe.com/date-report/1361-the-crazy-things-women-do-on-facebook-true-or-false.

186 **why Facebook might be ruining:** Available at http://www.howaboutwe.com/date-report/1603-5-ways-facebook-is-ruining-your-dating-life.

186 **the crazy things guys do:** Available at http://www.howaboutwe.com/date-report/1375-the-crazy-things-guys-do-on-facebook.

186 **terrible for new relationships:** Available at http://www.howaboutwe.com/date-report/1172-the-worst-thing-you-can-do-in-a-new-relationship-gchat.

186 **the elements of digital style:** Kristina Grish, *The Joy of Text: Mating, Dating, and Techno-Relating* (New York: Simon Spotlight Entertainment, 2006), pp. 54–58.

187 **coined such behavior bluffting:** Elizabeth Bernstein, "Why Texting Turns Us Back Into Teenagers," *Wall Street Journal*, Nov. 1, 2011.

Chapter Nine: Let's Keep This Fucker Coming Back

193 **"If you succeed":** Anand Giridharadas, "Dating Site for Married Couples," *New York Times*, Mar. 9, 2012.

194 **then-CEO Tim Sullivan told:** Bob Tedeschi, "E-commerce Report; In quest for financial payoff, online dating services are expanding to do more than find you the love of your life," *New York Times*, Aug. 11, 2003.

197 **"highly concerned" about unethical practices:** "Dating & Matchmaking Site Benchmark Report," p. 92.

199 **Two whistle-blowers said:** Geoff White, "Fools for Love: How an Internet Dating Firm Duped Clients," *Channel 4 News*, Nov. 1, 2012. Find article at:

http://www.channel4.com/news/fools-for-love-how-one-internet-dating
-firm-dupes-clients.

200 **In 2009, a fifty-eight-year-old man:** See Jonathan Leake, "Police target lonely hearts fraudsters," *The Sunday Times* (London), Nov. 27, 2011; Jim Dubreuil, Gerry Wagschal, and Rena LaFaille, "Online Dating Nightmare: N.Y. Woman Scammed Out of Thousands by Soldier," *ABC News*, June 22, 2011; Bill Tyson, "Smart Consumer: The lonely heart mum who lost €300,000 in an internet scam," *The Independent*, May 27, 2010; Harriet Alexander, "Police arrest suspected romance fraudster who posed as US soldier," *The Telegraph*, May 1, 2010; Harriet Alexander, "British victim of 'romance fraud' tells of ordeal," *The Telegraph*, May 2, 2010.

200 **including a sixty-nine-year-old woman in Minnesota:** Tad Vezner, "Love at first scam? Rice County woman defrauded on Match.com," *Pioneer Press*, Feb. 28, 2012.

201 **"Why You Should Never Pay for Online Dating":** The article is no longer available on the OkCupid site, but it's available here: http://www.scribd .com/doc/48916912/Why-You-Should-Never-Pay-For-Online-Dating-%C2 %AB-OkTrends.

201 **Match was sued in its home state of Texas:** "Customers sue Match.com," *Dallas Business Journal*, Jan. 4, 2011; Robert Wilonsky, "Yet Another Federal Deceptive Trade Practices Suit Filed Against Match.com. Wink!" *Dallas Observer*, June 22, 2011.

202 **The language in Match's user agreement:** See *Robinson, et al. v. Match.com, LLC*, U.S. District Court for the Northern District of Texas, 10-cv-02651, pp. 15–16.

203 **OkCupid announced it was selling itself to Match for $90 million:** "IAC's Match.com Acquires OkCupid," *IAC Media Room*, Feb. 2, 2011. The stated acquisition price was $50 million. Several sources informed me that the actual price, including payouts, was $90 million.

204 **he back treaded:** Brenna Ehrlich, "OkCupid CEO: We Will Not Charge Users Following Match.com Acquisition," *Mashable*, Feb. 2, 2011. See also Adrianne Jeffries, "OKCupid: We Didn't Censor Our Match.com-Bashing Blog Post," *New York Observer*, Feb. 2, 2011: "I know everyone wants to make a big deal out of this," Yagan said. "They didn't tell us take it down. I wanted to do it . . . We obviously believe in a free model but there are also paid models and I didn't think [the post's] continued existence served much of a purpose. People will say, 'Oh my God, they've sold out and they're censoring it,' that's fine. When we put our next blog post next week and keep being awesome and the product keeps being awesome and free, people will just realize they're overreacting." He added: "In general the totality of data that we have become exposed to leads us to believe that yes, the subscription sites are probably more successful than the post made them out to be."

204 **In due time:** "IAC Announces Management Changes at Its Match Segment," PRNewswire, Oct. 23, 2012.

204 **alleged that she'd been raped:** Rachel Quigley, "Tired of hiding: Match.com 'rape victim speaks out about ordeal at the hands of convicted sex offender she met on dating site,'" *Daily Mail*, Apr. 19, 2011.

204 **Match announced that it would be checking:** Leon Watson, "'If I save one woman I'm happy': Sex attack victim drops case after Match.com agrees to screen its members," *Daily Mail*, Aug. 24, 2011.

204 **"a joint statement of business principles":** Press Release, "Attorney General Kamala D. Harris Announces Agreement to Strengthen Consumer Protections for Users of Online Dating Web sites," State of California Department of Justice Office of Attorney General, Mar. 20, 2012. Available at http://oag .ca.gov/news/press-releases/attorney-general-kamala-d-harris-announces -agreement-strengthen-consumer.

206 **interviewed eHarmony's Dr. Gian Gonzaga:** "Love at First Byte: The Secret Science of Online Dating," CNBC, Feb. 9, 2012.

207 **described it like this:** Tedeschi, "E-commerce Report; In quest for financial payoff, online dating services are expanding to do more than find you the love of your life," 2003.

207 **Between 1998 and 2005:** Revenue growth statistics come from *IBISWorld*.

209 **The need to connect deeply:** Baumeister, R. F., and M. R. Leary. "The need to belong: Desire for interpersonal attachments as a fundamental human motivation," 117 *Psychological Bulletin* (1995), pp. 497–529.

211 **led a bust of two American women:** Jessica Fender, "Brighton mom-daughter team accused of $1 million online dating scam," *Denver Post*, June 19, 2012. Available at http://www.denverpost.com/recommended/ ci_20892031, indictment attached.

Epilogue: Dating Starts Here

215 **a CBS game show:** Clip is available here: http://www.youtube.com/ watch?v=lmIC7VFyE4M.

216 **Ginsburg withdrew the nomination:** Steven V. Roberts, "Ginsburg Withdraws Name as Supreme Court Nominee, Citing Marijuana 'Clamor,'" *New York Times*, Nov. 8, 1987.

218 **"that Japan is so worried about the low birth rate":** Aki Ito, "Japan's Government Plays Matchmaker," *Bloomberg Businessweek*, Aug. 26, 2010.

219 **a right to engage in such conduct was "facetious":** See Justice Byron White's majority opinion in *Bowers* here: http://www.law.cornell.edu/supct/ html/historics/USSC_CR_0478_0186_ZO.html.

219 **To hold otherwise:** See Chief Justice Warren's concurrence in *Bowers* here: http://www.law.cornell.edu/supct/html/historics/USSC_CR_0478_0186 _ZC.html.

219 **Now the Constitution did protect sodomy:** See Justice Kennedy's opinion in *Lawrence* here: http://www.law.cornell.edu/supct/html/02-102.ZO.html.

219 **the Court's scrappiest member threw a fit:** See Justice Scalia's dissent

in *Lawrence* here: http://www.law.cornell.edu/supct/html/02-102.ZD .html.

221 **"I'd like to think of myself":** Stern, "Brandon Wade."

221 **explains the genesis of WWW:** Wu, *The Master Switch*, p. 282.

224 **"The illusion of scarcity is what makes us so possessive and jealous":** See Ryan, C., and C. Jetha. *Sex at Dawn: How We Mate, Why We Stray, and What It Means for Modern Relationships* (New York: Harper Perennial, 2010), see, e.g., p. 145: "For most human beings, reality is pretty much what we're told it is. Like practically everything else, jealousy reflects social modification and can clearly be reduced to little more than a minor irritant if consensus deems it so."

224 **"from his baser unmediated impulses":** Wu, *The Master Switch*, p. 38.

INDEX